The Stressless Home

A Step-by-Step Guide to Turning Your Home into the Haven You Deserve

by
Robert M. Bramson, Ph.D.
and
Susan Bramson

ANCHOR PRESS / DOUBLEDAY
Garden City, New York
1985

Library of Congress Cataloging in Publication Data

Bramson, Robert M.
    The stressless home.

    Bibliography: p. 213
    1. Family—United States.   2. Stress (Psychology)
I. Bramson, Susan, 1940–   .   II. Title.
HQ536.B73   1985   646.7′8
ISBN 0-385-18289-9
Library of Congress Catalog Card Number 82-45390

THE STRESSLESS HOME:
A Step-by-Step Guide to Turning Your Home into the Haven You Deserve

*This book is dedicated to our children,
with whom we learned*

CONTENTS

ACKNOWLEDGMENTS

We are indebted to many for both the substance of this book and the courage to write it.

Wilson Yandell has been our counselor and consultant for many years. He encouraged us to write, helped us to discover ways of easing our own lives and then to determine why we weren't using them—after which we did.

Of the many writers of organizational lore whose work has seasoned our minds through the years, the following deserve special mention. To Stuart Atkins, Allan Katcher, and Elias Porter, Jr., we owe our first serious acquaintance with the strength-weakness irony, to use their words, that keeps us all from the perfection of character that we deserve. The work of C. West Churchman was a major foundation for our study of styles of thinking (with Allen F. Harrison and Nicholas Parlette). The writings of George Morrisey (Chap. 2), Charles Kepner, and Benjamin Tregoe (Chap. 3) first brought to our attention a number of priority-setting and decision-making methods which we later adapted to a variety of home situations.

Our first encounter with the phased character of the developmental process (Chap. 9) was a presentation by Allan Katcher. We have added to his formulations and have been pleased that subsequent evidence has supported the validity of the concept.

From friends, neighbors, clients, and colleagues, we have acquired many ideas on ways and means of containing chaos. We appreciate each of these bits of shared wisdom and are very pleased to pass them on.

Carol Mann, our agent, and Loretta Barrett, Executive Editor at

Doubleday, had faith that a book with the goals of this one had a place in the world, and that we could and would deliver. We received valued editorial assistance from Loretta, Jay Wurtz (in San Francisco), and Felicia Abbadessa at Doubleday.

Rita Kilstrom, friend, neighbor, and colleague, read the manuscript in varying stages of completion and offered many helpful comments.

Without our family, and we cherish every member of it, there would be no book at all. We have marveled at their forbearance when we at times marred the household tranquility with our "creative tension." At different times, and in different ways, they have helped us test and refine —not always with their consent, to be sure—a large part of the substance of each of the chapters. Most of all, they have permitted us to showcase ourselves as parents and professionals with both faith, and expectation, that we would strike a note of appropriate reality. Therefore, we say thank you to Wendy, Marni, Rob, Sean, Patrick, and Jeremy, the basic six, to their spouses Don and Eric, and our grandchildren Guinevere and Hillary.

THE STRESSLESS HOME:
A Step-by-Step Guide to Turning Your Home into the Haven You Deserve

CHAPTER 1

The Less-stressed Family: Haven on Earth, with a Little Help from Your Friends

This is a book with a unique viewpoint, and a positive one. It's about your home and how to make it the haven it ought to be. First, it will show you how the same sort of team building that makes *some* organizations into great places to work can also do wonders for your own family. Second, it will show you that your problems with your touchy tribe are more likely problems of pattern than personality.

Finally, it is a book that offers a "no-blame" approach to family problem solving, an approach that has no losers, only winners. It offers concrete ways and means for doing things differently that call neither for superhuman willpower nor mutual psychoanalysis.

The theme of this book, simply stated, is that for the caring-and-loving part of your family to have a chance, the getting-things-done part has to work well. It's about how to contain the chaos that may have crept into your life under the guise of easy informality; about how to prevent solving the wrong family problem the wrong way at the wrong time; about how to prevent recriminations over "where the money's gone" or "If you'd only told me!" In other words, this is a book about unstressing your family, about how to make your home into the haven it can and ought to be.

What makes a home truly a haven, that warm, comforting place free of the tigers and dragons that chase us constantly outside the castle walls? Certainly, we all want our homes to be a refuge from the tensions and competition of a sometimes harsh world. We dream, as people have always dreamed, of a glowing hearth, pleasant and peaceful conversations around the table, and the tranquil quietness of late hours.

Too often, however, that peaceful portrait becomes a harsh, modern abstract—full of contrasting hues, clashing lines, and sharp edges. Relaxed informality erodes into overloading disorder, freedom to "be ourselves" is washed out by a hundred new chores to do. The caring and compassion that might have offered us solace has turned into bitter nagging, silent recriminations, or isolation and loneliness. The family dream has become a family nightmare. Our high rates of divorce, separation, alcoholism, and suicide are ample, if sad, evidence of that.

Saddest of all, much of this is preventable—even curable; and the key to both prevention and cure is a vision of the family as a special kind of working group and some hard-won but readily applied knowledge that will help any group anywhere to function more smoothly.

WHO WE ARE

Before we go much further, we ought to introduce ourselves. We, Bob and Susan Bramson, are like many other contemporary working couples. We built our family on the foundation of two others, "yours and mine," and added a third—"ours". We're a two-career family, which means that all too often few troopers are left to guard the fort. Our castle, in fact, at its uproarious peak, housed five (mostly) wonderful children, two dogs (who should have known better), two cats (who didn't particularly care), six goldfish (who wondered why no one remembered to change the water), and a tortoise named Turtle.

What differentiates us from most other working couples is our profession—we're management consultants. We're paid by clients—individuals and organizations—to help them solve a diversity of problems. Eight years ago it occurred to us that the methods and techniques that we as management consultants had successfully been recommending to others for years might be useful to us personally. For years we had helped organizations of all sizes learn to communicate, plan, decide, and perform better. More importantly, we had built enthusiastic teams from discordant, frustrated human beings, all of whom were angry with each other. Why, we asked, couldn't those same methods that brought so much to others, work for us in our own domestic miniorganization?

With parental high hopes, tempered by a professionally skeptical eye, we selected a surefire, handy-dandy technique from our consultant's kit bag and started out. It was a not too complicated method—one we'd used many times before on other people's problems (you'll read about it in Chap. 2)—and it worked! We tried another, and another, and yet another. The magic multiplied, and our "profits" from a business of decidedly unbusinesslike beginnings were these:

— We gained a *sense of control* over the stress producers that were wearing away our health, contentment, and sex life.

— We began to "fit" each other better—not with the broken-down resignation of a worn-out pair of shoes; more like the members of a winning basketball team. We became *less difficult* for each other as those situations which had previously evoked our individual contrariness were identified and changed.

— We co-opted our kids into a household chores system that produced less nagging, fewer threats, an end to speechless fury, and —even harder to believe—high-quality work! More importantly, the system maintained itself with a minimum of friction for five years. With frequent resuscitations, it is still going strong.

— We all became *more productive* as individuals and as members of a family group.

— We *improved our communications* to a point where we (adults *and* children) felt our important needs and wants were heard and acknowledged, the basic foundation of mutual respect and support.

In other words, we brought more and more of those "havenly" qualities into our home. It was no surprise to us, therefore, as we incorporated the ideas and methodology for unstressing the home into our consulting practice, that our clients and their spouses began to tell us of their successes at team building in their own homes. Several things about these successes were noteworthy:

First, they were not achieved at anyone's expense. Every member of the family benefited to some extent.

Second, they did not require massive changes in character or personality. On the other hand, when things began to fall into place and the general level of irritation subsided, everyone began to feel more fulfilled, *and* to treat each other with considerably more humanity.

Third, the level of painful and debilitating stress that had reverberated within the family was noticeably reduced.

Finally, the changes were invariably accompanied by an increase in everyone's ability to have fun with each other.

These successes, ours and those of the clients and friends with whom we shared this new way of enhancing family life, were too dramatic to be simply enjoyed and then forgotten. Clearly, a book was in order, and this is it. We've addressed this book particularly to single-parent and two-career families—they now comprise over 65 percent of all household groups. For while any family can become overloaded with both problems and opportunities, these special "work groups" lack the room to maneuver the others may enjoy. When all of the business of making a home is crowded into the hours of five to nine, the opportunity for pleasant inefficiencies and procrastination just isn't there. For when the wrong problems are solved the wrong way at the wrong time, recriminations will surface like sharks. Lack of agreement on (or even awareness of) the standards by which each family member is privately judging the others will invite too high hopes, disappointment, and resentment. And of course, poor lines of communication will keep the tangles going.

FAMILIES ARE ORGANIZED FOR THE "BUSINESS" OF LIVING

If you think of organizations as groups of people working toward a purpose, you can see that families have a lot in common with any of them, from corporate giant to neighborhood grocery. Families have goals, toward which they hope they're moving. They have a budget within which (hopefully) they must plan and decide how their limited resources will be used. There are leaders and those who, with or without their consent, are led. There are agreements about who's supposed to do what and when in order to keep the ship afloat. There is praise for good performance and punishment for those who are thought sluggish, slovenly, or sinful. In other words, *any* group engaged in a joint enterprise, whether a family or a superconglomerate, must somehow find ways to meet basic needs for communicating, storing things, acquiring resources, dividing up the work, and maintaining morale. How it meets those needs will determine how well it does its job and—this is a big "and"—whether it enhances or diminishes the lives of those involved. The point is that when you leave the office (or the plant, or school) and head for home, you are not getting away from the confinement of organizational life; you are simply leaving one workplace and going to another.

Most of us don't think about our homes as "minicompanies" for several reasons.

First, we've confused ourselves by giving different names to the same function, depending on whether it occurs at work or at home. Here are some examples:

WORK	HOME
Raising Capital	Saving Money
Increasing Revenues	Getting a Raise
Marketing and Selling a Service	Earning a Living
Warehouse	Pantry (or cupboard)
Motor Pool	Our Cars
Employees	Us (Mom, Dad, kids)
Accounting Office	The Desk (or whatever you call that place where you stuff all the bills)

The functions, and the problems that go along with them, are much the same, only the names are different.

Second, for many of us, work is a place where we're bombarded with projects, slaves to a constantly ringing telephone, beset by impossible deadlines. We rush home to get away from it all, dreaming of peace, order, and blessed decorum. That is, until we stumble over whatever is scattered just inside the front door. (The moral is, of course, whether at work or at home, too much—or too little—organization adds to the stress quotient of any situation.)

Third, many of our workplaces *are* very nonsupportive places to be; the tasks are unrewarding and the atmosphere demeaning. Home, however chaotic, may look idyllic in comparison—any implication that the home we escape to is just a workplace in disguise smacks of heresy.

But the major reason why most of us don't understand that our families, regardless of their size, are also tiny organizations, is that from inside it just doesn't look that way, especially when things go wrong.

When an organization's or a family's gears don't mesh as they should —warmly and productively—we often overlook the causes for the symptoms. What catches our attention are the things that hurt: the messy house; the budget that defies control; the surly, resistant kids; or that feeling of resentful, helpless frustration when our helpmate explains away his or her most annoying behavior. How easy it is, and how understandable, to ascribe these irritants to personality conflicts or breakdowns in trust and communication. They are not. Rather they are the bitter by-products of nonexistent, inappropriate, or poorly implemented ways of doing business. Understanding and accepting this reality can work miracles for you, as it did for us.

Recipe for an Unstressed Family

We've always believed that anyone who is part of a family or household should have a list of chores for which he or she is responsible. What we *didn't* know was that the assignment and acceptance of these chores should be explicit, written down if necessary, but never assumed. We know it now.

Our route to this simple knowledge was tortuous. We had tried all the alternatives, but nothing worked. We'd been deeply disappointed in each other, and in our children, for walking away from work that "clearly" ought to have been shared. We fumed over slipshod jobs that *"anyone"* (especially those bright and alert kids of ours) could have done better and faster. Our sole profit from these agonizing trials was a surefire recipe for dank disappointment. If you are inclined to self-induced misery, here it is, with sympathy:

Ingredients: 1 pound of good intentions
                  7 parts of continually judging one another
                  7 different assumptions that everyone would know
                     how we thought things should be done

Stir in a husband, wife, and children merrily doing things the way they believe they should be done. Season to taste with disapproving frowns and mutterings about how nobody cares; bake in a heated argument and cool overnight in the deep freeze of martyred silence.

When we finally set ourselves to poke around in the stew we'd made, we came to several conclusions that now seem obvious, but at the time were not:

1. On the surface, at least, it seemed to all of us that every *other* member of the family was uncaring, overcritical, or supremely selfish.

2. When we found this same self-righteous anger in any of our clients' organizations, we could usually trace it to three poorly answered questions:

   a. "Who's supposed to do what around here?"
   b. "Who's supposed to tell whom what to do?"
   c. "How will we know if it's been properly done?"

   In other words, the tasks to be done were not sufficiently described or delegated, and standards of performance were vague, or the best kept secret in the place.

3. We were faced with the inescapable conclusion that we were running a very shoddy "organization." What was worse, we knew better. We had only to apply to our own family work group the methods that had worked so well—often startlingly well—with our clients.

The end result was a much more savory recipe for preventing family stress. Its secret ingredients are the six *sub*systems—what we call the *understructure*—of a systematically unstressed family. We call them secret because, while they've always been there, few people have taken the time to hold them up to the light and call them by their names. Here they are:

The Goal System
The Keeping-in-Touch System
The Tasks-and-Roles System
The Decision System
The Trust-and-Confidence System
The Methods-and-Mechanisms System

The recipe? Jell these precious ingredients through thoughtful negotiations; top them off with heaps of love and kisses; and serve them up with firmness, flexibility, and—blessedly—no nagging.

While we're offering you a few prize family recipes like this one, we're not trying to write a cookbook for eternal bliss. Our own experience has taught us that a little bit of a good thing goes a long, long way; too much can swamp the boat. In other words, we have not tried to write an encyclopedia for living.

What we *have* tried to do is present, in practical terms, the methods and perspectives that have actually worked for us, for our friends, and for our clients.

WHAT YOU CAN EXPECT FROM THIS BOOK

Even the best magic needs help from a magician.

First, read this book all the way through. You'll find exercises at the end of each chapter; they will help you apply what we've suggested to your own home and family. However, you may want to simply glance over them on your first read-through, returning later to those that seem to offer the most.

Then share what you've read with your significant others: your spouse, partner, and children. Discuss it honestly, do the exercises together if you can, and adapt at least *three* of the techniques it offers to improve your family's ways of doing things. You'll find, often after a surprisingly short while, that your family life has changed in five remarkable ways:

1. You'll feel more in control of your life, especially over those events that are most stressful.
2. You'll make better decisions and implement them with far more confidence and cooperation than in the past.
3. You'll understand and better anticipate those breakdowns in the family subsystems that leave your loved ones—and *you*—feeling misunderstood and uncared for.
4. You'll see fewer family discussions turn into arguments, and fewer arguments deteriorate into riots (we're counting this as a benefit although we know that shouting and hitting do provide a certain amount of inner satisfaction and sheer fun—especially if you're bigger).
5. You'll experience a welcome *decrease* in tension as you walk up to your own front door and, on more and more occasions, enjoy that feeling of positive elation once you've passed inside.

As an added bonus, you'll find that your new work-group skills can improve your relationships and problem-solving abilities at the office.

We hope, in short, that you'll find these simple, proven methods your road to a havenly home. As a couple who has made the trip before, we welcome you on your journey.

CHAPTER 2

Goals and Priorities;
or, Cleaning Out the Damned Garage

Weekends are hazardous to your health.

A 1982 Mayo Clinic study of male heart-attack victims, noted that the two most dangerous days of the week are Saturday and Sunday, in that order. To anyone who has awakened on a Saturday morning to an overwhelming list of chores, this finding is no surprise at all.

Oh, it's not the number of things to do that causes stress; it's the sinking feeling, even as you lie there with good intentions, that the weekend will slip away with most of the jobs undone.

Equally intriguing is the fact that the peak heart-attack days for women are Wednesdays and Fridays. They have seen the week slip by with that ever mounting list of chores drifting further and further out of reach, and with their own depressed assuredness that the next week won't be much better.

In this chapter, with a few embellishments, we'll show you two techniques that are guaranteed to reduce the stress of "overloaditis."

Most people have more goals than they know what to do with. Their problem comes from not making much progress toward any of them. Our experience with work organizations, and certainly with ourselves, suggests that most goal-related problems are the natural outcomes of some inexorable realities.

Work Reality #1: The amount of work that can be done is endless. Even the most elementary task can go on forever. Take the simple job of repainting the bedroom. You need only to buy some paint from the neighborhood hardware store, roll it on, wipe up the spills, and proceed to the next assignment, right? A three-hour task at most (you say confidently). But Bob points out that the house has settled a bit and there are a few cracks that need repair. Susan comments (now that she takes a look at it) that the previous occupants didn't do such a good job of preparing the wall for painting—the wallpaper behind it is coming unstuck and our own fresh coat would look like a woolly sweater before it too peeled off. To do a first-rate job, we decide, we'll have to steam off the old wallpaper, resize the walls, repair the cracks, then go out and purchase the paint. But wait a minute, Susan says, isn't there a sale on the kind of paint we want at that new shopping center outside of town? Sure, Bob says, but a mail-order catalog would be even cheaper. Of course the room won't get painted today!

So the drama goes on; in other words, any job can be expanded or refined into a lifelong career.

Work Reality #2: Too many priorities means no priority. Making lists is the great American pastime, and quite properly too. We've found that jotting down what needs to be done helps clear the mind, removes the clutter, and allows us to concentrate on one thing at a time. So, we're inveterate list makers. Bob because if he doesn't get it down, he'll forget everything in five minutes. Susan, too much aware of an endless roster of tasks to be done, writes them down because she needs to relieve the clutter in her mind. Fairly early in our efforts at havenly home building, we began keeping lists: A for important, B for less important, and C for the nuisance items—all, of course, with their own internal priorities. The problem with this method was that once we had listed everything we had to do and we saw how important each of them was, we determined (quite rationally) that it was impossible to do them all. Therefore, we decided that the logical thing to do was fiddle with the lists sporadically, convince ourselves of our good intentions, then go off on a picnic. Of course, the decision to do this was never made openly. What we said were things like, "I guess we'll have to do all those things someday." This led us to discover the third work reality, the inevitability of priorities.

Work Reality #3: Fate will set priorities if you don't. Since there is never enough time or energy to do everything, some things just won't get done. The only real question is whether you or fate will decide which get done and which don't. Take a look at this hypothetical excerpt from a list of January chores and you'll see what we mean:

1. Service the furnace. (Yes, of course it should have been done in September, but you forgot.)

2. Pay the monthly bills.

3. Send hurried notes to those people who sent you Christmas cards, but received no cards from you (the ones you met at a party that you really liked but were sure would never remember you).

If you do not, with determination and forethought, decide which of these chores to do first, fate will step in and do it for you, thusly. On January 10, dunning letters will begin to arrive on your pre-Christmas shopping bills. Obviously first priority, until January 12, that is. On that day a lint fire in the basement dramatically moves servicing the furnace into first place. Naturally, this shoves bill paying to a poor second place, therefore accruing a few more dunning notices. Those Christmas notes, which seemed so important January 3, have now been shoved so far back you'll decide it's too late to send them at all without embarrassment. Our point is this: It's never a question of whether priorities will be set, only who or what sets them.

For years we had seen these three realities, like Macbeth's three witches, gleefully foretell havoc at office, plant, and school. For almost as long, we had prescribed remedies for that havoc and had the smug satisfaction of seeing them work. How then could we let weekend overload and "someday" thinking creep unnoticed into our house and surround us with undone projects which we really wanted to do? It was only when we recognized that our home, that wonderful retreat to which we scampered (or, on some days, dragged) was no less a workplace than those we had just left, suffering the same ills and receptive to the same cures. The remedy with which we treated our own feelings of being swamped was a technique for taking charge of the priority-setting task before the three reality rules take their toll.

For ourselves and our clients who have tried this miracle cure in their own homes, there have been two enormous benefits: first, you will regain control over a part of your life; second, you will find that the right kind of priority list gets work out of people that they didn't know was in them. Both will result in your feeling less swamped and therefore less stressed.

THE MAGIC OF WORKABLE PRIORITIES

Strangely enough, the most important part of a priority list is its *bottom* half—the part that tells you what to do last, not first. Here's why.

Priorities Tell Us What Not to Do

Imagine a little mouse in your basement, a female mouse, it happens. (We've chosen a mouse rather than a human example to illustrate the peripatetic priorities problem for a special reason. We'd like to keep your attention on priorities and the dilemmas that ensue from a lack of them, and away from the necessity of doing everything that's on the list.)

If the mouse turns to the right, she'll find the pantry and earn a bit of cheese. If she goes left, she'll find that leaky old waterpipe and get a drink of water. If she scampers straight ahead, she'll find a crack in the molding that leads directly (we'll presume) to her little mouse spouse who, having arrived home before her, is quivering with mousely anticipation to greet her at the end of her little mouse day. Now assume that your mouse is hungry, thirsty, and starved for affection in equal parts. What will she do? Everything that we know about mice, and people, suggests that she will do nothing but sit there, immobilized by the pull of three equally strong internal urges. Suppose now that the mouse looks at the water and says to herself, "I'm thirsty, but I'm not *that* thirsty!" Now she relaxes a bit. Only two choices are facing her now, and she's capable of thinking more clearly about her own internal state. Too much stress, she has learned, sets the mind whirling, while a little stress sharpens the wits. Whether she decides in favor of food or frolic, she is freed now to move into action. Notice that her liberation came not by trying to decide which need was most important—food, thirst, or sex—but which was *least* important with respect to the other two. It is the recognition of what is of least value to you that enables you to choose *not* to do something even when everything on the list is clearly something you want or ought to do.

"Ought" points to the second reason that the proper kind of priority setting has an energy-releasing quality: It diminishes feelings of self-blaming and the enervation that follows any sort of self-directed anger.

In other words, *deciding* not to do something, even an important something, rather than simply not doing it, substantially reduces both the blahs and the blues.

Now on with the method that has been so useful to us: the Noah's Ark Paired-Comparisons Method.*

The Noah's Ark (Two-by-two) Method of Paired Comparisons

The inspiration for the Noah's Ark approach was the quietly desperate realization that our household was dissolving into chronic confusion. All of our available time—that is, time not spent planning for or meeting with clients—was taken up with the important job of parenting (which to us was *very* important) or in maintaining our home's position on a shifting sea of accumulated newspapers, household debris, and grass clippings that threatened to carry it off to parts unknown. "Where were the genteel amenities of life?" we asked with shaking heads. "Where was all our time going?" Examples of irritations showed up on all sides. We both enjoyed gardening very much, and yet the colder months would slip by without our ever having planted the winter vegetables. Going into the garage without a hard hat violated commonsense principles for staying alive, given the artful collection of both useful and over-the-hill paraphernalia perched on everything else. The boys' school papers lay everywhere unread—no heartless parents we, to throw them away without at least a glance, a nod, and a word of encouragement for future scholars. Our (home) office outdid the Library of Congress in the number of unfiled manuscripts—mostly projects brought home from work—and our family financial folders were kept from blowing away only by those strategically placed books which, fortuitously, had overflowed their bookshelves by a factor of two. We were, we noted, in an advanced state of dissociation. It was, if not yet a mess, well on the way to being one.

And the worst part of all was that we knew exactly what needed to be done to make things better. After all, hadn't we spent endless hours discussing just what we ought to do? Our only problem was, we were not doing it. Like our love-starved, hungry, and thirsty little mouse in the basement, we were thoroughly incapacitated. *That's* when we de-

* Application of the Paired-Comparisons Method to priority setting was first called to our attention by George Morrisey (see the reference list).

cided, out of sheer desperation, to try the priority-setting method we'd been preaching to our clients for years.

Putting a list of ten projects into priority (that is, ranking them from one to ten against some decision-making criterion) can be a lot of work, which is probably why most people, knowing better, don't prioritize their lists. The best thing about the Noah's Ark Paired-Comparisons Method is that the kind of thinking required to do it is of the easiest and most natural sort. Psychological research long ago established that the most accurate kind of measurement that people can make is whether one thing is more, or less, than something else. Take a group of people and give them two rocks, A and B, and you will get an extraordinarily high level of agreement on which of the rocks is heavier, lighter, rougher, smoother, or more throwable, even when that difference is quite small. It is when you ask them to tell you how much heavier or lighter A is than B that their wonderful agreement is lost. If only all of life's decisions could be reduced to simple "more-or-less-than" judgments, how much easier things would be. That little miracle, as you might have guessed, is precisely what wise old Noah's Paired-Comparisons Method does for you. Here's how you do it.

Step #1: Make a list. Before you can prioritize items on a list, you must make one. The size and scope of your list will depend on the purposes you have in mind. Here's the project list we used when we first applied this method in our own home several years ago. It will serve as our example as we walk through each step. If you'll refer to it from time to time, the instructions will be easier to follow.

1. Install bulletin board in breakfast room.
2. Buy odds-and-ends basket for front hall.
3. Put up message center board.
4. Clean out garage.
5. Plant winter garden.
6. Paint trim in breakfast room.
7. Clean out basement.
8. Build office shelves.
9. Build garage shelves.
10. Paint the deck.
11. Build shelves in Patrick's room.
12. Buy new mattress and springs.

PAIRED COMPARISONS
DECISION MATRIX

VERTICAL ITEMS

		1	2	3	4	5	6	7	8	9	10	11	12	13	14	SUM OF H's	
		Bulletin Board	Odds + Ends Basket	Message Board	clean out Garage	Plant Winter Garden	Paint Trim	clean out Basement	Build office Shelves	Build Garage Shelves	Paint the Deck	Build Shelves Pat's Rm.	Buy Springs + Mattress				
H O R I Z O N T A L I T E M S	1 Bulletin Board		H	H	H	H	H	H	H	H	H	V				10	1
	2 Odds + Ends Basket			V	H	H	H	H	H	H	H	V				8	2
	3 Message Board				H	H	H	H	H	H	H	V				8	3
	4 clean out Garage					V	H	H	V	V	H	H	V			4	4
	5 Plant Winter Garden						H	H	H	H	H	H	V			6	5
	6 Paint Trim							V	V	V	H	H	V			2	6
	7 clean out Basement								V	V	H	H	V			2	7
	8 Build office Shelves									H	H	H	V			3	8
	9 Build Garage Shelves										H	H	V			2	9
	10 Paint the Deck											V	V			0	10
	11 Build Shelves Pat's Rm.												V			0	11
	12 Buy Springs + Mattress															0	12
	13																13
	14																14

	1	2	3	4	5	6	7	8	9	10	11	12	13	14
ITEM NUMBER	1	2	3	4	5	6	7	8	9	10	11	12	13	14
SUM OF V's	0	0	1	0	1	0	1	3	3	0	1	11		
SUM OF H's (from right side)	10	8	8	4	6	2	2	3	2	0	0	0		
TOTALS	10	8	9	4	7	2	3	6	5	0	1	11		
PRIORITY ORDER	2	4	3	8	5	10	9	6	7	12	11	1		

Step #2: Enter the projects on a Paired-Comparisons Decision Matrix (PCM for short). First, of course, you'll need a matrix. A matrix is a grid or checkerboard pattern of intersecting lines. (At the end of the chapter you'll find blank PCM forms for use with your own project list, or you can make one with a blank piece of paper, ruler [or steady hand], and pencil.) Now, having somehow acquired a blank matrix, enter the project list twice, first in the numbered lines to the left of the matrix and then in the numbered lines at the top. You *must* enter them in the same order in both places, otherwise the confusion will be monumental. Your items are now paired ready for comparison on your matrix.

Step #3: Pick the right question. Your paired-comparisons matrix is like a Ouija board. Ask it the right questions and it will give you interesting and often surprising answers. Questions we've asked our PCMs in the past are: "Which activity will reduce our stress the most?" "Which one should we do first?" "Which would get worse if we did nothing about it?"

You'll notice that these questions tend toward the specific. The one question you should avoid, however, is "Which is the most important?" —especially if you're trying to arrive at a group decision. Why? Because most people who feel overloaded will insist that all the chores facing them are important. And in a sense, they're quite right. Certainly, if a job lacked significance, it probably wouldn't be on your list. The problem arises from the fact that different things are *important* to different people at different times, depending on their needs of the moment. To Jennifer, a socially aware teenager, a cosmetic facelift to the family room might be considerably more "important" than putting up new shelves in Mom's kitchen. Both would rightly insist on the "importance" of *their* favorite project. A little careful listening in on the discussion would quickly show that "important" means different things to them both. Not only that, what people want is often quite distinct from what any sensible person (you, for instance) can see that they need. For example, to you, painting little Rita's bedroom is merely a question of whether or not the walls need protection from deterioration. To her it has many other meanings. *Not* painting her room, for instance, can mean (1) that she is not very important, (2) that her brother has won another round in the ongoing sibling competition, or (3) that he or she is doomed to be permanently shamed in front of her playmates.

Because of this muddiness of meaning, it's better to ask action questions of the "What shall we do first?" variety; most people can agree on what such questions mean without (literally) endless discussion.

We think you'll find, as we did, that finding the right question will not only get you started, but will also generate some real excitement in the process.

Step #4: Compare the pairs. Having labeled the matrix and chosen the question you want answered, your next step is to compare each project to each other project on the list. Start with project 1 and compare it with each of the projects in the vertical columns. For example, "Will installing a bulletin board [horizontal item 1] decrease our stress even more than an odds-and-ends basket by the front door [vertical item 2]?"* If the horizontal project is "more" of what the question asked—more stress-relieving, more urgent, more damaging, etc.—than the project in the vertical column, place the letter *H* in the intersection box. On the other hand, if the vertical item has more of what you're looking for, place the letter *V* in the box. Thus, since we agreed that a bulletin board would ease our lives more than a catchall basket by the front door, we gave that comparison an *H.* Now continue in the same way across the page, comparing "Bulletin board" with each vertical alternative. A word of caution: You may find a tendency to forget the question that you originally asked and drift away to a more general question, such as "Which do we want to do the most?" or "Which is easiest?" You'll also be tempted by such interesting but sidetracking questions as "How much will it cost?"; "How long will it take?"; or "Haven't we waited long enough for this?" Remind yourselves that these very important issues will all be dealt with in their turn, and steer back to the problem at hand.

By way of example, here is the reasoning we used in our first trip through the matrix with horizontal item 1, the new bulletin board. In this case, the *H*'s made a clean sweep in every comparison but one. We agreed that a catchall basket, message center, clean garage, pleasant winter garden, dressier breakfast nook, clean basement, handy office and garage shelves, attractive desk, and Patrick's convenience (even Patrick agreed on this one) should *all* take a backseat to ending the frantic searches we'd experienced for misplaced papers, notices, etc., caused by the lack of a well-placed bulletin board. The only exception was the new spring and mattress, voted in by parents who recalled more than a few sleepless nights and morning backaches.

Now continue down the list, weighing each horizontal item against the items on the vertical list until the matrix is filled with *H*'s and *V*'s. You'll notice that the blocked-out portions of the matrix keep you from comparing any item with any other item more than once.

Step #5: Count the H*'s in each line and enter the totals for each item in the sum of* H*'s column at the right of the matrix.* Now transfer these totals to the appropriate boxes in the sum of *H*'s row at the bottom of the matrix.

Step #6: Add the V*'s in each vertical column and enter the sums in*

---

* You cannot compare horizontal item 1 with vertical item 1 because they are the same.

the appropriate boxes at the bottom of the matrix. (You'll always have zero *V*'s in column 1 because that column is completely blocked out.)

Step #7: Total the totals. In each column, add the vertical sum (sum of *V*'s to the horizontal sum (sum of *H*'s) and enter the results in the "Totals" row at the bottom of the matrix.

Step #8: Let the PCM tell you the priorities. Noah's computer will now tell you the priority order of your projects. The project with the highest total (in our matrix it was "New mattress and springs") will be priority number one. Similarly, the next highest total (in our project, "Bulletin board") is priority number two, and so on. If two projects turn out to have the same total scores, don't worry. You can resolve the tie by comparing the equally ranked items with each of the others, using the same principle.

Step #9: Relist your projects according to priority. Now list your projects in their proper priority order. Having done that, we urge you to sit down together and jointly gaze at this product of your communal effort. Do you feel a definite surge of energy? Do your feet tap and your fingers tingle? What you feel is an overpowering desire to grapple with project 1, now identified as the chief intruder on peaceful nights and weekend tranquillity.

Here's how our final prioritized list turned out:

1. Buy new mattress and springs.
2. Install bulletin board in breakfast room.
3. Put up message board.
4. Buy odds-and-ends basket for front hall.
5. Plant winter garden.
6. Build office shelves.
7. Build garage shelves.
8. Clean out garage.
9. Clean out basement.
10. Paint trim in breakfast room.
11. Build shelves in Patrick's room.
12. Paint the deck.

Fine, you say, but did it all help Noah build the Ark?

Yes indeed. Within three months we had completed all but three of the tasks. The three left unfinished were shelves in the garage, shelves in Patrick's room, and painting the deck. Here's the history of those undone three: In ten minutes of glorious abandon, we had thrown away most of our accumulated garage junk. Shelves, we cavalierly decided, would only tempt us to collect more, so no shelves. The deck we painted two years later as a small part of a considerably larger job. The shelves, however, are still not up in Patrick's room.

Which brings us to an important point. New tasks often arise, even before all of the old have been accomplished. In that case, a new priority list is called for, in which any yet undone tasks will take their place. If they are onerous enough, they'll work their way to the top of the list and be done with dispatch. If not, like Patrick's shelves, they will be resolutely *not done* with no guilt at all.

Why Do Priorities Work?

Priorities—well-thought priorities—get things done for several reasons.

First, they help untangle those complex, conflicting feelings that muddle up the brain, binding up precious energy. Nothing gets a job moving faster than a dumb and dependent slavery to a list, especially one that answers the hardest question of all: "Where do I begin?" The PCM has told you in no uncertain terms. No back talk, please!

Second, the list reduces stress caused by too much ambiguity. A mass of jobs that crowd for your attention with no order apparent can jangle nerve endings without your knowing just what is causing that "restless" feeling. To people especially susceptible to this kind of stress, even relatively unimportant chores can be severely overloading.

Third, making priorities, an *activity* in itself, is a very seductive first step for those who would really rather not do all that hard work anyway. After all, who can complain about sitting down and playing a little game with pencil and paper? It beats cleaning out the garage, doesn't it? Then there's the listing of the items, the brainstorming of their significance, and all that arithmetic—why, what a delicious way of evading any real work. Too late they find that they have been caught. For once having come near to its siren call, most people find themselves doing what the PCM tells them to.

Fourth, the bottom of the list lets you know that it's okay *not* to do some tasks that your Puritan conscience tells you are important. This reduces guilt, that most inhibiting and unproductive of human emotions. It reminds you that *your* criteria are what's important, not your mother's, and considering those criteria it makes perfectly good sense to paint the walls of a room and leave the woodwork undone.

ALLOCATING YOUR TIME AND MONEY

When there's more to be done than *can* be done, the important thing is to spend your time and money where it will count the most. Your priority list provides a solid foundation for doing this. Here are the steps to take:

Step #1: Estimate the total amount of time and money you can spend on the entire batch of projects. Don't think incrementally at this point. Decide only how much of your resources you can and are willing to commit to the whole list.

Step #2: Estimate the cost of the top-priority project. The economic principle that underlies this method is powerful—priority should determine the *quality* with which the job will be done; do the top-priority jobs well, scrimp on the bottom. This is a deceptively simple notion. However, it can dramatically increase the benefit you receive from scarce time or money. Of course, if your resources are unlimited and you can satisfy all of your lesser wants and needs to the full, you needn't concern yourself with priorities. But few of us can do that. When there is not enough to go around, your choices are limited. You can opt to not choose at all and let your hard-won time and money dribble away. Or you can do *none* of the projects because you can't do all of them equally well. You can opt for perfection, use all of your resources to do *only one* superbly, eliminating the others. A better option, we propose, one that most people don't often use, is to budget time and money in a way that matches your previous priority judgments. We think the latter makes the most sense and we'll tell you why later. But first, here's an example of how this system for allocating your resources works.

Sara and Jack had created the following four-item priority list and now they were deciding what to do with it.

1. Wallpaper the living room.
2. Plant the rose garden.
3. Have the car undented and repainted.
4. Replace the worn-out sofa.

Prudence, and their bank balance, had convinced them that they could allot no more than $1,000 to these tasks in total, and that no more than three days of their precious annual vacation would be used to accomplish all the projects. Here's how their planning conference went:

Jack: Hon, I think we can wallpaper the living room ourselves. We'll only have to buy the paper—we can get the prepasted kind—and an inexpensive set of wallpapering tools. Since this is our hottest project, though, we should do it right and get the best paper we can.

Sara: Sounds good to me, and since it's our highest-priority item, we *really* want to do it right. We ought to scrub the walls and steam off the old wallpaper and spackle the cracks. That alone will take two days of our vacation.

Jack: Just a minute, let me write that down. Two days, and $200. That's a lot of time gone. But I think it's worth it.

Sara: How about the rose garden? We've been going on about that for an awfully long time, and it *is* second on the priority list.

Jack: True. But being second means it isn't first. If number one on the list rates a super job, number two rates whatever we can muster to do a decent job, maybe not terrific, but at least adequate.

Sara: "Adequate" sounds pretty mediocre to me.

(Long silence from both parties.)

Jack: Maybe we should wait until the garden becomes our number-one priority. Then we could give it the money and attention it deserves. Is a magnificent living room worth giving up the garden of our dreams?

Sara: Hold on, Jack, you're getting us sidetracked again. We went all through this when we set our priorities, didn't we? That was too much like work to waste it.

Jack: Well, there's my old war wound.

Sara: What?

Jack: My old war injury. Remember how I strained my back lifting the TV while that John Wayne movie was on? We're looking at a day or so of frantic digging. That means we'll have to hire the neighbor's kid to help us out.

Sara (taking control of the notepad now): Okay. But we can do the actual finish work ourselves. Let's figure about 50 bucks for digging. Then we'll have to run down and buy the roses. Twenty bushes will run about $200. Can we put them in in about six hours?

Jack (rubbing his back thoughtfully): Sure, with your muscle and my brains six hours should do it.

Sara: All right! Now we've only got two more tasks on our list.

Jack: Yes, but we've also got less than a day left from our original three, and only 650 bucks in the kitty. Even if I knew how to do it and had the tools, I couldn't get the car done in that amount of time. And take another look at that sofa.

Sara: Now don't get ornery on me. We just need to proceed onward and downward.

Jack: You mean, apply the principle "the lower on the list, the lousier the job"? It doesn't sound very American, but if it gets the work done . . .

Sara: Okay, okay, let's split the effort. I'll ask around about cheapy body shops. Then I'll call till I find someone who'll do a quick and dirty job. That shouldn't take more than half a day.

Jack: You're on! I'll bet we can find a shop that will bang out the worst dents and slop on a coat of paint for $400. That leaves $150 to re-cover the sofa—more than enough.

Sara: You're joking!

Jack: Too low, huh?

Sara: By about 500 percent, I'd say. And with only a quarter of a day left on our schedule, I can't possibly do it myself. But I could buy a slipcover with that $150.

Jack: You mean one of those baggy things like your mother had?

Sara: Just shut up and take another look at the sofa, my friend. I don't like the idea, but with what I've got to spend, it'll have to do.

Let's recap how it all worked out for Sara and Jack.

They wound up with a resplendent living room that will keep its looks for a long time, and they finally have their rose garden. True, it was without some of the intriguing varieties they had seen in the wishbook catalogs, but it was there, *and* it could grow. Their formerly battered car is now respectable, at least from a distance. Although it may need another paint job in a year or two, it no longer draws snickers from passersby. The slipcover "needs a little tailoring"—that is, it looks just as baggy as Jack thought it would. But the eye is not offended by stuffing leaking from gaping wounds, and the "tacky" quality is gone. Before you decide that you could never put up with a barely presentable car and a baggy sofa, read a bit further about why we think this approach to the perennial budgeting puzzle works so well.

First, the method taps the strength of a fundamental reality of life known as *Pareto's Law.* This principle may irk some perfectionists, but it certainly seems to describe how the world really works. In essence, Pareto's Law says that in any endeavor, 20 percent of the effort produces 80 percent of the results. In an office of 100 people, it suggests that 20 employees are doing 80 percent of the work. Sound familiar? Even though $150.00 is only 20 percent of the total cost of a first-class reupholstering job, Sara and Jack realized much more than 20 percent of the satisfaction they were looking for—freedom from that awful "poor" feeling that hit them each time they spotted Augie the cat's handiwork. Whether the 20/80 split is always applicable, we have our doubts, but we've found the idea behind it to be true more often than not—*some* of a good thing can give you much of the psychic reward you're looking for. A few days in a nearby mountain retreat might never be as wonderful as two weeks in a tropical paradise, but those two days in the cabin can provide a much-needed interlude of fun and relaxation. And the added cost of tasting the romance of a tropic moon, that last 20 percent of fun and frolic, might seriously impede your ability to enjoy it.

Second, the method focuses your resources (time and money) on ends rather than means. Life can be full of seductions. A momentary urge, a shiny bauble, a fit of martyred anger, each can lead you to the rueful contemplation of time and money spent without satisfaction. For the greatest cost of that shiny new car you impulsively bought the day your neighbor drove by in his will not be tight money and possible financial hardship down the road. It will be the lost opportunity to get for yourself those things that you truly want.* Your glorious new car will lose its psychic luster as that tattered sofa in your dingy living room taunts you for another two years. For it was not the new car you most wanted, nor even to play "keep up" with the neighbors, it was relief from a sense of leading a shabby life. Had that been the question you put to your handy-dandy PCM, it would have shown you how best to get to it.

We have both experienced these scenarios ourselves and never found them pleasant. What we have discovered is this: It is only when we use the ends toward which we wish to go as guiding principles for allocating our resources that we at length gain deep and lasting satisfaction.

---

* Economists call this kind of cost "opportunity cost"—every expenditure of time or money has as its result some forgone opportunity. In other words, if you spend it here, you don't have it to spend there.

EXERCISES

1. In the spaces below, list five reasons why you would rather not use the Paired-Comparisons Method for priority setting; for example, "It seems too gimmicky," "Would take too much time."

1. _____

2. _____

3. _____

4. _____

5. _____

2. Having gotten that off your chest, in the spaces below write down five situations in which you have thought of tasks you want to do, or ought to do, but haven't; for example, "No room in my closet for new clothes—should have cleaned it out."

1. _____

2. _____

3. _____

4. _____

5. _____

3. Now, list five jobs that have been hanging fire for more than a year, but less than two years.

1. _____

2. _____

3. _____

4. _____

5. _____

4. Now list the five tasks that have come to your attention during the past six months that you'd like to get done "someday."

1. _____

2. _____

3. _____

4. _____

5. _____

5. You are now ready to prepare a list of jobs for prioritizing. Using lists 2, 3, and 4, which you've just completed, select no more than sixteen items for entry into your PCM. Choose equal numbers of items from each list if possible. If you only work on the oldest jobs, the newest ones soon get to be the guilty ogres sitting in the back of your mind. Don't worry about those that don't make it to the PCM list; eventually, they will, or they really aren't that worthwhile regardless of what your parents, neighbors, friends, or dog think. Prepare your list in the spaces below before transferring it to the blank PCM on pages 28–29. That way you can erase, cross out, and substitute without messing up the form itself.

1. _____

2. _____

3. _____

4. _____

5. _____

6. _____

7. _____

8. _____

9. _____

10. _____

11. _____

12. _____

13. _____

14. _____

15. _____

16. _____

6. In the spaces below, jot down three possible questions which you might put to your PCM. For example, "Which tasks, if done, will most relieve our feelings of overload?" "Which do we need to do first (so that we can get on to the next—we can't repaint the house till we've gotten rid of the pigeons)?"

Start off with the question that seems most important to you. However, you may find that you'll use more than one. For example, "First, which jobs will decrease the stress in the family?" followed by, "Which shall we start with?"

1. _____

2. _____

3. _____

7. Now, using the instructions that start with step 4 on page 16 complete your own PCM priority setter. We've provided two blank forms for your use. Feel free to draw a larger one if you need to, or to copy it.

8. Having completed your PCM, resist those strong impulses to get up and charge at the first task on your list. Instead, reward yourself for your effort, then post a copy of your priority list in a conspicuous place. It will remind you that a part of your next day off has been planned.

**PAIRED COMPARISONS
DECISION MATRIX**

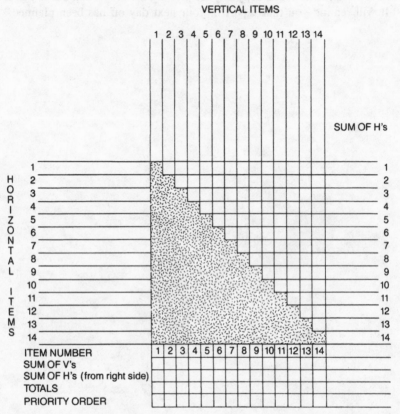

VERTICAL ITEMS

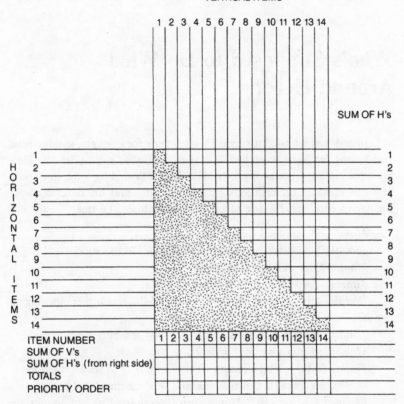

**PAIRED COMPARISONS
DECISION MATRIX**

CHAPTER 3

Who's Supposed to Do What Around Here?

Leonard was an alligator lizard with a taste for crickets, mealworms, and having his back scratched. His tour of duty as eight-year-old Timmy's pet included bouts of playful attention followed by long, dry spells between meals. Conversations between Timmy and his parents about Leonard's care and feeding often went something like this:

Mom: Did you feed Leonard, honey?
Timmy (busy with his stamp collection): He has food.
Mom: When did you feed him?
Timmy: Yesterday or this morning.
Dad (looking up over his newspaper): Well—was it *this* morning or not?
Timmy: I don't remember. But I know I fed him.
Mom: Did you give him water?
Timmy (after a long silence): Yeah—I think. I'm sure I must have.
Dad (voice rising): Get upstairs and feed Leonard right *now!*
Leonard (to himself): Hunger isn't enough—I've got to put up with shouting?
Timmy (clumping up the stairs, mumbling to himself): Nobody *ever* believes me around here.
Dad (to Mom): I *told* you who'd end up taking care of that damned lizard.

Sound familiar? No? Well, not everyone likes lizards. Perhaps this example will strike closer to home:

"I'm sick and tired of all the crap around here! *Especially,* I'm sick and tired of being the only one who cares!"

So saying, Joanna stalked out of the cluttered living room—leaving her husband Todd and their two children blinking in amazement—and stormed upstairs to soak away her resentment in a hot bath. As she settled with a sigh into the comforting, warm water, she tried to sort out her muddled feelings. How could she get so angry over a messed-up living room, she wondered, as the heat eased its way into her body. It wasn't as though Todd was a complete nothing when it came to doing chores. He made the breakfast toast every morning and helped clear the table afterward. He stacked dishes in the dishwasher at night and took willing part in handling the kids. What more could any wife expect? "It must be me," she announced to the empty bathroom. "I'm going through some kind of mid-life crisis—and not very gracefully either."

If you have guessed that both Leonard's dining schedule and Joanna's "illogical" resentment are but symptoms of deeper concerns, congratulations—you are acquiring the knack of looking beneath the hurt and into the heart of the problem. The actual villains are some seldom expressed, usually unresolved, and often invisible questions about how the family work is to be parceled out. Ignoring these miscreants is a sure cure for low blood pressure. In this chapter we'll look those querulous questions in the eye and lay out methods for answering them.

Before we begin, however, a few words to emphasize, once more, the urgency with which we have come to view the necessity for spouses, partners, lovers, and family members to deeply and fully understand what each expects of the other. In Chapter 1, we told you of the mutual disappointments that followed from our assumption that what each wanted from the other was obvious, having deftly floated into our minds on currents of love. The discovery, with the help of our own team-building consultant, that our assumptions of omniscience were as false as most such untested premises, was the starting place for the solid and satisfying relationship we've been working at ever since.

We rediscovered in our own home the same truths we had so often seen on the job: (1) If you don't tell others what you expect from them, you are likely to get what they expect from themselves; (2) When they fill their own expectations (or come close enough so that they can explain away their shortcomings) they feel smug—while you, on the other hand, feel disappointed because you expected something quite different from them—and (3) comments about unmet expectations delivered after the fact are potentially volatile—for your disappointment will add an accusatory edge to your voice—and in the aftermath of the explosion the accused will feel misunderstood, misjudged, and at length, misanthropic. There is no escape from these realities of interpersonal life. But there are ways to head off the resentment and bitterness that can result when they are disregarded, the very subject of this chapter—how to find out and understand what others expect from you, and what you can expect from them. Specifically, it arms you with some concrete methods and mechanisms for answering three very important questions:

1. "Who's supposed to do what around here?"
2. "Who can tell whom what to do?"
3. "How will we know if it's been well done?"

In short, we'll take a closer look at everyone's least favorite pastime: the art and science of getting things done around and about the house.

Who's Supposed to Do What . . .

Family roles have a way of changing with the times. Not too long ago the question "Who's responsible for what?" seldom needed asking. The father did (or knew that he was *not* doing) everything that fathers did: earn the daily bread, repair the house, act as the disciplinary "court of last resort," and generally pass on to the children the wisdom of the workaday world. Fathers were also characterized by what they *didn't* do. Breadwinners usually didn't cook the meals, and they certainly didn't clean the bathrooms. Mothers, of course, did "women's work" (or knew when they were not doing it). They cooked, cleaned, and cared for the children, and provided the moral support a husband needed to face the world and earn the living. They also passed on to the children the wisdom they had learned, most of it centered around what enhanced family values. The children did what they were told without question or discussion. The point is not that everyone did what they were supposed to do; in fact we are suggesting that they often did not. But they knew what was expected of them, and everyone had a rather clear notion as to whether or not it was done well.

Today we live in a time when these traditional family roles have been challenged. Not that the business of living has changed; it hasn't. Groceries must still be purchased, meals prepared, and bathrooms cleaned; but the once clearcut notion of who should do each of these tasks has been blurred by the impact of changing social values. While we are not always directly aware of it, we must all live within a vacuum of common understanding about just which roles are valid. If both of us are breadwinners, we must now decide for ourselves who bakes the bread—and cleans the crumbs from the table every night.

Most of us have tried to fill that vacuum with wonderful intentions, optimistic expectations, and high hopes that it will all work out. An approach, we suggest, that's sure to keep Joanna in her tub and Leonard looking for his dinner for a long, long time.

. . . And Who Tells Whom . . .

There is a moderately funny quip among management consultants to the effect that you can never go wrong telling clients that they simply lack the authority needed to carry out their assigned responsibilities. Harassed on all sides by second-guessing bosses and do-nothing subordinates, your clients will be amazed at how quickly you have gotten to the heart of the problem. To our chagrin, we discovered that this truism was equally true for family life. That is, we found little agreement among our troops on the important question of who could rightfully tell whom what to do.

As parents imbued with a pre-1960s view of family life, we simply *assumed* that the parents had all of the authority and the children had none. Not surprisingly, we found our own children—products of their own era—did not automatically share this view. We found, for instance, that they had the impertinence to believe that they should have some say about which television programs were to be watched. Similarly, they believed that they had a right to spend money that they had earned any way they wished, and that they could choose which kinds of foods they would eat, so long as they satisfied acceptable nutritional requirements.

The more we began looking at our assumptions about authority, the more interesting it became. We found that each child had a different idea about which things should be done and how, a lot of it depending, not unexpectedly, on whether they were big or little kids. For example, the younger children readily accepted the authority of the older ones when the parents were away, especially at night. The moment the parents stepped in the door, that authority vanished—at least in the eyes of the younger kids. Of course, people in a position of power—in this case, the older kids—are often loath to give it up. In such ambiguous situations, the stage is set for dictatorship-of-the-fist, anarchy, or other forms of family mayhem.

We handled this confused array of opinions in a way that some parents might think was radical itself: We negotiated agreements among all of us. Later in this chapter we'll describe just how we did it, but first, we'll address the question of how anyone knows when they've done a job well, poorly, or so-so. We'll start with the example of Maryann and Mom.

. . . When It's Well Done . . .

Envision thirteen-year-old Maryann picking up her room.

First she tosses her clothes onto a convenient chair. Then she dumps assorted school papers into a large box that sits on her unmade bed and kicks two-and-a-half pairs of shoes under her dresser. (The precise location of the last shoe will be left to a future generation of archaeologists.)

"I'm finished with my room, Mom," she calls on her way to the movies.

Ten minutes later dear Mom walks blithely into the room. How will she react to what she sees? Will she be angry? Will she be pleased? Or will her feelings fall somewhere in between? The answer all depends on Mom's expectations, on the standards of performance she has in mind. If Mom thinks "picking up your room" means getting most of the debris off of the floor and out of sight, she will feel quite contented. If, on the other hand, it means putting everything away in its place, making the bed, sweeping the floor, and dusting the furniture, she will be more than a bit annoyed. Our point is this. If Maryann clearly understands what Mom considers a "good job" and deliberately doesn't do it, then Mom's problem is one of discipline and enforcement. What's far more likely, however, is that Maryann was simply doing the job in a way that seemed perfectly okay to her. As we'll see, the cure for Mom's frustrated mumbling is an agreement with Maryann on just what a "well-picked-up room" really looks like. Simple as that sounds, it is the most likely step to be forgotten, or dismissed as obvious and unimportant.

In the rest of this chapter, we'll look at some ways to hammer out answers to the three essential questions we've posed: Who does what? Who tells whom? How do we know it's well done? The purpose of each of these methods is resolving—or better yet, preventing—problems of mismatched expectations. We'll start with a detailed look at the chore lists.

Right about now, you may be wondering if you really want to make a tiresome situation worse by organizing for family chores. After all, what makes a warm heart cool faster than hard-headed, concrete discussions about tasks and lists? We think you'll change your mind quickly once you realize that well-defined chore lists:*

1. Clear up ambiguities in roles and expectations.
2. State clearly what the job components are.
3. Tell everyone exactly when they must be performed.
4. Provide criteria for evaluating the jobs that must be done.

Chore lists are exactly what their name says they are: lists of the chores for which each family member is responsible. Their primary purpose, in fact, is to ensure that the necessary work of the household is done well enough to satisfy both practical needs (someplace to put today's garbage) and aesthetic values (escape from the aroma of yesterday's garbage). Here are some pointers that will help you get the most from your own chore lists.

Pointer #1: Write Them Down

Most people have better memories than your experience might lead you to think. The problem is, they all remember somewhat different things. In the emotional atmosphere that often surrounds assigning chores (why doesn't anyone ever volunteer to do the cat box?), memories of what was said are often distorted. We have found that the best way of preventing frayed tempers is to jot down the essence of what was said and display what you have written in a place particularly hard to avoid (ours was the refrigerator door). After a decent interval, file it, don't throw it away (turn to Chapter 8 to find out what to do when your overstuffed files explode).

Pointer #2: List Them All

It's tempting to list only the more significant or disagreeable tasks. We think, however, that it's better to err on the side of recording too much rather than too little. People tend to focus on what's written, and forget the myriad of other, lesser tasks that keep your ship afloat. It's

---

* In a work setting, we call these task lists. Their value, and the rules for doing a good job of writing them, are much the same as in the family setting. We have found managerial task lists and performance standards to be the single most valuable aid to improving the functioning of any organization.

important not to lose sight of the smaller jobs, because, as you'll see later, it is the *totality* of each member's portion of work that will be considered, as well as who has which particularly noxious job, in balancing out the work for fairness.

Pointer #3: Agree When the Chores Will Be Done

People often have very different ideas about when some things should be done. They do things at certain times for a variety of reasons: for their own convenience, for the convenience of others, or because the situation requires it. For example, on weekends George pauses for coffee at ten-thirty in the morning rather than ten o'clock because he prefers to get most of the morning's work done before the morning break. Sally would like to have her coffee at ten, but she waits for George so they can both have freshly made coffee. These arrangements work out beautifully as long as Sally and George understand *why* they have been made and agree that they're appropriate. If Sally didn't know about, or care about, George's special dislike of "taking a break" when half the morning's work remained, she would simply brew coffee at ten o'clock, the "proper time" for a break. At ten-thirty George would sip overheated, bitter coffee and feel aggrieved. While it may be obvious to you that the trash must be in the garbage cans on Tuesday because the refuse collectors come on Wednesday, it may not be as odorously obvious to others, especially younger children. It may suit their convenience to empty household trash containers when they think about it (never). Therefore, make sure everyone knows why things must be done on time, and publish the due dates with your list.

Pointer #4: Allow as Much Agreed-upon Leeway as Possible

If it is Bob's job to provide the dinner on Thursdays, does he have the option of bringing home a pizza in lieu of cooking? If so, what are the limitations, if any, to this option (cost, kind of food, etc.)? The answer to questions like these define the leeway, or latitude, the responsible person will have in completing a chore. We have found it advisable to build as much leeway as is practicable into every job. Permission to the doers to use a variety of methods adds interest to most jobs and gives them a measure of control over their fate. In addition, it says to them, "We understand your competence and respect your value as an important member of this family"—a message not often delivered but really appreciated when it is.

Pointer #5: Have Contingency Plans

Sometimes circumstances will prevent even the most dedicated family member from keeping his or her commitments. Unexpected illnesses, business or school trips, and weekend vacations all raise the question, "Who will do so-and-so's work while he or she isn't here?" The crisis of grumbles and sharp words so often precipitated by having to take on "someone else's work" can be prevented by a little forethought and a lot of "what-ifing." Our own family policy on "chore absences" wound up looking like this.

When someone must be gone or cannot otherwise do chores:

1. The absent person must take on three extra chores for two days before going or for three days after his return.
2. Except in the case of sudden illness, the responsible party must see that his or her chores will be done by other family members.
3. Any deals for future trade-offs (for example, one dog cleanup equals two cat box changes) must be written down to avoid future arguments.
4. If takers for chores cannot be found, report this to Mom or Dad for a nonnegotiable command decision.
5. Griping or complaining, or not doing the extra chores, will rate the same negative consequence as not doing your own original chores.

Specific contingency plans prevent the tendency of more responsible family members (namely Mom and Dad and singularly willing siblings) to do undone jobs themselves while resenting every minute of it.

Pointer #6: Be Specific and Concrete

The chore list's most important function is communication. While even the barest list can ensure that an important task will not be completely neglected, only specific, concrete, and detailed lists convey what a satisfactory completion of the task ought to look like. This is neither as simple nor as obvious as it seems. As consultants, we are often amazed (sometimes amused) at our otherwise capable clients' dependence upon vague and confusing terms—"coordinate" is a chief offender—to describe activities they assign to others. Invariably, the boss, the "coordinator," and the people who are "coordinated" had quite different conceptions of what that ubiquitous word means, and just as invariably they didn't know that they did. What was equally amazing (but not nearly so amusing) was the discovery that we were guilty of the same sin—using a general job description when a more specific one was needed. After all, as we justified to ourselves later, "they were such obvious and simple jobs." For example, everyone (we assumed) knew what "set the table" meant. We found out that it could mean any number of ways to put things on the table.

The dialogues went this way:

We (a half hour before dinnertime): You haven't set the table.

They: You didn't say how.

We (with a sigh): Put the plates around, and the silverware on, and napkins around the table.

We (ten minutes before dinnertime): You just piled everything on the table.

They (patiently): That's what you said to do.

We: That is not the way to set the table. You're supposed to give each person a knife, fork, spoon, plate, and napkin.

They: Oh.

We (at dinnertime): Where is the salt and pepper? Where are the glasses—and the milk?

They: I'm only supposed to set the table.

Our next try was better; it looked like this and it worked well.

To Set the Table Means the Following:

Lay out mats or tablecloth; check with Mom or Dad if these are not already on the table.

Lay out plates and silverware like this: (Sketch of our desired table setting was included).

Set out glasses.

Put milk on the table.

Put salt, pepper, or other seasonings in center of table.

Place a napkin to the left of each fork (check with Mom or Dad to see if company is coming and which napkins should be used).

You may, at times, find yourselves tempted to neglect the step of laying out your expectations in detail. You may see such kindergarten-teacher tactics—spell out so simple a task as setting the table?—as demeaning to your children. Besides, you may wonder, is it really worth the trouble, given the other important things you have to do? If such thoughts are crossing your minds, we proffer the conclusion that came echoing back to us as we noted our own whining complaints about partially set tables, intermittently and half-washed autos, and unfed pets. If detailed chore descriptions do nothing more than reduce your feelings of tired frustration ten minutes a day, they will be worth all the effort you put into them.

Pointer #7: Never Forget that Miscommunication Is the Rule

Most people, in spite of many stubbed psychic toes that should have disabused them, persist in believing in a number of communication fables. They are, therefore, often surprised when supposedly simple conversations produce more confusion than clarity. As reminders, here are six of the worst offenders. You can probably add a few more of your own.

Fable #1: People pay attention when you speak to them. (Some people are quite accomplished at looking very attentive while their minds are many miles away.)

Fable #2: People are paying attention when they say they're paying attention. (Everyone knows that the proper response to give, when you've just been asked "Are you paying attention?" is "Oh yes.")

Fable #3: Saying it over and over ensures understanding. (Attentive listening is the only thing that leads to understanding. Repetition discourages attentive listening on everyone's part.)

Fable #4: Saying it loudly over and over is even better. (A variation on Fable #3, it will only ensure that your neighbors will not have to strain so much to hear what's going on.)

Fable #5: Everyone will remember if it's important enough. (The question is, important enough to whom? While spouses, partners, and kids may or may not remember what you want *them* to do, they will nearly always remember what they want *you* to do.)

Fable #6: Hearing someone say "I know" means, in fact, that they do. ("I know" is a splendid tactic for ending an unwanted discussion. It ranks with "Are you through?" and "Can I go now?" as a surefire conversation stopper.)

Pointer #8: Use Chore Lists as Checklists

Chore lists can serve as substitute memories, or checklists. For younger children, especially, it's wise to provide a check-off space for the doer to mark when the task has been done. The status of the entire list may be taken in at a glance, and the checkoff itself gives one a certain sense of accomplishment. Above all, checklists can be potent stress relievers. Remember Leonard and his intermittent nutrition—a checklist would have relieved Timmy's memory strain, Mom and Dad's nervous twitches, and Leonard's digestion.

Pointer #9: Gain Commitment to the System

Small business owners often assume their employees share their own personal commitment to the business. They express surprise when their workers show more interest in the coming weekend than in improving product quality or customer relations. "How can they be satisfied with such careless work?" is a common refrain. Hearing ourselves make the same remark about our children's first efforts at chore completion helped us track down a major cause of our own "labor problems."

Just as a small business is created by a single entrepreneur (or several entrepreneurs in partnership), so a family is created by adults. Like all craftspersons who are proud of their handiwork, the family creators take pride in their creation. The adult, or parent, says, "This is my family," and thinks not only of a group of well-cared-for people, but of a little enterprise that may succeed or fail based on the efforts of the creators. While children, like employees, have great emotional and economic involvement with their "enterprise," they are *not* its creators. The fact of the matter is that except as it helps or hinders them personally, they seldom feel a proprietary "stake" in the success of the family enterprise. They *expect* their families to be there, ready to give them what they need, but providing for those needs is really someone else's business. In a small business that "someone else" is the proprietor. In the family enterprise, it is the parent.

Here are a few parental facts of life we had to learn before we could get down to the real business of de-stressing our havenly home:

1. Kids simply *don't care* about many things that are important to adults. Children who say, "Who cares which side of the knife the spoon goes on?" are not being impudent; that's exactly what they mean.

2. Most of the jobs kids do around the house have few intrinsic rewards. There simply are not many thrills in putting the dishes away or setting the table. Even superconscientious parents must admit that cleaning up after the dog is not most people's idea of an aesthetic experience.

3. Kids figure, and rightfully so, that your love is not conditional on their doing chores. Unwashed dishes may produce angry bellows, but when the ranting runs down, they assume that you'll still care for them just as much as before. The fact that your sense of losing the battle may make you harder to live with simply escapes their attention.

With these basic realizations, we freed our minds from such moralistic mutterings as, "Why do we have to remind them all the time?" We learned instead that what we really needed was a straightforward system of incentives ranging from a graduated set of highly prized rewards to a variety of negative consequences, our euphemism for punishments. Here is a list of rewards as it finally sat on our family bulletin board:

REWARD LIST

If chores are done willingly for:
1. One week, choose one from list A.
2. Two months, choose one from list B.
3. Four months, choose one from list C.
4. Six months, choose one from list D.

List A	List B	List C	List D
Large sundae at ice-cream parlor	Go to ball game	Trip to Great America theme park	Trip to Disneyland
Movie	Go to stage play, circus, etc.	New sweatsuit, ski pants, etc.	Large-cost equipment—e.g., down sleeping bag, musical instrument
Low-cost outing (picnic, kite flying, etc.)	New swim suit, jeans, etc.	Fishing trip on a party boat	

At the end of six months we all took a trip to Disneyland (a five-hundred-mile trek!) to celebrate: for the kids, six months of doing what didn't come naturally while swallowing grumbles; for the parents, five months (well, it took one month of hard work to get things going) of relief from nagging and tired disappointments.

Years of research have shown overwhelmingly that rewards and positive reinforcements shape behavior much more effectively than punishments. This does not mean, however, that there is no place in the havenly home for some of the latter. We prefer the term "negative consequences" instead of punishment because we believe it important to minimize the retributional aspect most of us associate with punishment. Perhaps the best way to think of it is to visualize your child literally traveling along a path. Positive reinforcements, praise for a job well done, for example, provide a boost and a renewal of energy, because they feed inner urges toward competence and recognition. Rewards (that trip to Disneyland, for example) provide a promise of fun that makes the effort worthwhile. But at times, rewards and reinforcements are not enough to keep your child from stumbling off the path and, more importantly, to ensure that he *knows* when he has gone astray. Negative consequences, therefore, are the "bumps" on the shoulder of the road, the rough terrain that signals that your child has wandered from, or run from, the desired (by you) track. In addition, they provide a means for canceling out transgressions and so set the stage for a new try at virtue. Finally, they provide a nondestructive way to dissipate offenders' guilt and parents' anger, which might otherwise interfere with turning over a new leaf.

Here, then, are some ground rules for using negative consequences in a positive way. We have drawn them from research carried out in children's institutions and with problem employees, and from our own experience as parents.

1. Negative consequences should irritate rather than hurt. If consequences are too painful, the receiver will think more about avoiding punishment than getting on with the job at hand. Besides, really tough punishments are hard to enforce. Most of us are reluctant to impose anything truly painful on our children, and deferred or watered-down penalties confuse recipients and donors alike.

2. Negative consequences should follow from unwanted behavior; unless doing so is completely ludicrous, they should have an invariable quality. For example, if Laura leaves the house on Saturday before vacuuming her room, she should be "doomed" and know it. Sure, the gang had unexpectedly dropped by to pick her up, from Laura's point of view a quite compelling reason. It ought not, however, mitigate whatever negative consequence might apply. By all means, take the time for a later conversation with Laura about how she might have handled the situation in a more responsible way. Remember, the meaning of negative consequence should always be, "You have slipped in carrying out your end of the bargain—pay attention!"

3. Don't confuse negative consequences with denied rewards. Think

of young Randy, whose family has worked out a system of rewards for tasks done willingly and monetary fines for tasks not done at all. Assume that one morning Randy forgot to take out the trash. "Fifty cents down the drain," Randy groans that afternoon as he drops his quarters in the fine box. Then with a shrug and a whistle he hustles the very full garbage can back out of the door without complaint. Without doubt, the fine was fair and Randy knew it. However, having paid it, he should not lose his place in line for future rewards. Remember, negative consequences should not stop forward progress, merely steer you back on the path. If Randy had been told, "You've slipped, so no weekend trip for you," he would simply lose interest in following the path at all, his attention turned to figuring ways to beat the system. The underlying principle is this: Negative consequences should work *with* the reward system so that living up to agreed-upon obligations becomes the most desirable alternative, and certainly the path of least resistance. While negative consequences should be predictable, fair, and administered with a firm, even hand, none of these qualities call for a solemn or sour-faced approach; humor helps a lot. The following announcement, conspicuously posted on our bulletin board, occasioned rueful smiles and an immediately improved appearance in the most lived-in rooms of our house. (It's hard to believe that a five-cent fine would deter anyone from anything, but in preinflation 1978, a nickel was still 20 percent of a weekly allowance.)

NOTICE: Effective June 5, 1978

From this day forward, be it known that a money fine in the following amounts shall be levied for each infraction:

Dirty socks left in the family room or living room .... 5¢/sock

Shoes left in family room or living room .... 5¢/shoe

School books, bags, etc., left by front door 15 minutes
after you are home .... 5¢/item

Dirty glasses, plates, etc., not returned to kitchen, rinsed out,
and put in sink .... 10¢/item

Pots used to cook snacks not rinsed and put in sink .... 10¢/item

This order signed by THE HOUSEHOLD ADMINISTRATOR, Susan J. Bramson

The first principle for successful fining is this: Never levy fines that you can't or won't collect. This means that they should be collected on the spot or as soon as possible after they've been earned. If you don't insist that the coins be immediately dropped in the fine box, you may later be tempted to forgive and forget, especially if the culprit looks penitent or loving, or both. Uncollected fines undermine the system and leave everyone uneasy and confused. Remember, it's the matter-of-fact inevitability of the whole business that does the job. Agreements to "withhold" fines from allowances or future bank deposits have additional drawbacks. By the time next month arrives, the penalty will be so far removed from the infraction that it will not make much sense to anyone. Similarly, inordinately high fines not only have the above collection problems, but they violate the first principle we proposed and motivate the child to concentrate on avoiding the punishment instead of completing the job as scheduled.

While rewards keep your eyes fixed on where you're going, a few properly placed "well dones" will make you feel good about staying on the path that gets you there. Best of all, they can work on both a thinking and an emotional level. If I say, "You did it just the way I hoped you would," I've told you that you have met my expectations for the task *and* I've given you an emotional "stroke" for your effort. Both will encourage you to do again what worked so well for you before.

As effective as it is in influencing others to continue doing what you want them to do, this raises some important questions. If you reinforce your child's behavior with praise and hugs and kisses, aren't you confusing the expression of bedrock parental love with approval or disapproval of specific actions? And if that's true, wouldn't such planned shows of affection amount to manipulating another person to achieve your goals?

To many conscientious parents these are not idle questions.

Perhaps the best way to answer them is to point out a few of the things we know about human beings in general, and families in particular. First of all, we doubt, as practicing consultants, that the reinforcement alone can influence anyone to do anything he or she doesn't already truly want to do. This is because the *power* of reinforcement, as the name implies, comes from the reinforcement of an *existing* motivation. Secondly, parents, with rare exceptions, have the best interests of their children at heart. Reinforcing affection, then, is merely an extension (and a positive one, too, we think) of parental love. The crux of the

issue really ought to be, "Is the end result something everyone understands and agrees upon and is it beneficial?" If it is, and the parent *also*
achieves a happier state of mind from the outcome, then the methods
used are not only ethical, but highly recommended as proper acts between loving people.

There is another issue surrounding positive reinforcement that is of
equal concern. That is the question of well-intended but unearned
praise. Here's an example.

> *Paul:* Okay, Mom. I'm finished with the dishes!
>
> *Mom* (entering the room, to herself): *Ye gods—look at this mess!
> He calls this finishing the dishes? The pots are still on the stove and the
> counters haven't been wiped and . . . Still, he did work in the yard
> most of the day. . . .* Well, Paul, it certainly looks like you did a lot
> of work. I bet you're tired from working on the lawn today.
>
> *Paul: Here it comes. Off to bed with no TV.*
>
> *Mom* (giving him a kiss and picking up the dishcloth): This looks
> just fine. Why don't you go out and watch your show now?
>
> *Paul:* Thanks, Mom. See you later. *Who is she kidding? I did a
> fifteen-minute job in eleven seconds flat. What's going on here? Maybe
> I've been overdoing this kitchen thing in the past. I hope I'm not this
> dumb with my kids.*

As you can see, while hoping to do the best, Mom couldn't have done
much worse. Now Paul has not only lost respect for the value of the
task, but he is genuinely confused over what the standards for his work
ought to be. What's more, the value of Mom's reinforcements in the
future will be weighed against two factors, at least in Paul's mind: (1)
"Is Mom really much of a judge of my work?" and (2) "Why should I
value praise for work that I know to be substandard?"

Like it or not, and whether or not we know it's happening, everyone
in the family is actually reinforcing everyone else all the time. The
trouble is, we may be reinforcing just the behavior we don't like.

Understanding the way that the reinforcement process works can
help you to make sense of some otherwise puzzling and highly frustrating situations. The essence of reinforcement is simplicity itself: When
something nice is experienced, it almost automatically ensures the repetition of the behavior that just preceded whatever it was that felt good.
For example, dog owners often bring about a curious sequence of events
that tends to hammer in the behavior that the owner is trying to pre-

vent. Picture Charlie trying to train his dog Fido to stop jumping on any available human. Fido starts the sequence by jumping up on Charlie, muddying his clothes, and being a general nuisance. Charlie responds with an angry "Stop it, Fido!" and pushes his eager dog down with his hands. Has Fido been discouraged from jumping up in the future? Not at all. He has just been treated to a caress from his owner's hands—always a huge satisfier to dogs. To make it worse (for Charlie, that is), Fido heard his name shouted with enthusiastic volume, an unquestioned reward for animals with limited vocabularies. Unfortunately, it works the same way with human beings—of any age. Let's take a look at little Johnny, bored and, at the moment, in need of a little attention.

First, Johnny tips his little sister Jennie's carefully arranged tea set onto the floor. Immediately, his boredom has been triumphantly assuaged: satisfier number one. Next, Jennie cries and screams for Momma, leaving Johnny feeling superior and strong. So far, he is two-for-two for satisfiers. Enter Momma, having been forcefully "summoned" by Johnny's action: satisfier number three. If Momma spanks him, the slap may sting for a moment, but—and especially if she has had to restrain or hold onto Johnny to whack him—a mother's touch is ever a potent satisfier. Even the angry lecture on "kindness to those smaller than yourself" is a winner—for Johnny, not Momma. Wasn't she attending to him, not Jennie? Who could ask for more?

At first glance, Momma seems to be in an impossible situation. If she ignores what happened, little Jennie will feel unprotected and justifiably insecure. Worse, Johnny may be forced to escalate his attention-getting actions to get the satisfiers he wants. Has Mom no recourse but to go outside and kick the dog (thereupon reinforcing whatever it was the dog was doing just before being kicked)?

Well, it *is* a rather tricky situation. However, if you will keep in mind four reinforcement rules, you should be able to avoid unwitting complicity in fueling your own frustrations.

Reinforcement Rule #1: When Disagreeable Behavior Persists, Look for Unplanned Reinforcers

When your best efforts at stopping some disagreeable behavior in yourself or another haven't been successful, take a moment to think through the sequence of events. What happens immediately after the behavior you are trying to stop? Try to identify any subtle satisfiers that have found their way into your own reactions to the behavior. Remember to look at it from everyone's standpoint—yours, the dog's, and Johnny's.

Reinforcement Rule #2: Use Reinforcements Judiciously

For a variety of reasons—some of them not clearly understood—a little reinforcement goes a long way. Experience shows that it's better to recognize a job well done at a few right moments than to lay down a continuous or consistent barrage of hopeful reinforcements. In other words, it works better to say, "It is great when you do your chores without complaining," every once in a while, than it does to say it every day. Similarly, vary your targets for praise. Being told you have done a superlative job of sweeping up loses interest rather quickly.

Reinforcement Rule #3: Reinforce Any Movement in the Right Direction

Even when the person whose behavior you hope to modify seems to show little progress, look for *any* positive step and reinforce it. For example, if Nan has yet to wash the car properly but *has* endured your careful explanation of what's required, you might say, "I'm really pleased you heard me all the way through this time," or "I think you've really listened to me this time; let's have a cookie and you can tell me what you think about it." If nothing else, this rule gives you something to do other than fret and fume.

Reinforcement Rule #4: Don't Confuse Rewards and Reinforcements

So far, we have discussed rewards and reinforcements separately, as if they were mutually exclusive ways of influencing behavior. This most definitely is not the case. Rewards, especially interim rewards, have a powerful reinforcing effect, and satisfiers such as those we've been describing can become rewards in themselves. The difference is that rewards ought to be attached to *achievement,* to the successful completion of the task, while reinforcements should be aimed at *efforts taken toward that achievement.* For example, Charlie should be commended for remembering that he forgot to do his chore last week (definitely a move in the right direction, albeit a small one), but a reward for having done the chore without reminder should be denied him.

Building Skills Through Delegation

The family's work system can provide a splendid opportunity for developing hidden talents and expanding everyone's horizons. Many husbands, for example, brought up with the traditional assumption that "wives do the cooking," have discovered latent abilities as *chef de cuisine* when finally pressed into the kitchen because of Mom's absence or illness. But you don't have to wait for such special circumstances for this to happen. Consciously plan a program for broadening the family's "coping powers" by switching or alternating tasks. Those with little cooking skills might begin by slicing vegetables or following simple, packaged recipes until confidence is gained. Having a different family member prepare a meal once a month or once a week not only gives the regular cook a break, but increases the household skills of everyone involved. What was once "black magic," or a dreaded chore, might even turn out to be fun. Up to now, at least, no one in our house has succumbed as a result of father's cooking, though they may have become a little tired of hearing him brag about it.

Up to this point we have been concerned with assigning tasks in a way that minimizes family struggles and provides for an equitable distribution of all the work. Although we have suggested ways for listing chores clearly, and defining what is to be done and when, we have not yet addressed the sticky question of *how well* those chores should be done. This most common source of all family disappointments will be discussed in the remaining pages of this chapter.

PERFORMANCE STANDARDS: YARDSTICKS FOR JOBS WELL DONE

Most work takes place in a vacuum.

This vacuum is formed when a subordinate starts off to do a job without any clear idea of what constitutes "poor," "average," or "superior" performance. This is not to say that the employee doesn't have his or her own ideas about what constitutes a job well done, or that the supervisor is without standards either. The problem—the vacuum of mismatched expectations—occurs when there is no communication between subordinate and supervisor about which standards will prevail for a given job. It's a vacuum that is very much worth filling.

In a family setting the conversation might go something like this:

> *Dad:* Young man, why didn't you clean up your room?
>
> *Billy:* But Dad, I *did* clean up my room. Look—the stuff's off the floor and my bed is made and my things are in the closet.
>
> *Dad:* Billy, the stuff is off the floor because it's been kicked under your bed. Your bed has *not* been made, you just pulled the covers up to the headboard. And your clothes are in your closet all right, but not on their hangers. You call that a clean room?
>
> *Billy* (quiet for a moment): I *thought* it was clean.

If Dad isn't sidetracked by his conviction that "anybody" ought to know what a clean room is like, he now has a great opportunity to show Billy just what a clean room means to him. He can, in effect, *set standards* that will move the clean-room controversy out of the vacuum of subjective guesswork into the realm of a self-policing chore that has an observable, mutually agreed upon outcome.

Here are some fundamental principles to help you achieve this kind of result.

While any standards are better than none, those that show gradations in performance are vastly preferred. Why? Because standards that focus only on do's and don'ts tend to assume the only choice is compliance or noncompliance. That is, they accuse the doer of mediocre intentions from the outset, discourage initiative, and make visualizing a really good job almost impossible. Try instead to communicate what a poor (unsatisfactory), okay (satisfactory), and superior job actually looks like.

Remember, performance standards are communication tools used to synchronize expectations. Their value does not depend on finding the "right" way to do something, or even the "best" way, but rather the way in which the person judging the work believes it should be done. Try to keep this perspective in mind, since it may help you accept another person's criteria without suffering a blow to ego or self-worth. It certainly served one couple well in solving this very problem:

> Janis and Roger had agreed that three nights of the week Roger would be responsible for cleaning up the kitchen. The morning after Roger's first cleanup night, however, an argument broke out that

threatened to scuttle their efforts to equalize the household responsibilities. Janis took Roger to the sink and grimly pointed to three rather "scudgy" pans left soaking in the water. He countered by ticking off with offended vehemence what he'd done. He'd stashed the leftovers in the fridge, wiped off the countertops, loaded the dishwasher, and cleaned up any major spills. That, he sanctimoniously pointed out, was what he had been required to do when called upon for kitchen duty in his parents' house. "Mom used to say," quoted Roger, "that pans left soaking overnight are always easier to clean in the morning." He just assumed, naturally, that washing any uncleaned pans was a normal part of "getting ready for breakfast," a chore which was not on his list.

Luckily, Janis did not get hooked into "setting him straight." Instead, she allowed the truth of Mom's pronouncement. "But," she said, "I have a little different notion of what cleaning the kitchen really means." "For example?" Roger asked, and they were over the hump. Janis explained that to her, dishes in the sink, the dishwasher not turned on, and a spattered stove top all indicated a *poor* job of evening cleanup. An okay job, she said, would be everything Roger had done plus cleaning up the pots and pans. And anytime that all of this was done *plus* putting the scrubbed pans in their proper places, returning spices and other cooking ingredients to the shelves, and sweeping the kitchen floor, why then they both would know that an absolutely terrific job had been accomplished.

The next night Roger tried out the new system. He completed his list, including scrubbing the pans. Janis duly thanked him the next morning. The third night—their anniversary—saw spanking-clean countertops and a freshly swept floor. Janis showed her appreciation with a kiss and a back rub. She knew that a superior performance should always receive a superior reward.

These examples demonstrate something that studies of performance standards have convincingly shown: The more observable they are, the easier it is to hold others (or yourself) to achieving them.

For one thing, if something can be looked at, touched, or heard, there is simply less chance of disagreement. Dirty pans are either in the sink or they are not. Condiments have either been returned to the spice shelf or they have not. While our familiarity with them often leads us to think otherwise, agreement on the meaning of such terms as "neatness," "tidiness," or "properly," is much harder to come by (unless we first go through the same clearing of minds as Janis and Roger).

Descriptions of what constitutes poor, adequate, and superior performance needn't fill an encyclopedia. Several examples will usually do to communicate the quality level desired. You can always add more indicators if those you've originally selected don't seem to be enough. By starting out on the lean side you avoid wordiness (a sure cure for interest and attention) and unnecessary work. If you have left gaps, you will likely find out soon. For example, our initial performance standard for taking out the trash described only the okay level; there just didn't seem to be any way that a person could mess up such a simple task, or earn a medal for outstanding trash dumping.

We were soon disabused of that notion. For instance, it is quite possible to take out and empty the inside wastebaskets and then leave them sitting outside to keep the garbage cans from getting lonesome. Not quite as bad were the wastebaskets thrust through the front door so as to greet the next visitor with a bit of homey ambiance. Better, but still irritating, the kitchen wastebasket could be shoved back under the sink without its paper-bag liner, at times necessitating a quick run to the paper-bag drawer with a hand full of something wet and dripping.

At the next family meeting, indicators of these and other potential malfeasances were crammed into the poor-performance page (they were crammed in because we had not left room on the paper), and a standard for a superior performance was even suggested: searching for litter not yet placed in a wastebasket before taking it out for emptying.

To keep motivation up it's important not to take superior performance for granted; in other words, a better-than-all-right job ought to rate some special recognition. Sure, for some people knowledge of something done exceedingly well is sufficient reward. Others may enjoy doing things superbly because it gives them a greater sense of power or control. Some are even motivated chiefly by the desire to be helpful. These, however, are internal rewards, far more likely to be tapped by jobs that have been self-selected—not exactly the circumstance in most household work arrangements.* Their motivations need some carrots, or sticks, to carry them through, and these, at best, will be tied very closely to how well the jobs are done. Thus, inadequate performance

---

* Kids, even teenagers, are not likely to derive much intrinsic satisfaction from chores unless they are fun (for ours, cleaning up the yard was fun, cleaning up their rooms was not).

rates an appropriate negative consequence, while outstanding performance should deliver some special bonus. To do otherwise is to tell them that okay is all that counts with you.

NEGOTIATIONS ARE A FAMILY AFFAIR

As important as they are, chore lists and performance standards are not the only benefits derived from collaborative family planning. The process of participation and agreement itself can contribute enormously to the workability of the list and the quality of the standards achieved. Here's an approach to negotiating those agreements that can help motivate those doing the work while retaining control for those who must oversee their efforts.

Time Is of the Essence

First, always set a special time to discuss important family matters, especially if different viewpoints or emotional reactions are expected. Spontaneous conversations are informal and often fun, but the informality tolerates short attention spans and allows people to leave when they're tired of listening, when their feelings are hurt, or when they just want to show what they think of you. This is not the stuff from which great dialogues are made.

Establish an Agenda

Second, tell everyone involved what the meeting is about and where you hope to be when the dust has settled. For an initial planning session you will want to have achieved an equitable distribution of all the family's chores, an agreement on how the work will be done, and a clear understanding of what rewards and negative consequences the doers can expect for various levels of performance. If the family group will decide on certain points by voting or consensus, then make that ground rule clear. If one or both of you will finally decide that issue, make sure everyone understands that as well. Either way can work, depending on the maturity and the chronological and emotional makeup of the group, and your skill at leading meetings. But if you're unwilling to live with the group's consensus come what may, always choose the latter decision process. Acting as if the group were deciding, when you have kept last rights of refusal in your own hand, always ends in distrust.

Conduct the Family's Business in a Businesslike Meeting

Once the crowd has assembled, be prepared for hoots, groans, elaborate shows of disinterest, nervous fidgeting, and some well-thought-out excuses concerning other important things that need to be done. Listen calmly and remind everyone that you made an appointment two days ago to meet with them at this time, and then firmly tell them to shut up and sit down. Point out to them that this is probably the most important hour or two they will spend in a very long time (don't bat an eye when they hoot, smirk, or giggle).

Once the meeting has been convened, ask those who will be doing the jobs to describe them as they think they ought to be done. Have them include in their comments any equipment, tools, or other assistance they think they will need in those jobs, and any sort of authority over other members in the household they think they will need to fulfill their obligations. Expect some of the dears to seem completely disinterested in having anything more to say about it. They will acerbically aver, "Just tell me what you want me to do and I'll do it, but let's stop all this phony fooling around." Don't be lulled or intimidated into stopping. Remind them that when it comes time to actually do the tasks themselves, their interest may be keen. If some should persist in bowing out of the conversation, try not to panic. Calmly state that you interpret their lack of participation to signify complete agreement; that should get them back into the discussion. Whatever happens, do not allow anyone to leave the group before the negotiations have been completed (barring short recesses, of course, for personal necessities).

Other useful topics to bring up (if others do not do this for you) are when the tasks should be done; how the more unpleasant tasks should be apportioned so that the work load is distributed fairly; how the chores of an absent or sick family member should be handled; and of course, what the components of the reward system should be. Before everyone scrambles off after the meeting, be sure you review your notes and obtain everyone's agreement that you captured the essence of the discussion accurately.

When the family meeting is over, hold an "executive session" with your spouse or significant other (or any other mature person who will be a supervisor over subsequent activities) and review the results of the meeting. The goal of this session is to identify any problems that may be expected in implementing any of the proposals. For example, your teenagers may have cavalierly proposed buying a $350 minitractor to dig out next year's garden in your ten-by-ten-foot yard. Or the reward system everyone voted for in the heat of the moment may actually be too rich for the family exchequer. Or you may simply believe that assigning lawn-mowing duty to six-year-old Debbie instead of her fifteen-year-old football-playing brother is an improper use of resources.

The final negotiation step is an important second family meeting at which you'll work out any differences between the initial proposals and the modified executive plan. Make it clear from the beginning that where possible, compromises will be sought, but final say for all arrangements rests with the adult(s). The care you've taken to involve the children in this process, your demonstrated desire to listen to and learn from their opinions, will make the final plan reasonably acceptable to them (in Chapter 4 we'll differentiate between accepting it and liking it) and thus ease its implementation. You should reassure them, too, that although the plan has been solidified, it has not been set in concrete. Changes can and will be made if what's been decided proves to be infeasible, undesirable, or unfair. *But,* let them know that everyone, including you, will be held to whatever is written down and posted until it is changed and rewritten. We were reminded of this when our complaint about something improperly done was greeted by a chorus of "But it's not in writing!" Our responses were two immense grins; the system was at last accepted by those who had to live with it.

Prepare to Repair

Professor of Management Leonard Sayles has said that the job of any executive is to develop foolproof systems for getting things done through others, only to endure having to repair them when they don't work—for over time they surely will break down. When they do, your response should not be disappointment, but a kind of spit-on-the-hands optimism that things can and will be repaired. Unfortunately, a sad fact of family work life is that corroding systems don't announce their demise; they creep up on you. One bleak day you'll notice that you've begun (again) to turn a deaf ear to your partner's pleading about a task not yet done, or you'll hear your kids bickering over who's "really" responsible for the cat box, and you'll realize that the chore lists are hopelessly outmoded. By inches, not miles, the family's previous predicament has reappeared.

But your reaction at that time will be different than it would have been before you found your havenly home. Instead of reaching for a belt (in either sense of the word), you will reach for this book, review the pertinent sections for luck, and then simply schedule another family meeting. You will resuscitate all of the successes of the past, and out of them will rise, phoenixlike, a rejuvenated system built on the ashes of the last.

But one that's better suited to the changed needs of growing kids and wiser—if a bit more tired—parents.

A book like this is designed to touch upon a variety of techniques and methods. If we have implied, through the necessity of keeping our explanations and examples short and to the point, that putting them into place is always easy and straightforward, we can assure you that it was not that way for us. Family work contracts deal with important issues. Working your way through such matters with those for whom you deeply care will always be an emotional pilgrimage. What's more, changes in attitudes or behavior take time, and the course is neither even nor smooth. At times, we let our wishes for an easy time of it lull us into forgetting this fact, and paid for it with very discouraging moments. When you encounter your own rough places, take solace from your conviction that you are on the right track. Keep in mind that persistence toward your goal, in and of itself, will engender a sense of control over a part of your life whose seeming triviality masks its potential for family tension. Remember, even a small measure of control will reduce your stress, leaving a bit of satisfaction and contentment in its place.

EXERCISES

Formats for Chore Listing

This page and the two pages that follow provide formats for getting started on family chore listing. If there are more than five in your family, exclusive of pets, you'll need to duplicate the form on a blank piece of paper. Also, if your handwriting is large, you may find it more convenient to enlarge the form at your local copy center—you have our permission to do so (only for use within your own family, of course.)

Use the form this way:

a. At the top of each page, enter the name of the doer of the chores.

b. In the "What" column list each chore separately. Be as specific and concrete as makes sense; e.g., "Feed cat and empty cat box" is better than "Take care of cat."

c. In the column to the right, insert the day or date by which the chore is to be done: e.g., "Wednesday" or "January 15."

d. You'll notice that the wide column on the right side of the page is divided into three parts headed "Poor," "Okay," and "Superior." To the right of each of the chores, in the "Poor" column, jot down one or two circumstances that will tell the chore doer that the chore has been done *poorly.* Think of past moments when you felt disappointed with a job that seemed sloppy or only half done. What were the particulars that caught your attention? For example, "Water dish not filled" or "Cat litter spilled on the floor."

e. Next, in the "Okay" column list the basic conditions of a minimally satisfactory job: e.g., "Food and water provided every day without reminder."

f. Finally, in the "Superior" column, write in one or two examples of what a top-notch job might look like. It may take a bit of thinking to identify those indicators of excellence, but they are invariably there. Here are a few examples: "Cat's food dish and water dish scrubbed once a week" (or day or month, depending upon how finicky you and your cat are); "Floor swept clean of spilled cat litter and mopped once a week."

If possible, all the adults in the household should share this job of preliminary chore listing. It is "preliminary" because these chore lists are the start of the negotiating process, not the end of it. Your next step will be to organize a family meeting, display what you've worked up here (you may wish to make enough copies for each member of the family), and keep the discussion going. Explain the reasons behind every entry you've made, but accept modifications unless they really go against your grain. Remember, the goal is understanding and commitment, *not* rule by fiat. Then again, don't give up on high standards. No one is required to do anything more than the minimum—that's what "minimum" means—but if that's all that gets done, it should be clear that rewards and good feelings on your part may not be forthcoming.

CHORE LIST FOR _____

What	When	How		
		Poor	Okay	Superior

1. *What Negative Consequences.* In the spaces below, list ten negative consequences that you can, and would, impose. Keep in mind your ability to weather temporary distress in your loved ones, the kinds of penalties that will have a sufficient "irritation" factor if consistently levied, and your own general standards of appropriate conduct, one human being to another.

_____

_____

_____

_____

_____

_____
_____
_____
_____

2. *What Rewards.* Suppose that each of those dears in your family willingly, and competently, fulfilled their chore responsibilities for the next six months. In the spaces below, list five activities, or things (remember it is they who are being rewarded, not you—you've had yours), that would adequately reflect their increased contribution to family harmony.

_____
_____
_____
_____
_____

3. *Questions to Keep You Honest About Yourself.* Most of us have magnificent intentions, which, somehow, never get put into action. The purpose of the next few questions is to help you recognize those areas in which your behavior doesn't quite come up to your own expectations. Don't panic, however, we will confine ourselves to matters relating to chores and chore listing. Each question will have two parts. Part A will ask you to state a belief or a feeling about some aspect of family life. Part B will then query you about whether what you do is consonant with what you say. You are on your honor *not* to read Part B before you've answered Part A.

1. Part A. Is your family more important than your job, or at least equally as important? Yes_____ No_____ Maybe_____

Part B. How well, in amount and quality, does the time you spend thinking, planning, and talking about how to improve family operations stack up compared to the time and effort you spend doing similar work on the job?

2. Part A. Do you believe that people should know when they've pleased someone important to them? Yes_____ No_____ Maybe_____

Part B. How many times during the last week have you told a member of your family about good feelings you've had from something he or she has done?

CHAPTER 4

Decisions, Decisions, Decisions: Deciding How to Decide

"They want me to manage the new branch in Seattle. What do you think? Should I say yes?"

"What's for dinner tonight, honey?"

"The new TVs have so many features. Which one should we buy?"

"Repaint? Shouldn't we *remodel* this dingy old kitchen?"

"But, Mom—*all* the other kids can be home after midnight!"

Decisions, decisions, decisions—large, small, and in between; easy or hard, boring or fun—they're the rocks and ripples in every family's stream of life. *Decisions* affect our control over what we will do or fail to do, how we will spend our time or money, and what sort of commitments we will make today that we will have to honor tomorrow.

Making decisions in any group is hard work. Making them stick afterward is sometimes even harder. This is especially true in a family where everyone cares about everything that happens.

Sometimes, to be sure, *decision evasion* seems to have been elevated to a high art form. Yet most of us could benefit from the steadiness that timely and effective decisions can bring to our complicated modern lives —lives that often seem to be moved by currents over which we have little control. The rub is that solid decision making takes time, and even a little thought, just the ingredients hardest to come by when life's alligators are nipping at the heels. The escape route from this paradoxical situation is to acquire some ploys and fancy moves that will turn the alligators into pussycats, exactly what this chapter sets out to do.

In it we present a number of tested methods that can help you to purposively toss off many decisions with little thought, reduce most others to manageable size, and give the truly important the attention they deserve. You will make these decisions more thoughtfully, too, with less emotional strain and far less worry about their workability. And you'll do it in a way that encourages, rather than discourages, the will to carry them out. Finally, you'll learn how to ease the way for those decisions that are as unpopular as they are necessary. You'll also see how the decision-making process itself can bring out hidden wishes or fears that may be blocking communications or commitment to family goals.

At this point we would not be at all surprised if a touch of skepticism had crept into your thinking: "Is all of this talk about how to make decisions really necessary, and even if it is, where do I get the time for it?" We promise to come back to these not unreasonable questions further into the chapter, but for now we ask that you withhold judgment for a time. Examine the ideas and methods on their merits, think about how you might use them, and then return with us to the question of whether they're your cup of tea.

While the goal of most decision aids is to simplify as much as possible, we need to start out by mucking things up a bit. (You'll see how this process actually streamlines things by the time we're finished.)

Right now take a second to think about how you *really* decide. For example, do you approach each problem using rational, building-block methods, or do you rely on quick intuition to help you cut through the fog? If intuition has worked for you in the past, are you loath to complicate things with a lot of paperwork and bother? If you pride yourself on structured, quantified decisions, do you wonder what good a lot of emotional handwringing will do for any situation? These are important questions to ask; they are especially valuable if they cause you to begin to question the way you habitually make decisions. Our view is that there's a place for both of these poles-apart approaches to making efficient, quality decisions.

Like family members themselves, decisions come in all shapes and sizes. Some are so riveting and important that they seize your attention from the outset; they deserve as many decision-making helps as you can bring to bear on them. Whether to follow your career star to that dislocating cross-country transfer is one example. Others seem almost trifling—white or whole wheat toast for breakfast, for instance—yet someone has to decide or there'll be no toast at all for breakfast. Other decisions, while not momentous, can cause the family machine to skip and sputter if they're ignored or improperly made—what colors to paint the living room comes to mind. To point out that each of these decisions must be attended to in some way is not to say that they deserve equal attention. Moving to another city changes the lives of everyone involved, while deciding on liver for tomorrow's dinner menu will only affect the rumblings of a few family stomachs. Without understanding and acceptance the losses in family harmony from a drastic move may far outweigh gains to the exchequer, while an unpopular menu item will cost no more than a few complaints and a momentary grouch. In other words, some decisions are major, others minor. Both kinds affect the workings of the family organization, both deserve the benefit of an appropriately made decision. But both do *not* require the same quality or kind of time and effort, a point at once obvious, yet often overlooked.

Because of the sheer diversity in the number and kinds of decisions, it pays high dividends to match the *way* a decision is made with its complexity and importance. In other words, the first and most profitable decision to be made is just how you're going to go about deciding. Here's why.

DECIDING HOW TO DECIDE

First, big and complex decisions ought to have a different approach from small and simple ones. The fascinating fact is that, left to their own devices, most people spend about equal amounts of time and attention on decisions of distinctly different importance. While all very human and understandable, this share-the-wealth practice shortchanges the big ones and wastes valuable time on the small. Deciding in what neighborhood to look for a new home simply doesn't deserve as much time and attention as a far more important question—whether or not one can, or ought to, buy a house at all. Quite improperly, otherwise sensible people will wrangle indefinitely over what color to paint the extra bedroom or whether they should have plastic or metal garbage cans. (We know a very busy couple who made a library survey of the comparative lasting qualities of plastic versus galvanized steel trash cans. We've suspected that such thoroughness may explain a good portion of their "busyness.") While such thorough deliberations do have a place, the plain fact is that most of us don't have a surplus of time with which to make decisions. And even if we did, would we want to spend it that way? It is the important decisions that *deserve* to be pondered, and with a quality of pondering that is as good as we can make it. But from what source do we squeeze the time and energy required? The obvious place to find these resources in an already full twenty-four-hour day is to take them from the decisions that don't really matter that much— that is, from the decisions where the *penalty* for a mistake or lack of acceptance by the implementers will not be quite as costly.

What is needed is a not too complicated approach to sorting out problems by size. We've found that dumping them into three categories nicely fills the bill. We've labeled them: *Big D, Middle D,* and *little d* decisions.

Big D's are those decisions which matter a lot. Middle D's matter some, but the world won't come to an end if a few wrong moves result. Little d's are those decisions that somehow must be disposed of so that daily life can unfold, but the penalty for a bad decision is irritation rather than trauma. You can assign any problem to its appropriate category by answering two questions about it: how serious are the consequences of this decision and how important is it that it be accepted by those concerned. The consequences question breaks down into three subordinate questions:

a. How much of your available resources will have to be committed?

b. How rough will it be to escape the troubled waters that a wrong decision could put you into?

c. How emotional is the matter to be decided to those most affected by it?

The meaning of acceptance is a bit more complicated. Acceptance, in this context, is an active willingness to help implement a decision that one might not have taken if only one's own wishes needed to be considered. While acceptance does not necessarily imply enthusiasm, it is more than simple compliance. Little Kimberly, who loves circuses but is lukewarm toward family picnics, having been told, "If you don't shut up about going to the circus, kid, we'll leave you home," might *comply* with the family's decision to picnic. Her grudging acquiescence, however, is not acceptance, as she would show you at every opportunity— from being late to treating the family to a tearful narrative of each of her discomforts on the long ride home. While an accepting Kimberly might *prefer* to be at the circus, she would balance in her own little mind such things as fairness, the possibilities of future favors for herself, and her wish to please her parents. She would not allow her disappointment today to prejudice her chances of future fun.

While the seriousness of a decision and its acceptability are logically related, in practice they represent two fundamentally different considerations, each with its own effect. It's very possible for a decision to be high in importance, that is, to have very serious consequences, yet be easy to implement once it's been made, and the opposite is equally true. For instance, you may puzzle long and agonizingly over how to invest your precious savings, but once the decision has been made, a phone call or trip to your local savings institution may be all that's required to consummate it. Whether the bank clerk or stockbroker feels right about what you're doing is inconsequential since their acceptance is not at all needed. In contrast, where the family chooses to go on its longed-for summer vacation is not likely to be a matter of great consequence. But if there is not at least a modicum of acceptance, a miserable time is likely for all, creative complaining being an art seemingly instinctive to children and not unknown in disgruntled adults. Putting acceptance aside, however, it doesn't really matter much whether it's two weeks among the pines or on the sand dunes, as long as it's somewhere away from the push and shove or the boredom of daily life.

Here are some examples of the "seriousness" and "acceptability" considerations that might turn up in thinking about some typical family decisions (see Figure 1):

We would rate A, B, and C decisions as Big D, Middle D, and little d, respectively. Here's a caution, however. Some decisions, when additional light is shed on them, become more or less serious than you originally believed they were. For example, a hairstyle discussion that provokes innuendo or sniping remarks from Dad may apprise all, and hopefully himself, that he does indeed equate orange hair with "rebellion." Hair then become an instant Middle D, or even Big D, decision. In other words, sometimes people care more about a decision than anyone thinks they ought to. Ignoring—or smoothing over—that depth of feeling may secure a superficial agreement at the price of future resistance.

Here are some examples of how we sorted out some of our own past decisions (see Figure 2). These examples, by the way, illustrate a quite common occurrence—one major decision often gives rise to a host of smaller decisions that, while not insignificant, are not of the same magnitude.

FIGURE 1

Problem	How Serious Are the Consequences	Is Acceptability Important
A. Should we spend $8,000 out of a $25,000 income to buy a new car?	Heavy budget impact, requiring major lifestyle changes. Entertainment, eating out, will be seriously curtailed; clothing budget cut in half. Nice-looking car means a lot to Dad. Loss of Dad's or Mom's job might mean forced sale of car.	Very important that everyone concerned would accept the need for strict budget controls. Any unplanned spending after the car purchase could put us in financial hot water.
B. Shall we take on another family pet?	One more "live body" in an already busy household. Could end up as another chore for Mom. Relatively moderate budget impact. Our family value system will preclude returning a disappointing pet to the seller or ASPCA.	Not every member of family wants another pet. Need clear commitment for pet care so Mom doesn't get stuck.
C. What kind of hairstyle should our teenage boys have?	Minor budget considerations. Mom and Dad don't really care about length, style, or color as long as it's neat and clean.	If boys choose style, they might be willing to be more careful about keeping neat.

FIGURE 2

Big D's	Middle D's	Little D's
Shall we go into business for ourselves?	When will we go into business?	What color should we use for our business cards?
	Where should our office be?	
	How much capital will we have to borrow to get started?	
Shall we have another child?	When should we have another child?	Which kind of disposable diapers should we use?
	To whom should we send announcements?	
	Who should be told verbally?	
	When and how should we tell the other children?	
Shall we buy a new home?	How much can we spend on the new house?	Should we look for houses on Saturdays or Sundays?
	Should we buy this house or another one?	
	What realtor should we use?	
What family-life philosophy should we apply to procuring material goods?	How much can we afford to spend for household appliances?	Should our appliances have a white or colored enamel finish?
	With our limited resources, shall we buy a new stove or a new washing machine?	
	What kind of stove shall we buy?	

Here is how we applied the "deciding how to decide" criteria to the first item on this decision list. We never doubted that going into business for ourselves was a Big D decision—the potential consequences to our economic life were great, and each of us needed to be fully committed to the effort. We knew there would be many times when resentments over budget pinches and working (rather than recreational) weekends could wring an "It's all your fault" from a lukewarm decision maker. Once both of us were fully committed to the Big D decision, the other choices, while important in their own right, didn't seem as earthshaking. Funding questions and office geography seemed clearly to be Middle D's, needing hours or days to consider, rather than months or years. Mistakes in assessing them, however, we did make, but the recriminations were far less severe knowing that our overall direction was the right one.

Having read this far in the chapter, we hope that you've brought yourselves up short with the realization that perhaps you've frittered away an inordinate amount of time on little d decisions. If so, console yourself with the knowledge that you have much company. Your friends do it. God knows your boss does it. Your parents and their parents did it. It is so common a human failing that *some* scheme for helping you resolutely turn away from spending a lot of time on those ubiquitous little d's is almost essential. True, some people are more prone than others to getting bogged down in a multiplicity of minor league decisions. But all of us can gain considerable amounts of thinking space by more efficient handling of own little d's. With some confidence, we can assure you that even a modicum of attention to the way you use your deciding time will help. Expect to slip at times. After all, arguing about inconsequential matters can be a pleasant pastime, a distraction from harsher realities; certainly, it is a habit of mind into which one can easily slip. What we predict is a sudden realization that you have just spent ten minutes discussing at which store to purchase some needed garden tools. You will then stop your conversation and dispose of the question with dispatch. The next few pages will describe a straightforward approach for doing just that.

MAKING BETTER LITTLE d DECISIONS

Remember, little d's are decisions which must be made but (1) are not very consequential in and of themselves, (2) do not rely on acceptance for their success, and (3) are not tied to any of the family's emotional triggers.

With this in mind, let's consider two rules of thumb:

1. Little d's should be made *intuitively, quickly,* and with a *minimum of discussion.*
2. Authority for making little d's should be clearly *delegated* to a single family member.

Here's an example of how these two rules worked for Cindy and Jim.

Cindy and Jim decided to devote a third of their small front yard to flowers. Although both of them liked a bit of color in the yard, neither cared particularly about gardening as a hobby. A first-rate, full-fledged formal garden, therefore, was not the objective (cross out Big D). How or where the flowers were planted didn't matter much either, so the decision wasn't even Middle D. For convenience's sake, they delegated to Cindy the job of deciding what kinds of flowers to plant and just where in the yard the garden would be. Armed with this understanding, she went to a local nursery and asked the nurseryman to assemble some inexpensive plants that would produce colorful flowers that would look well together. She accepted the nurseryman's recommendations, bought the flowers, and took them home. The next weekend, working under Cindy's direction, they planted the garden. While they worked and chatted, signs of doubt began creeping into Jim's conversation.

Jim: I didn't see any red blossoms on the packages. Hope we'll get some red flowers. Did I ever tell you how much I like the color red?

Cindy: The nurseryman said we'd get plenty of color, and I assumed that meant red as well. Besides, I thought we wanted "cheap" as well as "good."

Jim (after working awhile): Do you think we should have planted these closer to the fence? Maybe we should've analyzed the yard a little more before putting the garden in next to the wall. After all, a thing worth doing is worth doing right—

Cindy: Hold on, there, Lovey, I thought we decided this was a little d.

Jim: Well, I was only . . .

Cindy: I mean, we decided that this was a little d job, right? Planning the living room and dining room—those are Middle D's. We're going to lay everything out and plan it together, right after we finish this little chore. If we spend all our time getting this just right, we'll end up doing a slapdash job inside the house.

Jim: Yeah, I guess you're right. This outdoor stuff's for lumberjacks anyway. Let's just stick the rest of these in and spend the afternoon at the furniture store.

Cindy: You've got yourself a deal, sweetheart.

Of course, things don't always tie up in such neat packages. Halfway through the job Cindy herself might've discovered an unrecognized wish for a perfect garden, or Jim might have started sniping at Cindy about the dumb way she layed out the flower bed. Either event would call for a reclassification of the "garden affair" to a higher-level Middle D decision, starting a new cycle of events. With these later events in mind, Cindy and Jim could then have reviewed their paired-comparisons matrix (Chapter 2) to see if the garden job should indeed rank with the new living and dining room in priority. If so, they would schedule themselves for some serious planning. As it was, they enjoyed a satisfactory show of color in the spring, and the time saved by delegating the garden planning to Cindy was spent—with relish—planning, painting, and papering their favorite part of the house.

Delegate a Lot

As reasonable as all of this seems on the surface, we've found that it is all too easy to dump most decisions into the Middle D category. There are reasons why many choices seem to call up far more deliberation than they deserve. Foremost is the fact that decisions of any kind exercise power. They tell you what to do, when, and often how. Small wonder that they become—albeit much of the time unconsciously—convenient arenas for contests of wills. When the basic issue is "Who's really in charge here," trivial questions can evolve into long debates. Then, too, even minor decisions can be complicated. When Cindy arrived at the nursery, we can be sure that the number of choices facing her was immense; much time could have been spent selecting just the right kinds and colors of flowers. The important point to keep in mind, or to remind yourself of when you find you've slipped, is this: The distinction between little d's and Middle D's is *not* how *difficult* the decision is to make, but how great the consequences are of a poor decision. In a more obvious way, the motivation of the moment can add weight to a presumably minor decision. For instance, when you are hungry, where lunch should be eaten can take on major importance. Of course, if choosing the proper restaurant for lunch is the aesthetic high of the day for you, it may indeed be a Middle D and deserve to be treated as such. The point is, make it a conscious choice, otherwise what should be a quickie little d will blossom into weighty Middle D's.

When this oozing upward happens, be wary of your first impulse to simply chalk it up to forgetful human nature. Such slippage is always due to unclear or unconfirmed agreements about *who* has the job of deciding *what.* Once these basic delegations are made, the little d's can be handled with celerity and with confidence that they won't be second-guessed. Criteria to keep in mind in assigning responsibility for recurring kinds of decisions are:

— Individual talent, skill, and knowledge; quirks and "crazinesses."
— Who will be implementing the decision.
— Who has already been delegated what other kinds of decisions.
— Who has the most interest in the topic of the decision.

For example, we have delegated to Susan the task of deciding where we will eat lunch on those days in which our occupational paths cross at noon. Our considerations are these: We have about equal knowledge of the available luncheon places near our office; Susan's likes or dislikes for a particular kind of food are generally more pronounced than Bob's; and of course, Bob is such a sweet and wonderfully amiable person, always willing to follow Susan's inclinations.* Since these are little d delegations, they should be made quickly and without long discussion. Change them when it seems the thing to do, either permanently or on a "this once" basis, but do make the change explicitly. "You decide where to eat today" will suffice. Nondeciders ought to be free to throw any pertinent information into the hopper before the decision is made—e.g., "Nothing too spicy today, please." Once the person whose decision it is has majestically ruled, however, that ruling should stand, unless the consequences are an obvious physical or emotional bellyache. Otherwise, the whole point of defining decisions as little d is lost.

We are ready to turn our attention to Middle D decisions and some methods that we have found most helpful in making them.

* Susan: Read "always" as "sometimes."

IMPROVING MIDDLE D DECISIONS

Middle D decisions account for most of everyone's worrying time. They also provide the greatest opportunity for making better decisions and for feeling less doubt about them after you've made them. To understand this better, let's take a brief look at how most people approach the problem of solving problems.

The Leapers and the Lookers

Some years ago psychologist Egon Brunswick identified two basic approaches to solving problems (for the present we'll assume that problem solving and decision making are the same thing, though *problem solving* traditionally refers to finding solutions and *decision making* to choosing among them): Approach A, which we'll call the Leapers, and Approach B, which we'll call the Lookers.

Some Leap Before They Look. Leapers sometimes look, but it's usually over their shoulders, after the decision's made. Brunswick calls this the Intuitive Approach, wherein as soon as one looks at a situation, the solution leaps full blown into the mind. Instantaneously, the supercomputer in the brain has assessed the probabilities for the success of a number of possible alternatives and discarded all but the most likely. Unfortunately, these intuitive answers are seldom totally correct, even for the simplest of problems. On the other hand, such is the marvelous capacity of our minds to speedily integrate vast amounts of data that intuitive decisions are hardly ever way out of the ballpark either. This can be a source of both strength and irritation to the Lookers that Leapers often have to work with.

Some Look Before They Leap. Approach B, called the Calculating Method by Brunswick, is the one described in most books on how to make decisions. It's no surprise then that it is used mostly by those people who tend to think "by the book," namely engineers, accountants, auditors, and other analytic thinkers (we'll say more about Styles of Thinking in Chapter 6). When the Calculating Method is in play, one identifies the elements of a problem, searches for a proper method or formula, and applies that formula to the facts in the case. Hardheaded, concrete thinkers will try to tell you that the Calculating Method is clearly superior. This nettles Leapers, mostly because the Lookers are right much of the time. When all the data are known, when they have been accurately measured, when the formulas involved are relevant, then—and only then—those carefully calculated solutions are right on the money. However, although Lookers are often oblivious to it, if those facts are sketchy and the data hard to pin down, calculated decisions will not only be wrong, they will be *disastrously* wrong.

The best answer to this damned-if-you-do/damned-if-you-don't situation is the obvious one. When you need a rapid decision that will not be so wrong as to be disastrous, Leapers are your people. When most relevant facts about a problem can be nailed down, turn to those calculating Lookers.

Before you do this, however, you've got to know enough about your problem to see which method best applies. To find out you need ask yourself only the following three questions:

1. Do I know (or can I find out) most of the relevant facts?
2. Can the relevant facts be measured (or at least reliably estimated)?
3. Do I know of an existing method or formula that can solve this kind of problem?

Here's how these three questions can be applied to a pair of apparently similar (but actually very different) everyday problems.

PROBLEM #1:
My brother is having a family brunch at 10 A.M. He lives on the outskirts of Detroit. If I leave my home in downtown Chicago at 4:30 A.M., will I arrive on time?

ANALYSIS:
a. *Are all the relevant facts available?* They appear to be. I know the distance from my house in Chicago to my brother's home in Detroit. At 4:30 A.M. the traffic will be light, and should not delay me. I can assume I will travel at the posted speed limits all the way.
b. *Can the facts be measured?* Yes, I know the distance in miles and the speed my automobile will travel.
c. *Do I know an appropriate formula to apply to these facts?* Yes, the total time for the trip will equal the distance traveled divided by my rate of speed. Add the time spent en route to my time of departure, and I have computed my arrival time.

PROBLEM #2:
Gram is having Christmas Eve dinner for the whole family at her

ranch 250 miles away. If we leave when I finish work at the office, will we arrive on time?

ANALYSIS:

a. *Are all the relevant facts available?* No. While we know the distances to be traveled, we don't know just when I'll finish at the office; if Mom and the kids will be ready to go when I come by to pick them up; what moods they will be in, what the traffic will be like; and what we'll have forgotten because we rushed and then will have to go back for.

b. *Can the facts be measured?* No. We could reliably guesstimate our theoretical speed, but we can't determine the time our trip will begin, or how much we might be delayed by last-minute phone calls or bickering kids.

c. *Do we know the correct formula?* Are you kidding? What's the formula for figuring out how long it will take cranky kids to get ready for an overnight trip?

These two problems demonstrate a fundamental difficulty with both the Intuitive and Calculating methods. Leapers will confidently rely on their own past experiences to estimate their answer to problem #1, even though that past experience was based upon different times of day or alternate departure points in the city. While they probably won't miss their guess by over an hour or so, they might just be late or early enough to be an embarrassment to their hosts. Lookers, on the other hand, just *know* that the Time = Distance ÷ Speed formula always works, and will insist on applying it to problem #2 regardless of the holes in their data. They risk missing their target by a mile.

Perhaps we've convinced you now that you ought to apply both the Calculating and Intuitive methods in a way that gets the best out of both. We'll show you some of the ways to do this in the pages that follow. They've helped us reduce both Leapers' leaps of fancy and Lookers' "analysis paralysis" long enough to make some sound, important decisions. We call the first of these wise and friendly methods the:

Weight-Rate Decision Maker

At first blush, the Weight-Rate Decision Maker (W-RDM) may seem like a lot of busywork. If you've already leaped to this conclusion just from its name, a word of caution. Similar techniques have saved innumerable companies from disastrously bad investments. You can't afford to waste a hunk of your monthly income any more than General Motors can. We ask you, too, to remember the motivating effect of the Paired-Comparisons Matrix and to bear with us a little longer. The reward will be worth the wait.

The basic purpose of the W-R method is to dissect a large decision into its more easily handled manageable components before building it back up again to its proper size. Let's explore this method by showing you how we applied it to an actual decision with which we were faced— the purchase of a microwave oven.

To begin with, the Big D portion of the decision—did we want to give up our traditional way of cooking with genuine "hot heat" that one could feel and see?—was years in the making. It was interconnected with some fundamental values held by both of us that transformed a simple cost-benefit question into an emotion-laden issue. When we finally decided the answer was *yes*, we were faced with a less weighty but more complicated decision: which brand to buy. We perused the advertising literature and saw a number of models demonstrated, but we were still unsure which one would be right for us. Brought to a halt and starting to bicker, we were struck by the same thought. How about using the great Weight-Rate Decision Maker? In twenty minutes we had jotted down the essential criteria, taken it with us to the appliance store, and half an hour later we emerged with a microwave oven that has served us admirably ever since. We'll refer to our completed W-R Decision Maker as we walk you through each step we made. Two points before we start:

— If you are a Leaper by nature, the sight of so many numbers all in a row may set your teeth on edge. As two kindred spirits, we urge you not to skip ahead to more compatible fare, for it is such as you and we that need those numbers the most.

— If you can contain your impulse to dismiss this bit of method with "What a lot of fuss and bother—why take all the fun out of everything?" and stay with us, you'll find that each step is itself quite easy to do. The process has five separate steps: identifying important criteria; weighting the criteria; selecting and rating alternatives; multiplying weight times rate scores; and totaling the scores. In the following pages we'll first describe each step and then show how we applied it to our microwave purchase problem.

FIGURE 3

FACTOR	LEVEL OF IMPORTANCE	WEIGHT	Product A RATE	TOTAL	Product B RATE	TOTAL	Product C RATE	TOTAL	Product D RATE	TOTAL
Ease of Cleaning	High	10 ×	4 =	40	9 =	90	9 =	90	7 =	70
Feeling of Control Over the Monster	Medium High	8 ×	7 =	56	9 =	72	7 =	56	7 =	56
Need for Attention While Cooking	Medium	5 ×	7 =	35	7 =	35	9 =	45	9 =	45
Adequacy of Warranty	High	9 ×	5 =	45	9 =	81	9 =	81	9 =	81
Reasonableness of Cost	Low	3 ×	6 =	18	9 =	27	5 =	15	6 =	18
				194		305		287		270

W-R Step #1: Identify the criteria. Your first order of business is to identify which of the many factors that *might* affect your decision are worth considering at all. Oddly enough, this step—while crucial to an informed decision with or without the W-R method—is often skipped by all but the most patient decision makers. Its prime value is that it forces you to think through just what it is you're looking for. Three questions will help you pin it down: "What are we really trying to get from this decision?" "What would a perfect solution to our problem look like?" "What are the real differences among alternative solutions?" List any answers to these questions that come to mind, without worrying over priorities or the length of the list. Even after you think you've run out of ideas, keep working at it: You may force out some useful stray thoughts and embellishments.

Now review your list, eliminating, combining, or rearranging items that seem similar. Unless you're using a home computer to help you with your list, you'll want to reduce the number of factors to around fifteen. A personal computer, of course, can handle a virtually unlimited number of items, and speed up your calculation time as well.

As you can see from our example on page 74, ease of cleaning, a feeling of control over cooking operations, minimal need for attention while cooking, an adequate warranty, and reasonable cost were the five factors most important to us at the time. Notice that all the factors were stated in *positive* terms—the qualities that you hope to find—rather than as attributes that you wish to avoid. For example, even though your question is "How noisy is it?" the proper phrasing should be "Quietness of Operation." This is important in your eventual use of rating numbers because it allows a higher numerical score to indicate a better, more desirable choice. The ultimate length of your list will be a function of how much time you have, how complicated the decision seems to be, and the amount of patience you can muster to be "calculatingly rational" when your instincts may be crying "Leap! Leap!"

Now that you've identified the qualities in the decision that are important to you, you must decide just *how* important each of them is with respect to all the others. The way you do this is by assigning a multiplier, or weighting factor, to each item.

W-R Step #2: Weight the criteria. The best way to approach this particular task is to sneak up on it. Before trying to fit numbers to your items, decide in a general way if the quality under consideration is of High, Medium, or Low importance. Inevitably, some items will feel

"Higher than Medium" but not quite critical enough to be High. In these cases, or in similar cases where items are clearly more important than Low but less important than other Mediums, feel free to assign incremental values, such as Medium High or Medium Low, etc. The idea here is to start off with an easier discriminating task so that the next job—assigning numerical values—will be more easily done, and with greater accuracy. As you can see from our example, "Ease of Cleaning" was of High importance to us, while "Feeling of Control Over the Monster" was important, too, but a little less so, rating a Medium High. "Need for Attention" was less important than these other two, since prior to the dinner hour someone who could read would usually be nearby to make these adjustments that some ovens performed automatically. Still a mite skeptical that the age of electronic marvels is really here, we gave "Adequacy of Warranty" a very High rating. In our original "go or no go" decision to buy a microwave oven, we had agreed to an amount up to which we could spend without second thoughts. Since all of the models in which we were interested fell within this amount, cost became a third-level consideration for *this* decision.

Having now positioned the criteria in the proper order with a rough estimate of comparative importance, the task of changing these qualitative rankings into numerical values is relatively painless. Expect to be tempted to stop the process right here and make do with approximate weightings; however, we strongly suggest you persevere so that you can let the numbers and the power of mathematics do the work for you.

We've found the quickest way to proceed is to count the number of factors on the list, then use that number as the highest weight to be assigned to the most important of the High items. If you have less than ten factors, as is the case with our example, use 10 as the highest value in order to ensure adequate discrimination among your criteria. Thus, our highest High factor had a potential multiplier of 10, while our lowest of the Low could only score 1. In our chart, you'll notice we gave "Cost" a weight of 3 points to give an extremely low cost but still effective oven a better chance to compete. A reminder: Zero won't work as an anchor to the scale because anything multiplied by zero will be zero and might as well not appear.

The main thing to remember here is that the reason for assigning numerical weights is to enable you to intermix in the final decision the relative importance of each attribute you're looking for with the degree to which that attribute is present in each alternative.

If it seems too complicated, or time-consuming, we reassure you that it will, in practice, be neither and move on to step #3.

W-R Step #3: Select and rate alternatives. Before you can rate alternatives, you have to have some. At times, the situation will present you with a ready-made set. For example, you may have only received three job offers. More often, however, the number of potential possibilities will be much greater. For that reason, the first step is to rule out the impossible—for you, that is—and see what's left. We arrived at our microwave alternatives, products A, B, C, and D, by such an elimination process. We set price limits beyond which we would not go, we ruled out those too small for family needs, too large for available space, and too automated for our nervous systems.

Your next move will be to roughly apply your evaluation criteria to all of the possible alternatives remaining—use your rapid-fire intuitive side for this—to narrow the list still further. A rapid walk through the microwave sections of two appliance stores with notepad in hand produced our list of products A through D. Now you have a reasonable list of alternatives, all of which are potentially satisfactory, and a set of weighted evaluation criteria. You're ready to move on to rating each alternative.

Everyone's played the game of rating someone or something on a scale of 1 to 10: movies, restaurant meals, even passersby of the opposite sex. Athletic experts, such as the judges at a swimming or skating competition, make these estimates all the time. Your task now is to assess how much or how little of each attribute you're looking for is *actually* present in the alternative under consideration. You then quantify that judgment with a number from 1 to 10. (Using this scheme, a 1 represents "so little you can hardly notice it," and 10 means the product has "as much as we could want.")

Take another look at our microwave oven example.

You can see that we rated product A's ease of cleaning at 4; the feeling of control it gave us as 7; its need for attention at 7; the adequacy of warranty at 5; and the reasonableness of its cost at 6 (the less cost of the product, the higher the rating). Observe, those of you who have been skeptical, how the Decision Maker helps you keep an eye on yourself. It substitutes rather nicely for willpower to bring you to your senses *before* you sign off on that superbly engineered, elegantly sporty,

200-mile-an-hour car. It does this by forcing you to *separately* consider the super speed of that marvelous machine, its beauty in the eyes of your neighbors and yourself, *and* the fact that going 200 miles per hour is really not that important to you, while cost is. In other words, it can help you deal with the "halo" effect, that well-documented tendency of human beings to be so enthralled by a single striking quality that the negatives recede into the background. Because a car can go 200 miles per hour does *not* mean that it also has outstanding driving comfort, or even that it *will* put your neighbors' collective noses out of joint.

We are now ready to move on to the denouement of this drama by computing an evaluation score for each attribute and then for each alternative as a whole.

W-R Step #4: Multiply the weight times the rate. Now it's time to turn the handle of your decision machine and crank out some answers. For us this part of the process has a touch of wizardry, because we often find ourselves pointed in a direction we didn't anticipate. It uses numbers and the properties of the multiplication process to meld the qualities that you want with the particular characteristics of each of the alternatives that you were considering. Proceed this way: First, multiply the weighting score of each factor by the rating score which represents how much of that particular characteristic each alternative has. In our example, product A has some cracks and crevices, so it only earned 4 rating points for its "Ease of Cleaning" qualities. The evaluation criterion "Ease of Cleaning" had been weighted 10, our most important factor. So we multiplied the weighting value by the rating points awarded to get a total of 40 points. The same holds true for "Feeling in Control" ($8 \times 7 = 56$); "Need for Attention" ($5 \times 7 = 35$); "Adequacy of Warranty" ($9 \times 5 = 45$); and "Reasonableness of Cost" ($3 \times 6 = 18$). This procedure, made easier with even the simplest hand-held calculator, is then repeated for each alternative under evaluation.

Now we're ready to total the totals and see which alternative provides us with the best combination of the qualities we're looking for. Admit it now—the system is intriguing and you'd use it in a minute if it weren't so much bother. Read on, we'll examine the question "Who has time for all this?" in a moment.

W-R Step #5: Total the Weight-Rate scores. The last step requires you to sum the total of the Weight $\times$ Rate scores for each alternative. In our example, product A had a total of 194 points; product B a total of 305 points (applause, please); product C a total of 287 (a nice hand for the runner-up); and product D a total score of 270. A quick glance at the total showed us that product B would clearly give us more of what we were looking for in a microwave oven, so we wrote out a check on the spot with no further hesitation. Without, for once, the nagging suspicion that we had allowed ourselves to be done in by a skillful salesperson, a colorful brochure, or slick product packaging.

What happens if the scores are closer? This does happen, but in our experience, it has not been a problem. After all, even in a tie, the two or three best alternatives have been identified. According to your own criteria, *any* of them will serve your needs equally well, although in somewhat different ways. Simply relax and choose the one that feels the best, matches the color of your eyes, contains your lucky numbers, or has any of the other subjective qualities that you would have used without your W-R Decision Maker. The difference is that you will know that all of your needs and wishes were considered and that you've used the best possible combination of looking and leaping decision making.

Was It Worth All the Trouble?

Some of you, at this point, may yet be wondering whether it's worth all that trouble. We sympathize with that question because we often ask it of ourselves. The answer to that very sensible question depends on what you mean by "trouble." For us, *real* trouble takes the form of wasted money, missed opportunities, unsatisfactory purchases, and the hours of endless recrimination that can accompany any poor or unnecessarily arbitrary decision. Compared to these miseries, a few moments with paper and pencil on the front end of an important decision seems like a modest price to pay. (Actually, the W-R process is much easier to practice than to explain.) You'll also find that it has allowed you to think objectively about what you *really* expect from your decision, something you might not stop to do on your own. You will have described for yourself, or other concerned parties (your banker, for instance), a solution that will optimally fit your needs, functional and aesthetic, rational and emotional, practical and eccentric, all balanced just the way you want them. Finally, you'll have a written document of your decision-making process, a record that can be reviewed should your best-laid plans happen to go a bit awry. As a matter of fact, this is eventually what happened to us with our newly acquired microwave oven.

About a year after our purchase we came to realize that we had underestimated the value of electronic programmability for a family as busy as ours. All too quickly our calm, logical, and friendly conversation about this realization began to slide into a discussion about whose fault it was. As one, we stopped short and then ran for our original matrix, scrawled on a sheet of borrowed notepaper and handily filed away with the warranty. We confronted ourselves with the now hazy reasons for the original decision; end of discussion and back to our havenly home. It was, as a matter of fact, this particular incident that convinced us that we wanted to write this book.

But just as Middle D problems come in a variety of forms, so do their solutions. Certain decisions simply don't lend themselves to Weight-Rate quantification. For these sorts of problems, we use a well-seasoned method you may have used in your own household from time to time: the Pro and Con Technique.

Highlighting Pros and Cons

As the name suggests, the Pro and Con Technique is a dialogue approach to making a decision, a sort of "challenge and response" system that draws out onto a list both the positive and negative aspects of an intended course of action.

For example, suppose you ask the question "Shall we buy a sailboat?" On the Pro, or "yes," side, you might list things such as "Fun"; "Fresh air"; "Love of the water"; "Cheaper than power boat"; and so on. On the Con, or "no," side, you might consider "John gets seasick"; "Water is a hundred miles away"; "We already have a vacation cabin we hardly ever use"; etc. This procedure, of course, is highly rational. You have laid out all the reasons to take or forgo a course of action. What's more, you'll find that reasons tend to come in pairs. Once started, every Pro argument you think of will automatically call up an equally convincing counterargument. Through this process, an emotional or logical preference will begin to emerge, either Pro or Con, anticipating your decision. It is obviously a process *par excellence* for highly analytic Lookers.

But the clear rationality of this method, as valuable as it is, is not why we've included it. It is here because we have seen two important and useful side effects that stem more from the process itself than the products of it. First, identifying Pros and Cons and pondering over them can open a channel in your mind to the underlying wishes, values, or conflicts that may have kept you from being your usual resolute selves. At a crucial and much beleaguered time in our own family's history, one of us had to decide whether or not to leave a job that, while full of interesting work and variety, was essentially undemanding and without a future. The contemplated new job had undoubted attractions, but also great uncertainties and risks. Days of maundering discussions with friends and family did little except to heighten the anxiety of the decision maker. Finally, facing the deadline for a commitment, the baffled equivocator resorted to the Pro and Con Technique to bring a little order out of chaos. Ten minutes into the task of listing reasons for and against the change, a hidden issue came roaring into mind like a freight train: "I know I'm not the perfect human being I should be. Imperfect as I am, can I *really* handle this demanding new career?"

After jousting a bit with this rather unreal view of the perfectibility of human beings, the answer was a wry but clearly optimistic "Who knows, but I've got to try!" The secret fear having been faced, the choice was easy and obvious—and never regretted later.

Second, the Pro and Con Technique can often defuse an erupting argument into a matter-of-fact, if less spirited, discussion of the issues. Susan, an extraordinarily incisive decision maker, is not too open to new ideas once her mind's made up (Susan points out that she is that way only because she's always right). Yet she responds very well to this approach. When someone says, "Well, I suppose we should talk about the Pros and Cons before we decide," one can see a self-imposed damper close down over the fire in her eyes—well, perhaps a little reluctantly at times—as she listens to, and then joins in, the process of teasing out the positives and negatives.

IMPROVING BIG D DECISIONS

Middle D and Big D decisions differ in more ways than size. Big D decisions affect the quality and direction of all the lives they touch. They require persistent attention, ceremony, and a deep look beneath the surface of the issues to be resolved. They also require some maneuvering room, much more than can be obtained solely from the application of methods or formulas, as valuable as those techniques can be. Big D decisions, in short, require the best of both the intuitive and calculating approaches. They require Lookers who, once having looked, understand how to leap.

Big D and Middle D decisions often elbow into the same life situations, one on the heels of the other. Since Middle D's are more numerous, less intimidating, and usually more fun to deal with, it can be tempting to work at them and avoid more serious issues—or worse, to assume that they have already been resolved. This is *not* the path to a havenly home. For like your utility bills, Big D's not dealt with in the light will surely be dealt with later in the dark.

The key to addressing these monster-sized problems is the realization that the biggest decisions should not be *made* at all, they should *evolve*. Tending to their patient and reasoned evolution is what Big D decision making is really all about.

Within certain limits, the longer an important matter is talked about, examined, and otherwise mentally tried on without forcing a decision, the greater the chances for a satisfactory outcome. This means that your conversations in the early stages of Big D resolution ought to be loose and meandering, like a stream trying to find its way to the ocean. Your goal here is to chase out hidden issues, uncover subtle nuances, bring fears into perspective, and focus on the longings, dreams, wishes, and needs that might otherwise escape rational detection. At length, you should understand as specifically as possible everything that's involved in the decision. When that full appreciation of all that's involved has been attained, the right answer for you will be clear. But the road to that best resolution is not easy. Initiating Big D discussions can drive impatient people crazy. While this impatience can be a potent antidote to indecision, timidity, and "paralysis by analysis," it can also spawn half-baked solutions. "What the hell—let's give it a try," is not the sort of reasoning one should use to bring a new baby into the world or uproot the family to live in another state. For this reason you gain much by defining a problem as a Big D decision. When it is so defined, you will find it easier to hold in check your understandable impulses to "get on with it." You can then let all feelings and issues surface and run their course until the best possible solution has been found.

Here are some steps that can help you evolve your own important decisions:

1. Avoid ultimatums.
2. Check frequently for understanding.
3. Be wary of the primrose path.

4. Make conflicts explicit.
5. Sum things up frequently.
6. Set a time for the decision.
7. Nourish new ideas.
8. Nail down the decision.

We'll take them one at a time.

1. *Avoid ultimatums.* Major feelings are usually attached to major decisions; emotional depth charges can surface at any time and explode into nonproductive conflict. Ultimatums, such as "I *refuse* to be saddled with taking care of a bigger house!" can too easily invite counterultimatums or angry accusations: "Well, you've got nothing better to do with your time!" To head off such emotional escalations, try to anchor your feelings, reactions, or conclusions to the matter at hand. Instead of an adamant refusal, a better statement would have been, "Right now the thought of a bigger house feels like a ton of bricks on my back." No one ought to argue with that, true or not; it's how you feel. "Right now" or "At the moment" is relaxing. They say that your mind is not petrified on the subject and that, who knows, you might change. However, don't be too surprised if, in the heat of the moment, your significant other doesn't quite catch the "right now" part. Angry or hurt folks just don't hear very well. Be ready to say it again with extra emphasis.

2. *Check frequently for understanding.* Nothing better guarantees misunderstanding than your assumption that you've been understood. Assume instead that miscommunications are the rule in human relationships, a wary perspective that will reduce the time it takes to uncover and repair crossed messages. You can help prevent the worst mixups with a few simple aids to understanding.

Without making it sound as if it's a challenge to their basic brightness, ask other decision makers if you're still on their wavelength. By doing so you give them an easy opening through which to bring up any confusions they may have about what you're really getting at. If the issue is complicated, ask others to restate what's just been said. Test your assumption that you've likely been misunderstood by asking others to tell you what they think your point is. If it doesn't help in any other way, all this verbal clarification will give slower thinkers, and people who may have been thinking of other things, a chance to get back on the main track.

3. *Be wary of the primrose path.* Some situations have a way of leading you on, pulling you along one step at a time until you're suddenly

confronted with a choice that you find very hard to evade. The arche-type of all such decisions, of course, is the age-old invitation to "leave the party and go to my place for a quiet drink." Once the initial steps have been taken, it becomes more and more difficult to choose another course. The everyday variety of primrose path decision might be, "I know we haven't really decided to buy a house yet, but it can't hurt to see what's available," or "I know we don't need another dog, but it's such fun to go look in the pet store." About the only foolproof way to guard against being stuck with the results of decisions you didn't really choose to make is to:

a. Bring along a friend for that "quiet drink."
b. Take your kids along on your house-looking expedition (they'll get bored quickly and fuss you into making it a brief afternoon).
c. Leave your kids at home when you go to the pet store.
d. Always leave your checkbook at home.

4. *Make conflicts explicit.* A little conflict can be a good thing, even in a havenly home. No single factor has more immediate value in work-ing your way toward an important decision than uncovering conflicts in family members' dreams, wishes, or expectations that have previously been hidden or merely quiescent. When you've found them, especially in yourself, don't smooth them over. Talk about them simply and di-rectly, even when you're certain that no one else feels the same. It is a cruel kindness to be so "considerate" of others that you submerge your own needs and desires in order to fit in and be a good kid. If you don't give your own wants equal time they can easily fester for want of fresh air and attention. The time to raise such questions is the moment they enter your head. It may indeed turn out that what you wanted *was* unfair, or impossible to attain, or not as vital as other considerations. If so, those facts will emerge in the discussion, but only if you haven't first censored them out yourself. Here is a short, and sad, story about two people who tried to do just that.

Ed and Millie were in their early thirties, a bright and busy young couple, thoroughly enjoying the exciting life a two-career family can have in New York. They were concerned with each other's needs—perhaps a bit too much so—and an always agreeable relationship was clearly the order of the day. When Millie was offered a promotion to account executive in her agency's Philadelphia office, she was aglow with pride. Both she and Ed knew it was a great opportunity for her and agreed that there were no serious obstacles to prevent their following her star to Pennsylvania. "After all," Ed said, "I'm a top salesman with a national company—I can easily transfer to the Philadelphia district." Of course, there might be a temporary dip in his income after the move, but what Ed lost would be more than made up for by Millie's raise. Even so, Ed began to have a few sleepless nights as the date of the move grew near. He would be leaving a neighborhood he enjoyed, a very supportive work situation, and more than a few close friends. But Ed resolved never to let such childish feelings throw a wet blanket over his wife's enthusiasm. These minor obstacles, as he called them silently, were put straight out of his head, or so he thought.

The first few months after the move were spent catching up with day-to-day problems and soaking in the sheer newness of it all. When the season changed, however, Millie began to notice small differences in Ed. In New York he had always been animated and full of conversation as they relaxed before dinner. Now he often simply sat, downing his cocktails, frequently more than one, in silence. He began to drop subtle complaints about his new job, the size of their new condominium mortgage, and the coldness of their neighbors. His new district manager was "pushing him too hard" and his problems at work seemed to multiply. Ed spent several hours a week in long phone conversations with friends from their old apartment building, after which he'd report each bit of gossip to Millie, buoyed up and bouncy for the moment, only to sink back into his hole at the end of the evening.

Millie finally faced Ed with her concern over his new style of behavior. He denied that anything had changed between them and for a while made a great effort to seem lighthearted and pleasant, losing each time to a growing moroseness. Not long afterward Millie was startled to find herself enjoying her job more than Ed's company. She found new excuses to work late or to bring home assignments from the office. "I guess what they say is true," she thought, "no honeymoon lasts forever."

In his secret thoughts Ed now admitted to himself how much he missed his former life in New York. Of course, he rationalized, there was nothing that could be done about it now. They had made the right decision and he was stuck with it.

There are two morals to this tale of woe. The first is one to keep in mind every time an important decision is under consideration: Hard as it is to pour cold water on a loved one's ideas, the longer you wait, the harder it becomes. Well, perhaps Ed even knew about that bit of wisdom but just couldn't bring himself to risk Millie's potential anger. If so, it's because he forgot moral number two: A brief bout over conflicting ideas, wishes, and dreams early on can save months or years of disappointment and depression later.

5. *Sum things up frequently.* Any discussion can be helped along by occasional breathers in which someone sums up what's been said and who's taken what position. Such a summary might sound something like this:

"Well, guys, we've now spent two hours talking about moving to the country. As I get it, the move sounds exciting to you, Johnny, but Mom is worried about whether she'd miss the conveniences we're used to. As for myself, at this moment I'm for moving—partly because it would get me out of my long commute, and partly because I think I could do a bang-up job selling farm machinery. Sally, I can see from your face, and from what you've said, that you think you'd be pretty unhappy about leaving your friends. Can you say more about that?"

A brief recap, with the corrections or amplifications that follow, helps all parties feel that their concerns have been heard and understood, whether or not anyone else agrees with them. For what you want is not agreement but a deeper, more thorough exploration of each person's present thoughts, wishes, or expectations. As these precious ingredients are reflected upon and savored, new perspectives may form. Try for a tone that avoids drawing conclusions. By saying, "And you absolutely refuse to leave your friends, Sally," you might anchor her into a mental set she was on the verge of leaving. Sally's tearful accusation that nobody cares how she feels may have been more a shy preteen's fear of making new friends than a lament over leaving old ones, some of whom she doesn't like that much anyway.

6. *Set a time for the decision.* We have said that Big D's should be incubated with patient care and attention to the decision-making process—and that's true. Unfortunately, it is equally true that major decisions can be postponed only so long before some of the players involved will begin to twitch. The Leapers among you will grow edgy, willing to agree to *anything* that means more action and less talk. Their agitation becomes especially acute if there's a whiff of procrastination in the air—

that deadly enemy of even the best intentions—a suspicion that is often well founded. Wisely allowing big decisions to evolve naturally is not at all the same as foot dragging to sidestep disagreements or avoid facing painful necessities. So with care that you do not let the discomfort of living with an unresolved decision propel you into an unwise choice, you'll also need to find a way to keep it from dying on the vine.

Two precautions will help you deal with the need for both evolution and resolution: (1) Set a date by which the decision will have been made, and (2) If the matter has reached a dead end, agree in advance to end *all* discussion of the problem for a specific length of time.

In some cases, reality will step in and dictate a deadline for you—that exciting new job offer will expire on the twenty-fifth, or that lovable bargain of a Great Dane puppy might soon be sold to other buyers. Even so, set a preliminary deadline of your own ahead of the one determined by the situation, to allow you the luxury of a few postdecision steps that we'll talk about in the next section.

A present deadline will also ensure that you do not allow the decision to slip out of your hands without positive action on your part. For your own peace of mind you ought to actively decide that you do *not* want that job or that sweet Great Dane puppy (which shortly would have cost more to feed than you). Passive decisions, made for you by the expiration of a deadline, or by the toss of a coin, have an undoubted attraction—they avoid the necessity of facing nasty conflicts and putting opinions on the line. However, they also leave behind doubts and regrets that can later fuel a sense of being trapped.

What happens if the time for decision has arrived and you are still at loggerheads, unable to agree, but uncertain as to what's wrong? The first rule in this situation: Do not let the decision just decompose. Instead, bury it temporarily with a firm agreement on when it will be resurrected for another try. With luck, the issues and your wisdom concerning them will ripen during the hiatus, feathers ruffled by argument will smooth, and positions will soften. Your interim interment will sound like this:

"Well, family, we have just not been able to agree on whether or not to become a two-dog family. Let's stop beating on this thing for a while and take up the matter again in January, after the holidays. You're the one who seems to want another dog the most, Lisa. It will be up to you to bring it up."

7. *Nourish new ideas.* Creative decisions can pop up like bubbles in a

pancake once the heat of discussion reaches the right temperature. Or sometimes they have to simmer overnight, seeping into your consciousness when you least expect them. Such moments are exciting. When shared, they glow with the warm feelings of joint accomplishment. Enjoy them. For us they've been a most wonderful part of our living and working together. New ideas are not only valuable in themselves, they are hope-generating beacons that reduce the darkness that fate and ill luck can bring to any family. Cherish them with active listening, a supportive expression, and lots of amplifying talk.

8. *Nail down the decision.* Even first-rate decisions, made with sureness and the best of techniques, can end in disaster. In part, it is because the world has kept right on turning, changing the facts on which the decision was based. At times, sheer bad luck will bring the most brilliant plans to grief; certainly, that's how most of us tend to view our misfortunes. More often, however, disastrous endings to otherwise well-made decisions can be credited to two culprits: lack of commitment by those who must implement the decision, and a lack of contingent planning for picking unexpected flies out of the ointment. The balance of this chapter deals with ways to avoid these perennial troublemakers.

Don't Accept Silence as Assent. All organizations, families included, have some members that are more vocal than others. These more aggressive and articulate people can sometimes reduce the more timid to speechless frustration, weariness, and resignation. Such silence rarely means assent. More likely, it means they've been bullied into a kind of underground resistance, fed by unanswered questions, confusion, and doubt. Unfortunately, active solicitation of opinions from those who've been driven underground often results in more silence. You must insist, therefore, upon openly stated commitments from everyone when arriving at a decision of importance. Point out that commitment means acceptance as we've discussed it earlier in this chapter, rather than full agreement with the choice. It is particularly important to get a yes from those upon whose cooperation the success of the plan depends or those whose lives will be significantly affected by it. Work at making it easy for still hidden away reservations to surface. Couch your question in supportive, conditional terms to make it difficult for even the most recalcitrant or timid to evade your request for either an up-front "Count me in," or an open "I can't say yes yet, and here's why." Here's how you might sound:

"Sid, I think you agreed last night to live with your aunt while I go with your Dad to start his new job. How do you feel about that this morning? Any second thoughts?"

When a decision involves actual hardship and distress, those who will have to pay most dearly should not only choose to pay, they must *know* that they have chosen. This special kind of commitment helped us make and continue to cherish one of the most important mutual decisions we have ever faced.

For two years we had ruminated on, brooded over, and been ambivalent about whether to add a sixth child to a family life already fully entwined around the existing five. We had trepidations about the additional responsibilities. We were concerned about providing security for a child whose financial needs might compromise our retirement plans. (There were a myriad of other vital emotional questions that brought us alternately to anger or tears.) At length, with a stark and undisguised vision of all the problems as well as the joys that would be forthcoming, we chose to have our sixth child, Jeremy. Every problem we had foreseen did, indeed, confront us. Yet in each time of difficulty we were calmed and comforted by the knowledge that we had both, with full awareness of them, chosen the burdens, as well as the immense satisfactions, of having him. It is a decision we have never regretted.

Involve All of Those Affected. Although behavioral scientists rarely agree totally on anything, one thing they're virtually unanimous about is the value of involving participants in a major decision as soon as possible, and to the maximum degree appropriate to their place in the decision. Selling Big D decisions to people who feel that their wishes or ideas were ignored is an uphill struggle. Even tougher is forcing compliance on people who know they have the power to resist, sabotage, nag, recriminate, or get bad grades. (Self-flagellation can be an elegantly economical way of punishing loved ones who do not respect your wishes, as long as you're willing to hurt yourself in the process.) How much better it is to provide a forum in which each affected family member can toss out his or her own ideas about the problem early enough to really count. How early this should be, however, depends on many factors. Telling your kids you plan to move to a different city, for example, should certainly take place before the van arrives. While informing people after the fact may encourage their morbid curiosity and general wariness, it also fosters distrust and endless complaining. As soon as the problem becomes clear enough to demand some kind of resolution, get *everyone* together, explain the situation, and ask for ideas and reactions. This raises the sticky question of giving smaller kids their due in big decisions.

Perhaps the best guide to handling these "important subordinates" is to consider these two questions:

1. How mature and responsible are the people involved?
2. How important is their commitment to effectively carrying out the decision?

Because a five-year-old has the right to say "I don't want to move and leave my friends," it does not necessarily follow that his or her opinions should have the same weight as an adult, who bears the legal and financial responsibility for the household. Similarly, a teenager with a carefree attitude toward property (Why not? You're paying for it!) is probably not the best judge of how and when to buy a car.

Maturity means, among other things, that one is capable of making a decision that might not work out to one's own personal advantage. Is Mary Beth, given her age and temperament, truly able to agree that Georgie needs a new violin for his lessons more than she needs a new bicycle? If you're in doubt, give her an opportunity to be mature by asking her. If the answer is no, make the decision yourselves but inform Mary Beth *before* you buy the violin. Tell her the reasons for your decision and be prepared to listen—perhaps longer than you'd like—to hurt or anger or both. Above all, don't expect Mary Beth to like your choice because "it's good for the family" or because "you get to go to camp each year while Georgie stays home." In this respect, nearly all decisions involving immature people have a Big D flavor about them and they require special time and attention. At such times it may help to remember that if you have otherwise handled the decision properly, your wisdom will at length be recognized. ("At length" means that when you are sixty and your kids are thirty, they'll thank you for making them practice the piano.)

How Much Commitment. When people are committed to decisions, it means that, in spite of any leftover doubts, they will not hold back in carrying out the actions required of them by those decisions. You don't need commitment when "slave labor" is all that counts and you're in a position to supervise what the "slaves" do, with plenty of rewards and punishments to pass around if the bickering becomes too great. Johnny hates to wash the car, but if you stand over him, nagging, threatening, or cajoling, you may end up with a reasonably well-washed car without any commitment on his part at all. If, on the other hand, you believe you have better ways to spend your time than in close supervision, you will want to involve him early in discussing the weekend plans. You will get a better job done, and Johnny will know that his wishes, whether or not they ruled the decision, were not ignored.

Similarly, a decision to sell the house, invest the proceeds in the money market, and move into an apartment, *can* be carried out whether or not the kids agree. You might like to have their okay in the matter, but you don't really need it unless—and this is a big "unless"—you want them also to accept and be happy with the decision. Like everything else in the business of building a havenly home, building commitment requires earnest, early involvement, hard listening and a willingness to spend a little time at the start to save a lot of time at the end.

PLAN FOR CONTINGENCIES

When a decision has finally been made—and not before—stop all implementation action until you have put yourself through the sometimes frustrating, but always valuable, exercise known as negative, or worst-case, analysis. The purpose of this experience is to identify potential pitfalls you may encounter with the aim of avoiding them, minimizing their effects, or steeling yourself for any necessary pain you may have to go through to get exactly what you want.

Here are the rules for this most important game of "What if?"

First of all, everyone must understand that in this case "negative" means "realistic," a reminder of those unpleasant realities that sometimes happen to people en route to the fulfillment of their dreams. Neither mindless optimism that refuses to see potential dangers nor timid pessimism that sees them lurking in the shadows, *your* brand of positive thinking foresees possible obstacles and prevents or provides for them. A sound negative analysis involves five steps: (1) List the activities. (2) Identify what can go wrong with each. (3) Plan around those problems. (4) Build a "horror floor" beneath you. (5) Involve all those affected.

Let's look now at what each of these really means.

1. *List the activities.* As an unknown wit once said, "At some point all decisions must disintegrate into work." The work is comprised of the action steps needed to implement your decision. For example, here's a list of the important activities that would follow a decision to buy a house:

   a. Ask around about real estate agents.
   b. Select a real estate agent.
   c. Look at many houses.
   d. Choose a house.
   e. Make a deposit on the house.
   f. Find a source for a loan.
   g. Establish your creditworthiness.
   h. Sign papers.
   i. Move in.

2. *Identify what can go wrong.* Now's the time to play devil's advocate. Let loose the negativist in you to ferret out what *might* go wrong at every step. Don't be seduced by the brilliance of what you've planned; think rather of *unplanned* causes and effects (who plans disasters?). For example, visualize yourself applying for your loan. Suddenly, you become acutely conscious of a fact you'd somehow "forgotten"—lending institutions invariably check your credit. In your mind you hear the credit interviewer ask if your accounts have been up to date and paid on time. Enter a sickening realization that you've been a little cavalier about paying all of your bills on time—twice in the past six months you've had notices of overdue payments. "Uh-oh," you say to yourself, "better check out what that might do to our credit rating." Is it in fact a problem, or just an imaginary worry? Your negative analysis has done its job; your attention has been focused and you can do something about it if anything needs to be done.

3. *Plan around the problem.* Even the worst of problems can be planned around to some extent. Suppose that you have checked your credit rating and found that the goddess of finance does indeed favor the compulsively prompt—your credit is a bit tainted. Well, it isn't good news, but you can face it with a little more aplomb than if you'd heard it first across the table from a condescending loan officer. More important, with this contingency foreseen you are in a position to do whatever can be done about it. You might write letters to your lender and local credit bureaus explaining that your monthly payment schedule differs from the billing cycle of the companies involved (don't laugh—even if no one believes you, you've at least given someone who wants to help you an excuse for doing so). You could include a summary of your financial health over the year to show that you had the money even if you didn't send it on time. Or you might elect to put off your house hunt for six months, during which you will make all important pay-

ments on time. Why six months? Because that's the period most often used by lenders to determine a borrower's payment reliability—another important fact you would have learned as part of your contingency planning.

4. *Build a horror floor.* Unreasoning fear can be the most incapacitating of emotions. Therefore, before leaving the dock in a Big D decision, it's important to reassure yourself that no matter how bad things get— and they can get pretty bad sometimes—you will be able to stand it. This worst-case form of negative analysis puts a horror floor beneath your feet. It allows you to look at the worst things that *could* happen squarely in the eye and proceed across that floor to do whatever must be done.

Begin by reviewing the action steps your decision requires, just as you've done above. At each step along the way, dwell on the *worst* things that could possibly happen, including complicating factors. (This is your chance to get really morbid.) For each of those potential disasters, ask yourself, "And then what will we do?" The answers may surprise you. Here's an example that combines contingency planning and worst-case analysis.

Assume you are free spirits who have just committed yourselves to a hefty twenty-five-year mortgage. Here is what you are facing:

Major Activity: Make bank payments for twenty-five years.

Potential Unplanned Effect: A major recession—Frieda loses her job; Jack's pay is cut by 25 percent.

Contingency Plan: Make interest-only payments during that period (better make sure the mortgage allows that).

Worst-Case Analysis: We lose the house through foreclosure.

"Suppose we do? What then?" "Why then we'll find an apartment, or move in with your brother-in-law—awful, but not impossible— and start over."

After a moment of panic and when the heart palpitations subside, you'll find that you have given yourself the only bedrock internal security possible in the face of the risk that accompanies nearly all Big D decisions. In your imagination (usually more terrible than the reality), you will have faced the worst and moved beyond to the often elusive truth that no matter what happens, somehow, somewhere, there will be a life that can be lived. On the other hand, you may see that while you might *survive* virtually any disaster, you'd really prefer not to have to—an indication that you ought to, after all, bail out of that decision.

We have walked with you through a host of principles and methods which can be used by anyone who wants to make any life decision better. These methods have been good to us, not only because they have saved us time and money, but also because they have helped us and those we love to understand the value of melding the rational, realistic, and caring aspects of life.

EXERCISES

1. In the spaces below, list ten little d decisions that you regularly need to make. For example: what to fix for breakfast; where to eat lunch; when to have the car serviced; where to do your banking.

Decision	*Assigned to*
_____	_____
_____	_____
_____	_____
_____	_____
_____	_____
_____	_____
_____	_____
_____	_____
_____	_____
_____	_____

2. Now jot down the name of the person in your family to whom each of the little d decisions has been, or should be, assigned. Remember: It's not that each of these matters couldn't benefit from both conversation and cogitation, but that they're not worth the time and effort. If most family members really care about what's for breakfast, it automatically becomes a Middle D decision to be handled with appropriate ceremony.

3. In the spaces below, identify five Middle D decisions (refer back to pages 61 through 66 for criteria) you're faced with at the present time.

Decision	*Method*
_____	_____
_____	_____
_____	_____
_____	_____
_____	_____

4. In the space just to the right of each decision, indicate the decision-making method best suited to that sort of problem. For example: the Weight-Rate Decision Maker; the Pro and Con Technique; the Paired-Comparisons Matrix; any other approach you've found useful in the past.

Note: You've probably guessed that the purpose of exercises such as these is to get you to take the first steps, always the toughest, toward handling family decisions with the same care that you give much less important matters—to you, that is—at work. On the other hand, if you are not using this kind of methodology at work, try it; you'll like it, and so will your boss, clients, or customers.

5. If you have read this chapter with another family member (or if you can get him or her to sit still long enough for you to outline the suggested approach to Big D decisions), ponder together how you worked your way through the most important decisions you have had to make in the past. Regardless of the outcome, which may have been affected by the impossible-to-predict actions of others or by sheer bad luck, how well did you go about it? Might more time, deeper discussions, the earlier inclusion of others have affected the outcome? Think about the steps we've suggested for productively evolving such decisions. Did you touch base with any, most, or all of them? What internal or outside influences might have kept you from resolving issues as well as you could have?

The point: The purpose here is not to belabor a past which cannot be changed, but to better prepare you for the next time you're faced with a vital decision.

CHAPTER 5

Tracking the Problem to Its Lair

Sally and Ted were an openly affectionate couple. Friends envied them their outgoing, easy relationship and the fun they had together. One day, however, Sally confided to her friend Nan that she had come to feel a distance from Ted that both frightened and saddened her. "We talk together a lot, but always around trivial things," she said. "I'm afraid I'm losing contact with him, or maybe we never really had it." Nan suggested that she had a "communications problem" and what she ought to do is make a greater effort to communicate. "Why don't you take the initiative, Sally. Let him know how you feel. Start off some deep conversations yourself."

All the next week Sally went out of her way to do just that. She perused her favorite self-help book for hints on "how to communicate well," and armed with a firm intention to "make the connection," she apprised Ted of hopes and concerns that were important to her. Each time, Ted listened with patient attention, gave her advice on how she might solve her problems, and eased the conversation into a query about the dinner menu or what they might do that weekend.

"The more I try to talk with Ted, the more alone I feel," she finally confessed to Nan. "The only way I can get a human response from Ted is to yell at him or cry." Sally wondered, for the first time in their relationship, if they were heading toward separation—or worse.

If Nan had her wits about her (or happened to have read this book), she might have raised the possibility that Sally was trying to solve the wrong problem the wrong way at the wrong time. Sally's mistake, and it is an easy one to make, was confusing a distressing symptom—shallow communication—with the disease that might be causing that symptom. True, doing this did give her something to do and allowed her to feel beautifully noble. But it also allowed the real illness to continue untouched. No wonder the end result for her was bafflement, frustration, and the beginnings of fear for her marriage. We will return to the tale of Sally and Ted shortly, but for now let's pursue the question of why, and how, solving the right problem can be difficult.

As partners, fellow homemakers, and consulting professionals, we are ever dismayed at how easy it is to go barking up the wrong problem tree, energetically howling at the shadows of life's problems while the villains themselves rest easy in their lairs, thinking up new mischief.

This chapter is about tracking such problem bears to their lairs. In it we'll show you how to separate symptoms from the ailing family systems that spawn them, and then suggest ways to correct those systems that have gone awry.

Like all good trackers, you'll have to have a method. Serious family problems, like dangerous animals in the wild, have an instinct for avoiding detection through dissimulation and camouflage. We've found that the following five steps will smoke them out, however, on almost every occasion:

1. *Identify the Symptoms.* These are the hurts and frustrations that let you know a problem's prowling around your house.
2. *Diagnose the Problem Areas.* These are the iniquitous causes of those previously detected symptoms that sally forth to eat you alive. They usually involve malfunction in some necessary attributes of a vital family life:
   — Goals, objectives, and priorities which challenge, direct, and coordinate your family's energies
   — A process for meshing mutual expectations
   — A system for communicating and keeping in touch
   — A process for grinding out quality decisions that everyone can get behind
   — Means for maintaining or, if necessary, rebuilding trust and confidence
   — Methods and mechanisms for getting everything done
3. *Select a Solution and Try It On.*
4. *Check Your Progress and Modify Your Approach.*
5. *Evaluate and Celebrate.*

Before we take you for a closer look at each of these steps, a word of warning. There are three pitfalls on the path to revitalizing your own family's underpinnings that you'll need to be alert for; they are: skipping the diagnosis, giving up too soon, and not following through. Although we'll revisit these malefactors later in this chapter, they're sneaky enough to merit a few cautionary words.

The first hazard is the hardest to avoid—the tendency to skip directly from step #1 (Identify the Symptoms) to step #3 (Select a Solution and Try It On).

Since it's the symptoms themselves that hurt, it is they, not some yet undiscovered underlying issues, that you want to be rid of, and why not? A bee-stung big toe calls for careful removal of the stinger, aspirins, and antihistamines, not a lecture on wearing shoes while cavorting among the clover blossoms. Then, too, symptoms in a family setting often appear as if they *can* be simply solved. It seemed thoroughly good sense to Sally to remedy a lack of quality communication by simply communicating more. To make it worse, searching for causes takes time, effort, and attention, and is not immediately gratifying. No wonder the natural reaction of most of us is to skip the diagnosis in favor of immediate action.

The second hazard is an understandable, if regrettable, tendency to evaluate results too soon. If symptoms hurt badly enough, you want the medicine to act fast, and it's tempting to make pass-or-fail judgments on how well the solution is working before you've given it an adequate chance. Giving up too soon not only fails to solve the original problem, but saps your enthusiasm to try again.

The third swamp is the overleaf of the second one—premature congratulation. It swallows up those who are so properly pleased with the miraculous changes that their solution steps have wrought that they stop using them, assuming that magic spells last forever. These superoptimists are often seen smiling with satisfaction as their heads sink slowly beneath the surface.

Let's now examine more closely each of the important steps on the way to a more havenly home.

STEP #1: IDENTIFY THE SYMPTOMS

Like a fever or scratchy throat, disappointments and frustrations are *signs* that a disease has infiltrated the family's previously healthy body.

While they are not the disease itself, they point the way to it; therefore, your first step will be to identify and describe precisely what tells you that something's gone wrong. In other words, you must catalog the hurts that beset your family. Your list might contain items like these:

— Sam jumps into his automobile with barely enough time to get to an important sales meeting across town. As the engine roars to life, he notices that there's just enough gas to get to the end of the driveway. "Who was the last one to drive the car?" he seethes as he stomps into the house to telephone that he'll be late.

— Ann places the bulging kitchen trash container in the center of the floor and waits for someone to empty it. No one does. At length, Ann carries it out herself, muttering "No one *ever* does anything around here."

— Fifteen-year-old Ron is sent out to rake the leaves in the yard. Half an hour later his father notices a magnificent pile of leaves in the center of the yard, the rake casually thrust into the center of it like a flagpole. Ron flashes by, basketball under his arm. "Bye, Dad, I'm off to shoot a few baskets."

— Margaret burns with angry frustration as she turns on the kitchen faucet and a spray of water *again* hits her in the face. "Why hasn't Paul fixed that leaky gasket?" she fumes.

— Ten-year-old Robert sits sulking in his room. "Dad cares more about his office work than about me," he finally tells his mother. "We never do anything fun on weekends anymore."

— Thirteen-year-old Angie asks her mom if Ron, Mom's new "friend," doesn't like her. "Of course he does, honey," Mom replies. "Whatever made you think he doesn't?" "Because he never comes down for breakfast when he sleeps over," Angie says. Embarrassed for herself, sorry for Angie, and *furious* at Ron, Mom packs her daughter off to school.

The variety of symptoms of family stress is endless. Yet every irritation does not require an intensive search for hidden psychological monsters. A rough-running car may mean either a mistuned engine, or a chance bit of water in the gas line which will clear itself. So events like those above may indicate deeper, more troublesome problems or may be merely blips on the screen of your life that need to be lived through or simply waited out.

Here are some clues that will help you differentiate those of life's transitory "ouchies" that you can safely ignore from those symptoms that call for careful investigation.

1. Symptoms are distressing. Disorder, confusion, and general chaos are, by themselves, not always symptoms—they must bother someone. When daddy George walks into the living room and finds toys scattered all over the floor, a situation exists but not necessarily a symptom. George may gaze fondly at the debris of play because it represents to him the joys of fatherhood. He may even be one of those people to whom you'll be introduced in Chapter 7 who simply screen out much of their environment—George really doesn't notice the toys on the floor. The situation becomes a symptom only when George waxes bitingly sarcastic over a house that's "so wonderfully picked up," or storms around the house yelling at the offending kids. In other words, it's not a symptom because neighbors, in-laws (unless they live with you), or your latest how-to book (other than this one, naturally) says it is. It must bother someone in the family.

2. Symptoms don't just chafe, vex, or annoy; they hurt a lot, they leave in their wake helpless anger or frustration, and loss of self-esteem. The question here is whether you or your loved ones are *inwardly* boiling, even if you're not outwardly steaming. It's the inner hurt that counts, not whether or not you are expressing the feelings that flow from the hurt. Remember, however, that inner anger can show itself in ways other than yelling—boredom, depression, or an icy retreat into silence are common examples.

3. When a reasonable effort to rid yourself of the hurt doesn't work, you have likely identified a symptom that calls for serious attention. Before she sought Nan's help, Sally had asked Ted if anything was on his mind, a quite sensible and caring thing to do. It was his response— kissing her and then changing the subject—that might have led her to suspect that Ted's recalcitrance was a symptom of some, as yet undefined, problem. However, if he had, perhaps with a bit of urging, poured out a woeful tale of abrasive customers and unforgiving bosses, Sally could have safely assumed that Ted's withdrawal was no more than a temporary rough spot in his life.

Having used these simple criteria for separating routine tribulations from symptoms worthy of the chase, you next must identify and describe the most important indicators of something amiss in your own set of family systems. (In this section we'll suggest the general approach.

At the end of this chapter we've included some exercises that talk you through a diagnostic look at your own family.)

Symptom compiling is best done together with your spouse, partner, or significant other. Start by individually, and privately, listing symptoms. Your lists might wind up looking like variations on the one above, in fact, but with the names of the characters your own. What ought to appear on your list are hurts, miscues, rubbing places, communication dead ends. Don't try to make the list exhaustive. Stick to the things that are the most bothersome, especially if they've been going on for an unreasonably long time. After you've completed your own lists, exchange them with whomever you have been working for a thoughtful, but initially silent, perusal. Keep reminding each other that the symptoms are not the problems (we keep harping on this point—we'll do it again and again—because it's so easy to lose your way).

Now that you have identified your significant symptoms, your next step will be to follow them to their sources—the gaps, eddies, and whirlpools that are keeping your family systems from working as they should. Ask each other how long the troublesome events have been noticed. How frequently do they occur? What's been done to remedy them in the past? Refrain from explaining away any symptoms in which you are named as a guilty party, and don't allow your partner to do it. Remind yourselves that the point of this process is not fixing blame, an enormously attractive but quite futile activity. What you're after is an investigative frame of mind, a thoughtfully diagnostic look at assorted aches and pains, buttressed by the hope—and a realistic hope it is—that the underlying problem areas will emerge.

STEP #2: DIAGNOSE THE PROBLEM AREAS

To find the sources of those bitter pills that you have identified, you'll need to know something of how systems work and how they sometimes don't. Much of what you'll read in the next ten pages has been drawn from recently gained knowledge of the "systemness" of organizations. When you begin to look at your own family from this fascinating perspective, we believe that you'll discover, as we did, that you are much less mystified about how, and why, well-intentioned people can make such trouble for themselves without even knowing it. Even better, you'll be more able to remedy the sources rather than the symptoms.

Webster says that a system is "an organized integrated whole made up of diverse but interrelated and interdependent parts," a somewhat wordy but very apt description of any family. "Interrelated" means that everything in a family is connected to everything else. "Interdependent" means that success or failure in one part of the family affects every other part. It is this very quality of the family system that is both bane and boon to those of us who want to do something about our own, or our loved ones', behavior. The bad news is this: When one aspect of your family life isn't working as it should, the aches and pains may show up in an entirely different place. To illustrate, let's once again retrace the chain of events that plagued Sally and Ted but this time from a systems view. The whole mess began with a difference of opinion that was real, but not in itself devastating, over how much a man should "burden" others with his feelings. Sally—warm, intimate and open—expected Ted to be just like herself, free to reveal his deepest feelings. For Ted, stuck with a role image he'd acquired from his father, the manly way was to keep up a front, be always calmly in control and, if possible, pleasant. If Sally and Ted had known that they'd been imprinted with quite different notions of the ways in which proper husbands and wives should communicate, some thoughtful negotiating of what each was prepared to deliver, given these newly recognized facts about each other, would have sufficed. But because they did not know what the core of the problem was, they could not address it. Instead, they began to subtly disengage. As Sally tried to extract intimacy from Ted, he felt first puzzled, then uneasy. Aware that he was somehow disappointing her, he gave her more of what she seemed to want—conversation. When this failed, he felt irritated at being "pushed" and began to share her doubts about their compatibility. What will the final act bring them? Unfortunately, unless they get help from someone other than Nan, they will find themselves communicating less and less—certainly, neither of them wishes for more of an already frustrating activity —until at length, they do indeed have a "communications problem." The main systems point is that trouble travels. When there is a gap in your understanding of what to expect from one another, your partner's behavior will seem first incomprehensible and then "wrong." You'll assume that he or she knows what's happening and you'll invent a rationale that will make sense out of it—the "sense" will be laden with words such as "thoughtless," "stubborn," and "selfish." Down will go your trust and confidence, up will go your guard, and out will go future openness and honesty. You'll talk less and less about your true hopes and aspirations—after all, they might be used to ridicule you—bicker instead about how you've spent money, and, at length, wonder what happened to that sweet, understanding person you came together with five years ago.

Thankfully, this "everything affects everything else" property works for, as well as against, family serenity. Improvements in any aspects of your family life will have a positive effect on all of the others. To see how this happy property works, let's magically put Ted in a situation that strengthens his own set of personal goals and priorities. Imagine him in a career-planning seminar provided by his employer as a morale booster. As is common in such seminars, Ted is asked to list his goals identifying assets and liabilities and chart a future course for himself. Ted shows his new career plan to his boss, who surprises him by starting a long and very affirming discussion about some new assignments he will give Ted that will provide just the kinds of experience Ted will need. Great for Ted, you say, but how does it help Sally? In this way. As you may have suspected, Ted's smooth demeanor concealed nagging doubts about his ability to "make it." Now propped up a bit by his boss's interest, he has less to conceal. He can afford to open a tiny window into the real Ted that Sally had glimpsed and, because of her own nature, had wanted to touch. It was clarifying Ted's goals and showing him a path to them that gave Sally the intimacy she needed, not her well-intentioned campaign to communicate more.

Without this beneficial systems property, some kinds of family problems would be extraordinarily hard to solve—but more about that later when we touch upon breakdowns in mutual trust and confidence. Even better, family systems are very forgiving as to wrong guesses about where the problems truly lie. Any buttressing you do anywhere will at length begin to bring the rest of the system along. However, zeroing in on the major problem areas—the diagnosis approach we've been urging on you—is most valuable and can help you spend your time and energy well. Otherwise, you'll need to set yourself to wait, albeit impatiently, for the improvements to get around to the places that are hurting you right now.

In addition to an understanding of how systems glue holds your family together, you'll need to remind yourself of just what families are all about. To aid you, in the following section we've briefly described the ingredients that are always present in a family, what they do for your family when working well, and which signs and symptoms most often point to something awry. Use these sketches of family underpinnings as clues which, when put together with your knowledge of yourself and those with whom you live, will help you deduce which system needs to be shored up. You'll need the courage to look clearly at your own symptom list with an inquiring perspective as free as possible of guilt or blame. You will try to see, for example, that your feeling of frantic overload is due, not to a fate that has cast you adrift on horizonless seas of work, but to a family priority-setting system that is nonexistent or not working as it should.

The System of Goals and Priorities

As a ship needs stars to steer by, every family, whether it knows it or not, ought to have a vision of itself, a sense of "specialness," and an awareness of shared goals toward which it is striving. It is this fusion of dreams and goals which sets the general direction and tone for everyone. Without such a vision, any organization is easily lead astray by the chance winds of fortune.

We human beings are purposive creatures. We are full of wishes, wants, and needs that propel us toward goals as concrete as a new car or as diffuse as "a good life." From the start, each of us is full of desires which tug us along toward real or fancied satisfactions. When we become family members, these individual needs don't simply disappear. Sometimes they meld into larger family purposes to which we all subscribe—to stay together, for instance. These goals bind us; we feel like warm clusters of special people, belonging to each other and unique in the world. But at times there will be goals that attract some of us but are uninviting to others. For example, Dad and daughter Mary may want to become a boating family, while Mom and son Brad are drawn more to leisurely weekends devoted to music and art. To add to the complication there will always be goals that are avidly pursued by one family member but of little attraction to the others—the purchase of a high-powered motorcycle by a possibly high-risk teenager may fit this category. Picture these individual goals as magnets, pulling each family member in a variety of directions at once, potentially fragmenting the energy and resources of the family and ensuring that no matter which family course is chosen, no one will ever be fully satisfied. To work well, a family goal system therefore needs at least these features. First, a more or less well-articulated and agreed-upon concept of where the family as a whole is, or ought to be heading. Second, some workable means for setting priorities that will get everyone pulling together, at least occasionally. Third, a method for demonstrating to the principal players that their own individual wishes have been taken seriously by those others that mean so much to them.

Family goals are not the same as family values. Family values tend to be incubated by example, and they are taught, even when seldom articulated. Goals actuate family values by turning them into future targets toward which efforts can be directed. The power of goals to coalesce diverse energies comes largely from the fact that they focus our attention. The clearer and brighter they are, the more they beckon us on. Powerful as family goals can be in providing a unifying sense of direction, most of us are pretty vague about them—if we think about them at all. That's unfortunate, because it is when we talk about where we think we want to go, and what we want to be, that we have the best chance of creating that unifying vision of ourselves as a family that will help us over rough seas. Here are some goal-related (and value-related) questions that rattled around in our family for years:

— What kind of family is this going to be? Will it be child-oriented, adult-oriented, adult-career-oriented, etc.?
— What kind of household do we want? Well-regulated and spotless? Basically clean and safe with some untidiness accepted?
— Do we want to be rich (whatever that means to us) or just comfortable?
— How much precious time should we spend in community work? Is volunteer work as "important" as work for pay?
— Are we striving for a simple, pleasant life, or are excitement and competitive achievement the things?

As you might suspect, these questions, while frequently discussed, will never be fully resolved, for the answers themselves depend upon a perspective that shifts with each family accomplishment. We have found, however, that when we make the time to chew them over (and time for such ruminations is never "just there;" it has to be made), the goals that emerge from those discussions guide each of us in judging what is reasonable to expect of ourselves and each other, and just how and where family resources ought to be spent.

If goals for the family have not been articulated, the vacuum will be filled by the diverse and often divergent goals of the individual members. This is especially true when some family members are stronger or more active than others, parents versus children, for example or highly motivated children versus those whose purposes in life are less well defined. Here's an illustrative scenario:

Clifford, the father of several teenage children, has been offered a promotion. The new job, though well paid and full of challenge and opportunity, requires a move to a larger city, several years of nearly constant travel, and evenings filled with extra work from the office. Melissa, Clifford's wife, who knows her bookkeeping business is fairly portable—and might even do better, in fact, in a larger city—supports the move. Mark, the oldest son, however, sees it as a major blow to his three-year dream of becoming a varsity football star. "Can I hold my own at a new, big city school," he worries, "up against a crowd of two-hundred-pound jocks?" Small wonder that Mark angrily opposes any relocation until his high school years are finished.

On the surface, the issue seems to be cut and dried, at least from the parents' perspective. To them the advantages are irrefutable—the promotion means more money for the family and the prospects of new and wider horizons in an exciting city. These facts seem clear, but do they, in truth, promise a more satisfying life? It depends upon the answers to more basic goal questions which Mark's resistance is raising, although he is probably quite unaware of it: "What kind of family is this? Is rich and semifatherless what we want?" "Is this family only for you guys? What about me?" "Why do we need to be rich? Isn't comfortable enough?"

Suppose that these and similar questions had been regularly raised and hashed over at family meetings, over dinner, at overnight camp outs, or on long drives? Would his objections to the move have been prevented? The answer may surprise you. Much evidence, drawn from studies in many different kinds of organizations (including families), suggests that giving those whose lives will be affected a chance to raise, and be heard on, such questions does make a difference when it comes to working out and implementing important decisions. Mark will still be disappointed if the move proceeds, but he will not be as embittered by it; and at least he will not have been surprised. Remember that the predictability of stress-producing events lessens their capacity to erode self-esteem and the ability to cope. Mark would see the decision not as a diminution of himself, but as an action that carried out a clearly stated preeminent family goal: building and supporting the careers of the family breadwinners. He might not like it, but he will understand that first priority for his own goals will come only when he is out of the family unit and on his own.

Ideally, the achievement of a family's overall goals would also satisfy each individual. This is seldom the case, of course, because families, like the people who compose them, are living, breathing organisms, and their needs and desires change as they develop. In addition, at any given time most of us are loaded with so many goals that at least some of them are bound to be contradictory. We are quite aware of that in our own family, often bemoaning a lack of free time while simultaneously undertaking more and more ambitious professional tasks. A family goal that pointed us toward either greater glory or financial resources (at the cost of leisure) or escape from the rat race (at the cost of lessened fame or fortune) would provoke at least temporary resistance in one or both of us. To further complicate the problem of reconciling family goals with the wishes of individuals, at some stages of development contrariness itself, often as a step toward independence, becomes a chief goal in life. The naysaying of two-year-olds, thirteen-year-old girls, and sixteen-year-old boys comes readily to mind. Finally, the sheer number of goals that *might* be attained if diligently pursued is in itself overwhelming. Every event in each eventful day thrusts a hundred additional tasks at you, all leading to some possible satisfactions. Somehow choices must be made, and they always will be—by inertia, by a lack of time and money, or by simply taking care of that which hurts the most at the moment.

Given these true dilemmas, some potent means for reaching agreement on the blending of family and individual goals and for thoughtfully setting priorities are a necessity. That is precisely why we've included Chapters 2, 3, and 4 in this book.

Signs and Symptoms of Problems with Goals and Priorities

— Arguments about spending family money (How much and on what kinds of things should our money be spent?)
— Perceptions that others in the family are spendthrifts, or cheapskates
— Feelings that "life has passed you by"
— Arguments about how time should be spent on anything
— A sense that there are just too many things to be done all at once

— A feeling of being deprived of things, or attentions, that are rightfully yours

The Complex of Roles and Expectations

Most of us, most of the time, try to do what's expected of us. These
expectations may come from ourselves, from people we know, or from
the rules of our larger society. Expectations tell us what to do, and how
to do it if we want to gain the acceptance and approval of others.

When expectations tell us how to perform an entire job, we call them
roles, because they have a lot in common with the roles that actors play
—that is, they tell us how to act and what to say. Mowing the lawn is
really a task that anyone can do if they're physically able; but expectations about how it should be done can change if it's categorized either
as "man's work" (from a landscape gardener, for example) or "kid's
work." "Lawn mowing" names a task. "Man's work" describes a role.

A role, therefore, is simply a label we give to a set of expectations that
cluster around a particular occupation. "Mother," "father," "child,"
"boy," "girl," "manager," and "teacher" are examples of roles; simply
put, they are occupational titles followed by long lists of prescriptive
statements which describe what a perfect performer of that role would
look like. For example, the role expectations for a child might be:

1. A child is always jolly and never cross.
2. A child appreciates things that are done for him or her.
3. A child is dedicated to educational achievement, particularly
   homework.
4. A child is obedient.
5. A child is truthful.

Two qualities of this abbreviated set of role instructions may have
caught your eye: They paint an impossibly idealized picture of a child,
and they paint it from the perspective of what would most gratify a
parent or teacher. For it is an example of what has been called a "sent"
role—a set of messages that we send to others to tell them what we
expect from them. We write them down in children's storybooks, job
descriptions, marriage vows, prenuptial contracts, church pamphlets,
and scouting handbooks, replete with qualifying comments. Our own
heads have been filled with these sets of marching orders, each one
telling us how we, and those who are important to us, should behave.
One problem, of course, is that often we have taken quite diverse roles

unto ourselves which bombard us with instructions to behave in quite opposite ways. You are in a true dilemma when your "good mother" roles says "Give time to your kids" while your "professional" role tells you "Weekend or not, the report has to be in on Monday." While the result has got to be much tension, it will be lessened considerably if you are aware of what is happening to you. For that reason we've included an exercise at the end of this chapter which can help you sort through your own repertoire of roles.

Contradictory expectations within, however, are but a part of the problem. An equally great source of relationship problems is the exasperating fact that different people have very different sets of expectations filed under the same role title. You may go about your business thinking that you're the very model of a perfect helpmate while the mate that you are helping wonders where you ever learned to fold a shirt or balance a checkbook. A more effective means for generating conflict is hard to imagine.

Similarly, family members can have quite different ideas about who is supposed to do which jobs, or whether or not they need to be done at all: I think that kids should mow the lawn once a week; you believe twice a month is enough and its a job for anyone who is around—not just kids. Further, my expectation that I have a right to tell you what to do may not match yours. And when the lawn is finally mowed, we might have quite different ideas about how well it was done. Each of these differences in our expectations, of ourselves and of each other, can lead us to disappointment. It is a maggoty kind of disappointment that grows by eating away at the trust and confidence in which we hold one another.

Hidden differences in task and role expectations can be the most vexing of all because they are a part of every aspect of daily life: love, work, and recreation. None of us can escape from them. Therefore, for our own protection, we'd better get them clarified, and where possible, agreed upon.

Signs and Symptoms of Unclear Expectations

— Routine but essential jobs are done only on a last-minute or emergency basis. For example, the cat box is not cleaned out until visitors turn green.

— Jobs are poorly done or partially completed. For example, the exterior of the car is washed but the inside is left littered with school papers, dog toys, and moldy French fries.

— Two people wind up doing the same job, together or separately. For example, when I do the dishes, you come along and rewash all the pots.

— Nagging has become a primary method of job control.

— Unfinished jobs are viewed not as oversights or misunderstandings, but as signs of "resistance to authority."

— Conscientious family workers begin to feel like not so willing martyrs on the altar of domestic hygiene.

— Genuine surprise at a housemate's list of grievances or a complaint that he or she seems to be unappreciated.

— Resentment over apparent broken promises. Did you *really* promise to fix the sink or did you merely agree that it *ought* to be fixed?

— Constant mumbling about "spoiled kids."

— Lack of caring behavior (whatever that means to you) from someone who professes to care for you. Sally's consternation over Ted's lack of intimate communication is an example of this.

Communications: The Problems of Keeping in Touch

If we lived isolated lives—one of the advantages of becoming a hermit —this problem area would go away. But human beings are for the most part social creatures; certainly, that label applies to anyone reading this book. Whether or not people get pleasure from interacting with one another, anytime they work together in a coordinated way they must somehow be apprised of what each of the others is about. Keeping in touch is a necessity for successful accomplishment when vital human needs are concerned. Therefore, the "keeping in touch" system deals with the ridiculous *and* the sublime. It manages such mundane tasks as coordinating the dinner schedule and making sure telephone messages are delivered. It also is the means for sharing intimate feelings and personal anxieties. Key questions to ask in making sure that this system is working well include: Are the messages getting to the right person at the right place at the right time? Are the messages clearly understandable and understood? Does the sender of the message *know* that communication was accomplished?

Here are some clues that will tell you if you're getting the kind, quality, and quantity of communication you need.

Signs and Symptoms That You Are Out of Touch

—Confusion over what the other person is *really* saying or what their motivation is for "keeping in touch." For example, Charlie complains at length to his wife Frieda about his current business worries, then switches abruptly to talk about the current football season. Frieda is left scratching her head about whether or not Charlie is on the verge of bankruptcy or is merely having another bout with a late-paying customer.

—Family members feel that others cut them off while they are talking and aren't interested in what they have to say.

—Important messages about family relationships are indirect or confusing. Examples:

· Blanket accusations are made, such as "no one cares about me."
· Jack, a high school senior, complains about demands that he leave an intinerary every time he borrows the family car. His father replies that when *he* was in school, there wasn't even a family car to borrow. Jack is uncertain about just what he's being told: "Shut up," "Be grateful," or "Things were tougher in the old days."

—Messages from third parties are lost or not delivered.

The Decision-Making System

Anytime anyone does anything, it always means that somewhere a decision was made, whether or not those involved were aware of it. (Even as you read this book you are deciding not to do any of those other tasks that are nagging for your attention.) So the question is never *whether* decisions will be made, only if they will be made appropriately and well. Work groups must have some planned means for making decisions. In families, however, the decision-making apparatus tends to be less formalized. Nowadays, changing role definitions add to the confusion—it's not often simply assumed that the man has the right to decide for everyone. So decisions often just happen with family members not quite sure when they were finalized.

Rich walks through the front door, bubbling with high spirits. "Jeanie," he says, "remember that washing machine we looked at the other night? Well, I stopped at Dinkleman's on my way home from work tonight and bought the little beauty." Jean hardly pauses in her salad tossing: "All I know is that you're late again. Now wash up—dinner's on the table."

If you are saying to yourself, "How could Rich have been so thoughtless—making a decision like that himself?" or "Witchy, bitchy Jean should never have deflated her loving husband that way," then you probably should go back and begin this chapter again. Jean's disappointment in what otherwise should have been a pleasant surprise, and Rich's breezy assumption that he had a perfect right to make the final choice of which appliance to buy, reflect the same source of trouble: lack of some clarifying discourse about how, in what way, and by whom decisions in the Jean and Rich family will be ṃade. To Jean the washing machine question was still open. They had talked about which brand might be the best for them, but was that a decision? Jean wasn't sure about that, or who had the right to execute whatever decision was made. She evidently didn't think it was Rich.

Even supposedly simple decisions can breed a multitude of misunderstandings if the family system for deciding hasn't been put in order. As a case in point, let's look at the potentially awesome decision of buying a loaf of bread.

Duane, recently chastised for his lack of attention to family matters, vows to do himself and the family a good turn. He vaguely recalled hearing at breakfast that the bread supply was low, so he stopped on his way home and picked up a loaf of white sandwich bread to see them through the week. He proudly announces his clever purchase, only to be informed that both his wife and eldest daughter have just bought bread, and anyway there were already two loaves of sandwich bread in the freezer. What was *really* needed was a package of English muffins for Grandma and a loaf of bakery-quality rye bread to go along with the cold cuts being served for dinner. Duane, his sense of competence in family affairs torpedoed again, whispers to himself that "shopping is women's work anyway" and slinks off to his study.

Why did Duane's decision to buy bread—so full of good intentions at the outset—turn out so badly? First of all, his basic decision-making technique left much to be desired. He hadn't checked the facts: What was on hand? What was really needed? Second, he had concluded that bread-buying decisions were his to make without checking with his wife, who was responsible for the food budget. In other words, Duane (1) acted without enough real information to ensure a quality decision and (2) acted unilaterally without consulting more knowledgeable family members. To top it all, he then confused his faulty decision-making system with invalid role expectations (a convenient fall guy for many uncomfortable situations).

Decision-making problems show up most often in families where there is insufficient knowledge of how information is gathered, alternatives thought out, and choices put into action.

Here are some symptoms that will tell you if your decision-making system is malfunctioning.

Signs and Symptoms of Problems in the Decision-making System

— People find themselves wrangling over decisions they don't really care about.

— Problem discussions often end without a clear understanding of what was decided.

— Decisions materialize without anyone knowing when, or by whom, they've been made.

— After the decision discussions are frequently a forum for accusations and complaints.

— The implementers of your decisions habitually complain and drag their feet.

— Decisions are often made in haste, without considering available information.

The Problem of Trust and Confidence

Most people eventually realize that love, friendship, and trust don't necessarily go hand in hand. Liking may never blossom into love. Friends may still be friends, even though they lie a little. And unfaithful lovers have been the mainstay of romantic literature. Fortunately, perfect harmony is not at all necessary for an efficiently running, havenly household. As parents of battling siblings can attest, friendship, while fun, isn't an essential to keeping the family ship afloat. Even love, exalting as it is, can be dispensed with. What *is* necessary, however, is a belief on the part of family members that, no matter how obnoxious they may find a parent, child, sibling, or helpmate, no one in the family is consciously "out to get them." Also required is confidence that chores that have been entrusted to a family member will in reasonable likelihood be accomplished. In other words, each must *trust* the others' good intentions and have *confidence* in their ultimate ability to carry them out.

These two kinds of beliefs are interconnected, but by no means interchangeable. For example, we have known a physician—a surgeon by training, though he now seldom practices that craft, and for good reason. He has, over the years, developed poor motor coordination; in other words, his hands shake. Now we know that this physician has nothing but the best intentions for his patients. Yet we would never consent to have him operate on us or ours because zigzag incisions hurt a lot. (He has now confined his practice to diagnosis and consultation.) Similarly, we know of absolutely top-notch surgeons we would engage only after a fourth opinion. Why? Because we suspect their motives are more closely tied to their inflated fees than our good health. Put in the simplest way, trust is a belief on my part that you mean everything you're telling me, while confidence is my belief that you can deliver what you promise.

Building trust is a tedious and fragile business; putting it together requires care and patience. Yet trust must be the foundation of any deep relationship, and we all depend on it for security in a rapidly changing and sometimes hostile world. Once trust has been lost, it's devilishly hard to regain, simply because matters of trust depend on attitudes and beliefs more than hard, demonstrable facts. The question is not so much whether you do indeed mean what you say as whether *I believe* you mean it. That is why a crisis in trust and confidence is one of the most difficult to resolve. Let's take a look at a typical example:

Kate: Have you gotten any calls from the ad to sell your old motorcycle?

Hank: Uh, not exactly.

Kate: What does that mean?

Hank: Well, I wrote the ad, but I haven't called the newspaper yet.

Kate: What? You told me a month ago that you would sell that rusty old thing. Besides, we need the money for the baby's room. And you *know* you promised.

Hank: I forgot. I'll call in the ad tomorrow.

Kate: Sure—that's what you said three weeks ago.

Hank: Look, I said I'd send it in and I will. What do you want from me anyway?

Kate: I just want to be able to believe what you tell me.

Hank: Do you think I'm lying to you?
Kate: Well, I don't know what else to call it.

Hank and Kate have a problem, and the way this conversation is going, they'll never solve it. Sure, it had been hard for him to agree to sell his beloved motorcycle, even in the interest of a growing family, yet he had at length decided to do it. How unfair to well-intentioned Hank that his procrastination has convinced Kate that he can't be trusted. To make things worse, Kate will probably chalk up the eventual sale of the machine to her own persistence, and is likely to accuse Hank in advance the next time he makes a serious promise. What's worse, things may go on this way until Hank despairs of convincing Kate that he is worthy of her trust. It is the ironic essence of trust relations that once lost, they cannot be regained by dealing directly with them—that is, by vowing to be trustworthy. Once Kate has lost faith in Hank, any protestations to the contrary will merely be seen as evidence that he's not only irresponsible, he's also a liar. In any event, rebuilding that trust—rightly or wrongly lost—will be a slow process.

To rebuild a serious loss of trust and confidence requires an open acknowledgment that a breach of trust has occurred, a statement that your intention is to be trustworthy, and most importantly, zealous attention to each of the other problem areas discussed in this chapter. For when family members talk together about common goals, clarify what they expect of one another, maintain good and candid communications, and keep the mechanics of family life in good working order, breakdowns in the mutual trust network will seldom occur. So repairing a loss of confidence requires a conscious and sustained effort to discover and fix anything amiss in those same vital family systems. In sum, the loss of trust and confidence is almost always a by-product of failure in other family systems.

Here are some indications that trouble could be brewing in this important area.

Signs and Symptoms of Trust System Breakdown

— Disbelief that others are truthfully "calling them as they see them."
— Apprehension about the future of the relationship. Sally's worry about Ted's "drifting away" is an example.

— Derogatory comments or sniping about the other kids, or about relatives or friends.

— Unwillingness of parents to delegate tasks to the children, or of one parent or partner to trust the other with such tasks.

— Excessive or unrealistic worry that mistakes or unsatisfactory results will come from another's efforts.

— Frequent use of the statement "I just don't understand how he (or she) could . . ."

The Problem of Faulty Methods and Mechanisms

Gaze with envy on Jim and Cheryl.

They have always wanted similar things out of life—for themselves and for their family. They agree on sharing the family's work load, communicate often and well, and their level of mutual trust approaches sainthood. They even agree that all significant decisions should be made jointly.

What's that? You've noticed a decidedly unhappy look on their faces?

Well, it all started that afternoon when Jim forgot to give Cheryl an urgent message from one of her most important clients. "Call back *no* later than 5:30 P.M.," said the message. What a pity that the message was finally delivered at 6:15 P.M.

Jim mightily and properly castigated himself unmercifully for his poor memory, and Cheryl forgave him as charitably as she could.

On the following day, however, Jim waited an extra hour for Cheryl to pick him up at the train station. It seems Cheryl "forgot" that his car was being left for service in the city. Naturally, Cheryl apologized profusely for her awful memory, and Jim accepted as graciously as he could. Is this simply the balance of nature at work, one poor memory deserving another? Or did you silently suspect that Cheryl might be having her revenge—unconsciously, at least—for Jim's previous flub. Both may be true, but as is true of most symptoms, they distract our attention from the real culprit: the breakdown in the system of nuts and bolts that holds everything together. For good intentions, even full agreement on all the basic tenets of this chapter, are not enough to keep a household running smoothly. There must be a practical system for nailing down those agreements and smoothly putting them into action. Even though Cheryl and Jim want to communicate, *love* to communicate, and do communicate frequently in a positive, supportive manner, that alone isn't enough to avoid occasional (or more than occasional) run-ins with misfortune. What they needed, and didn't have, was a *mechanism* for focusing their communication on the matters at hand. They needed to better schedule their meetings so as to avoid irritating and time-wasting omissions or duplications of effort. And both need some handy-dandy methods for buttressing their faulty memory circuits.

In communications or any other area—from decision making to bed making—methods and mechanisms can speed up tasks, ensure higher-quality work, ward off mistakes, and generally lower the stress in any household. In a very real way, memory helpers, family meetings, and priority-setting methods are the "glue" that holds all the others together. If they are faulty or nonexistent in certain areas, trouble is bound to follow, often snowballing into bigger and tougher problems. In one sense problems in this area are not as basic to family life as others we've discussed. With enough trust, talking and love, Cheryl and Jim will get by, even if she does lose a client now and again because "Jim just can't remember anything." Yet living with inadequate methods and mechanisms can guarantee aggravation, more painful perhaps because it is so unnecessary.

Here are the signs of rusty family machinery:

Signs and Symptoms of Inadequate Methods and Mechanisms

— There is a lot of talk about tasks and goals but very little action.
— Messages are frequently lost or forgotten.
— Bills or important documents are frequently misplaced.
— Decisions seem to be made unilaterally, though everyone agrees they should be shared.
— Everyone agrees that priorities are important, but somehow they are never set.

Now you've become further acquainted with the essential foundations on which your family is built, and have identified which part may be the shakiest. Next comes the action—selecting some solutions that appear promising and trying them out.

STEP #3: SELECT A SOLUTION AND TRY IT ON

Your perspective about a problem largely determines the way you go about solving it. If you are ill, say with a serious bacterial infection, how do you define your problem? You may see it in immediate terms: kill the bug, get well, and forget how terrible you felt. Or you may view it from a longer-term perspective as staying healthy. From the first point of view, a proper solution is a shot of antibiotic. From the second, you'll view overcoming your current illness as only the first step to improved health overall, perhaps involving penicillin to start with, but moving on to a better diet, more rest, and a program of regular exercise.

This latter view is the perspective we take in outlining the solutions in this book. Each of its chapters contains methods that have worked for us, our clients, and our friends. Used singly or in combination, they can, like penicillin pills, cure specific ills. Even more importantly from our vantage point, they can also provide a framework for prevention. By regularly checking on the status of each of your family systems, you can renew and refurbish any that aren't doing as well as they might, before trouble starts. Whether or not your intention is cure or prevention, before an improvement occurs you'll have to select appropriate methods and mechanisms.

The following table will help match the solutions offered in the book with the problem areas we've outlined in this chapter.

PROBLEMS	CHAPTERS									
	1	2	3	4	5	6	7	8	9	10
Goals	X	X							X	
Roles and Tasks			X	X						
Keeping in Touch					X		X	X	X	
Decisions							X			
Trust and Confidence			X	X			X			
Methods and Mechanisms			X	X			X	X		X

Of course, since people differ in many ways, you'll have to adapt methods to your own family and situation. You'll find that the more you try these methods and the more you learn about your family, the easier such adaptations will become—and the more effective their result.

The hardest part of any new endeavor, particularly one that's unfamiliar, is getting started. Fortunately, that realization alone may be enough to get you under way. We have also found that it doesn't pay to try to get things perfect the first time out. Don't waste valuable time by trying to understand everything in advance. We've tried to lay out each method in a step-by-step fashion that will allow you to get started at once, even if the concept you're working with still is not completely clear. You don't need to know how aspirin works to let it cure your headache.

As you proceed through the steps, however, you'll find out for yourself what each method is about. By then, you'll be well on your way and less likely to be intimidated by the whole thing. In each chapter we've also tried to identify the more common pitfalls you may encounter on the way. If and when they occur, don't be discouraged. Yours isn't the first family to encounter and overcome them.

The main idea is to begin at once. If you follow the steps with reasonable care, the method itself will see you through.

STEP #4: CHECK YOUR PROGRESS AND MODIFY YOUR APPROACH

As you implement the methods that seem appropriate, don't forget to pause now and then and check your progress. Here are some questions you may find useful to ask during these periodic reviews:

1. *Did we do it as we intended?* Sometimes, especially if things are going well, it's tempting to skip a step. For example, an essential part of the chore list method is that it be written down. Did you, in the exultation of a surprisingly speedy family agreement, let that one particular detail slip your mind? If so, you're setting yourself up for trouble down the line and a return to the nagging and frustration. The idea here is to make sure that you applied the method properly.

2. *What actually happened compared to what we hoped would happen?* Suppose that after reading Chapter 4 you decided to inaugurate a program of family meetings. If so, what were the outcomes? Did anyone show up? Was there an agenda? Was the agenda followed or ignored? Were plans or decisions effectively implemented? Keep in mind that whatever methods you chose to use will have a variety of effects, some positive, some negative, some planned, and some completely unexpected. Getting a fix on these effects will provide the basis for modifying your efforts so as to get more of the positive and less of the negative.

3. *In the light of our experience to date, how should we modify our plan?* If your family is like most others, you will find that modifying your method will be the rule rather than the exception. Here are two such modifications that stand out in our memories. Our first attempts at chore lists weren't nearly specific enough. Oh, they were clear enough in our minds, but not where it counted—on paper. Fearing what might happen if we removed them from the bulletin board for even an instant, we simply scribbled the needed particulars in the margins and in any other available space, a minor modification that greatly improved the result. Similarly, in our first attempts to apply the Noah's Ark Paired-Comparisons Method (Chap. 2), we crunch.d all of the numbers correctly and neatly filled all of the spaces, yet we weren't immediately galvanized into action. Then we discovered that we were putting the wrong question—"What's most important?"—to it. The right question —"What will reduce the stress in our life the most?"—turned out to be the winner.

Don't be at all cautious about modifying the methods to suit the particular needs of your own family. For example, one of our clients found that while her children tended to ignore the family message board (writing is lots of work when you're eight), they talked with relish into the tape recorder. Subsequently, all family messages (and a few really superior animal imitations) were left on a recorder placed conveniently near the telephone. Just be certain that the modifications you make do not destroy the essence of the method you've chosen.

4. *Are we solving the wrong problem very effectively?* You may on occasion find, after energetically and persistently applying a given method, that the old aggravations just keep on occurring. You hope that will never happen, but if it does, you must ask yourself two additional questions: "Are we attacking the right problem in the wrong way?" or "Are we solving the wrong problem very effectively?" In the first case, you're on the right track, but you may have selected methods that simply don't fit the style of your family. In that case, select other methods to try, or modify those you are working on to fit your needs better. In the second case, you must make a new, and now better informed, search for the source of the problem. Here is an example of incorrect problem assessment:

Our family used to wrangle incessantly about who got to watch what show every time the TV set was on. In our first attempts to keep the peace, we made the simple (and, as it turned out, simple-minded) rule that each family member was expected to take turns in selecting among alternate shows. If there should be (perish the thought) disagreements, they were to be resolved without fighting. To put teeth in this plan, we even drew up a set of negative consequences for the negotiators to contemplate if the situation escalated toward the physical. The unplanned result of this logical approach was constant chaos. For a time, the wall of negative consequences held, then business went back to its old high-decibel level. We began to dig a little deeper. We gathered some data by individually "interviewing" the kids and then sat down to reassess the situation. Here is what we learned: We had incredibly underestimated the attachment each one of us felt toward favorite programs. Surrendering them to a sibling rival was not unlike giving hostages to a foreign country. It became, in other words, a test of power between family members as to who would watch what. Some kids, in fact, exercised their turns not so much to see their own favorites as to deprive their rival of the same opportunity. As for ourselves, we were confident we could take the tube or leave it alone. On the other hand, as we reasoned to ourselves, since we watched it infrequently, we had a perfect right to preempt anyone's turn whenever there was a "quality" program we wished to see. We were surprised to find that there was very incomplete agreement with this soundly logical and completely justifiable (to us) analysis. They, it seems, would have been perfectly willing to allow us to watch whatever we wished during those times when their favorite programs were not appearing; when our favorites competed with theirs, it was a different matter. With a strong feeling that our own logic had been turned against us, we fell back in some disarray. What we had taken to be problems of parental authority and unclear expectations turned out to be neither. We looked again at the symptoms: disagreements about whose preferences counted the most; no system for setting priorities; a sense of injustice and exclusion from the decision-making process.

How did we handle the situation? First of all, we admitted that we had devised a good solution for the wrong problem. We then determined that our real problem areas—the *real* lairs for the *real* bears in the situation—were goals, and priorities, and a poor decision-making process. We set ourselves to discard the previous TV monitoring system and try something else. The first step was to involve everyone in the solution to the problem. We therefore announced a family meeting three days ahead. Each family member was asked to review the television log and bring to the family meeting a list of favorite programs. Then at the family meeting we compromised, negotiated, and traded our way to an agreement in which each person was assured of an unquestioned right to watch his or her "absolutely most favorite" program. It became clear to us all that no one could expect to watch everything he or she wanted without the addition of three extra TV sets, an option that we had excluded from the start. Interestingly enough, there were fewer conflicts than we anticipated, and certainly fewer than there would have been under our previous system. The goals of the family (equitable viewing time for everyone) were synchronized with individual needs (the desire for specific programs) by establishing mutually agreeable priorities (reducing the need for power struggles). The key, again, was asking ourselves, "Have we tracked those symptoms to the right problem area(s)?"

STEP #5: EVALUATE AND CELEBRATE

If you follow our usual pattern, success will sneak up on you. The signs of your accomplishment will include the absence of irritations, a gratifying sense of control over what's happening in your family, and a gradual awareness that you're feeling better about things because the pain you *used* to feel is gone. Once you realize this, you will experience the additional satisfaction of knowing you've finally trapped those troublesome bears that so long eluded your grasp.

At this point you may want to sit down together as a family and compare life the way it is with the way it (groan) was. Is the getting-up-in-the-morning panic a thing of the past? Are you spending less time fuming while you wait for your partner to show up? Are household chores now being done routinely and well? Was the end result of your last major purchase quiet satisfaction rather than a fusillade of accusations and recriminations?

If so, let each other know it and have a celebration—you deserve it! But formally recognizing success is more than an excuse for a party. It provides the support that will help you through those instances that don't work quite so well, and the courage to try again and keep going until you find your way clear.

WHEN TO GET OUTSIDE HELP

It is always easier to see straight to the heart of other people's problems. For that reason it's sometimes well worth it to involve an outsider in helping to assess your own family situation. Here are some possibilities.

Friends

Some friends can help you to a heightened perspective. Others will pull you deeper into the quicksand out of which you're trying to struggle. Especially avoid those sweet souls who help you to deny that you're having any problems at all by saying, "Everyone has problems, my dear." Relinquish also the solace of friends who agree, with arid enthusiasm, that your prospects are ghastly, and then help you to understand that it's all someone else's fault. Instead, look for friends who will share their own experiences with you, those with whom you do not have to seem perfect and always in control. Best of all, talk to a friend who will ask questions rather than give prescriptions, and the more difficult the questions the better. At some point, usually near the end of your discussion, a person like this will ask you, "Have you told (whomever it is) just what you've told me in just that way?" Your answer very likely will be no, and you will have found the first step toward lightening your load. You can assist such a friend (yes, we know they're rare, but they do exist) by saying ahead of time what you expect from the conversation. If you want feedback on your ideas, ask for it. If you simply want a willing ear to listen while you blow off steam, ask for that, too. Above all, give your friend permission—if feedback is what you want—to be honest. Remember that social restraints run deep, and even close friends will think twice before offering views they think may hurt your feelings.

Finally, don't ask for their advice on what to do. What you hear may fit your friend's needs very well, but is less likely to fit yours. Use your friend as a sounding board for your own ideas, but never forget that old and very wise saying: "If I ask Peter (my friend) to tell me about Paul (me), I will learn more about Peter than I will about Paul."

Using Professional Therapists and Counselors

As consultants and counselors ourselves, we have seen many success-ful executives who, while truly believing they could benefit from our help, decline to ask for it. They are convinced that successful people should be able to solve their own problems by themselves. The fact is, as much research has shown, this position is largely false. One of the marks of top managers everywhere is a rich understanding of the tough-ness of life in general, and of their own limitations in particular, capped by a willingness to seek help wherever they can get it. A captain, per-haps, has the right to go down with the ship, but we think he ought to have a very good reason for doing so. To wait to seek professional help until driven to it by a life that is falling apart is not only unnecessarily painful, but rather stupid to boot. For it is always easier to prevent than to cure; even cures work better earlier rather than later.

Professional helpers are not superhuman—guardian angels who will swoop down and rescue you from your problems. Their most valuable commodity is a perspective from which you can look with momentary detachment at your own entanglements. Other aids are a "safe house" in which to express pent-up feelings which may be blocking your prob-lem-solving attempts; insight that can help you understand complicated emotions; and tough, realistic optimism that can support you through trying times. Some of which we hope you will find in this book.

If, simply from reading these pages, you find that you are able to formulate plans and get started on implementing them—great! You will have received your counseling via the printed word—not as personal as we both might like, but effective nonetheless, and considerably less ex-pensive than face-to-face consultations.

Suppose, on the other hand, that you've seen the point of what we're proposing and approve of the methods we've suggested, but you have not been able to translate your ideas into action. Then time with a professional counselor may be just the ticket for you. Our own experi-ence suggests that intermittent short-term counseling with the right professional can be extremely useful, and certainly a better alternative than enduring the needless pain of continued family problems.

Above All, Stay Optimistic—and Realistic

The evidence of our own experience and of that of our friends and clients says loudly and clearly: Be optimistic. It's not only possible that you can get a fix on your own family's problem areas, it is highly probable. The odds are that your miseries are not due to perverse personalities, but simply to an incomplete job of putting together or maintaining a cooperative family organization.

Yet even with this realization, the going will not be easy. A task as large as realigning faulty family systems is going to take some doing. Your brave optimism, therefore, must be tempered with a solid dose of realism.

Expect to try and try again. All systems tend to wobble and break down over time, even the good ones. Expect to wake up one morning to the kids wrangling over the TV set and your spouse or significant other bitching about last night's dishes in the sink. Remind yourself, as we did, that it has been a year or two or three since the system was first put into place, and that the time has probably long since arrived to rejuvenate it, recast it, or simply let it die a dignified death and give something new a try.

Keep an eye out for warning flags. If you live on one of our stormy coasts, you're used to seeing special flags that warn residents and skippers of approaching gales or hurricanes. Sailors, and other careful people, take them very seriously. Fortunately, family storms seldom blow in without first sending up signals of approaching heavy weather. You must, however, keep a sharp lookout for these signs, for they are often subtle. Our writing of this book, for example, began gradually, without formal declaration, to overstress our previously adequate household systems. Like hardy sailors in a strong ship, we resolutely ignored the signs, thrusting ourselves even harder at the achievement of our goals: to finish the book and keep both home and office fires burning. We gritted our teeth (to keep from yelling at each other) and nobly picked up the increasing number of loose ends. Thankfully, a fortuitous ten-day hiatus provided a pause in which to face the symptoms of impending overload.

We reassessed the status of our systems, retuned them, and committed ourselves to watch them frequently and with more care. It worked.

Keep always in mind that in times of stress, personal defense mechanisms are much sensitized and easily triggered. When stacks blow, therefore, it's especially critical to take a deep breath, a day off, and a hard look at what needs to be done to shore up the family's understructure for whatever lies ahead.

EXERCISES

1. In the spaces below, list ten troublesome symptoms that currently irritate, frustrate, or worry you, or others in your family (review page 99 for examples).

Symptoms	*How Long*
1.	
2.	
3.	
4.	
5.	
6.	
7.	
8.	
9.	
10.	

2. To the right of each symptom, indicate how many months or years it's been hurting. This should motivate you to continue on to the hard part, coming up next.

3. Now alternate your attention, back and forth, between your list and the lists of signs and symptoms that we've suggested are clues to a breakdown in a family system (you'll find them between pages 104 and 117). In the spaces below, note the three systems that could use the most strengthening in your family.

_____

_____

_____

_____

Insight: You're trying to identify those circumstances which tend to bring out the worst in each of the family members mentioned in your systems list. For example, unclear mutual expectations don't *make* Roger self-centered and thoughtless, but they make it mighty easy for that side of him to control what he does.

CHAPTER 6

Styles of Thinking; or, "Who's Who in the Family Zoo"

Josh slumped into an easy chair, a motion mastered only by disgruntled, perpetually picked upon sixteen-year-olds. "Mom, if Dad's s'pposed to be so smart at work, how come he's so *dumb* at home?"

Helen, Josh's mother, glanced out from the kitchen. "Josh, is that any way to talk about your father? What's the problem now?"

"Oh, nothing much. He just spent half an hour telling me how to change the oil in the car when I've already done it a hundred times myself. It's just dumb."

"Well," Helen said, "he just wants to make sure everything's done the proper way. That's why he's such a good engineer. Just try and understand him a little."

"Oh, I understand him all right," Josh tossed out. "He's a nitpicker, and not just about the car. He counts every nickel we spend and treats us all like we don't know up from down."

"That's enough, young man!" Helen said firmly. "I'm sorry you're so upset, but I won't let you insult your father that way."

She watched Josh stalk out of the room. "I guess every teenaged boy fights with his father," she thought ruefully, "but I'll have to admit that Josh has his dad pegged. I love that man but he can be *exasperating.*"

Her reverie was interrupted as her husband, Carl, came angrily into the kitchen. "That boy is completely hopeless, Helen. I tried to tell him how to keep the oil from spilling all over the garage the way it did last time, and all I got was his usual bored, smart-aleck look. What's the matter with him anyway? Why doesn't he want to do things the right way?"

"Well, Josh can be pretty careless sometimes," Helen agreed. "I'm *always* picking up after him. But maybe there's a better way to try to put some sense in him. I don't think lecturing does much good."

"What does?" rejoined Carl. "Helen, what in the world are we to do?"

"Indeed." Helen thought, "What am *I* to do—about both of you? Why do you two rub each other the wrong way so much when you're both actually pretty nice guys?"

Of course they're both nice guys, Mom. More's the pity that their perpetual wrangling keeps them from appreciating each other. Even sadder that their misery is not simply the result of a stubborn aberration of character. It's the product of an amazingly pervasive human characteristic called *assuming similarity*. We are all guilty of it much of the time, but we hardly ever know it; that's what makes it so dangerous.

Most of us, most of the time, assume that others are just like we are, but a little bit defective. (If we're having an attack of low self-esteem, we make the same assumption but conclude that *we're* the ones with the faulty personalities.) When they don't behave as sensible, proper-feeling people should, we label them dumb, dense, or difficult, and we've taken the first step down the road to unnecessary anger and resentment. Nine times out of ten, they are not especially difficult, they are just different, as unlike us on the inside as they are on the outside. The fact is that while everyone of us thinks, feels, and wants, we each think differently, want different things for ourselves, and are aroused by quite different sets of circumstances. That is why the wonderful people in your family, those familiar faces that you know so well, can often seem so hard to understand. You may be thinking to yourselves at this point, "Of course they're different. I know that." And so you do. The curious and fascinating fact about us all is that while at one level we "know" that others are unique, we continue to act as if they were not. Fortunately, there is a way out of this dilemma. The more you know about how you all differ, the less likely you will be to see differences as defects. Our purpose in this chapter and the next will be to introduce you to two of the most intriguing of the many ways in which people differ. First, we will take you on a brief journey into the varied ways in which your own and your hard-to-understand dear ones' minds work. In the following chapter we'll reintroduce you to the dolts and ditherers in your family who differ principally in their sensitivity to what's going on around them. From both chapters you will find a new kind of awareness of those curious creatures that share your home. Even better, you will have learned some ways to make differences delightful rather than demoralizing.

But before we can do this, we'll need to know a little more about the nature of thoughts in general, and the human beings who think them.

Thinking About Thinking

Thinking is invisible.

We know that it exists because we're aware of it going on in our own minds, and we see the products of other people's thoughts in the problems they solve and the decisions they make. What we don't readily see is that the wheels are turning in our minds in quite distinct ways. So pertinent was this fact to individual competence and the way groups work together that eight years ago we and our professional associates (Allen F. Harrison and Nicholas Parlette)—building on the work of many others—developed a framework for measuring and understanding differences in thinking styles.

How does understanding that people go about their thinking business in quite different ways, help you toward a more havenly home? Here are some of the specific ways that it has helped us and our clients:

— Knowing more about your own preferred Style of Thinking, its strengths and liabilities, will help you adapt the methods we have presented in this book more effectively.

— Understanding other Styles of Thinking will help you make sense (even if it's not your sense) out of the seemingly inexplicable behavior and attitudes of others.

— Knowing how to cope and collaborate with people with other Thinking Styles will help you communicate more clearly and to avoid unintentionally rubbing them the wrong way.

Gaining these benefits, however, requires an understanding of two basic ideas about individual styles of thinking.

First, there is a strong, if not invariable, connection between the way a person thinks and the way that person behaves. Even when you seem to act without thinking, or to think one thing and do another, your thinking machine is always involved.

Second, and this point may be a little less obvious, there are only a handful of ways we humans have developed for gathering data, mentally processing it, and then making decisions. These five modes of thought—we call them Thinking Styles—are the core of the human mind. How we each combine them, in fact, is what makes us unique.

Here's an example of what we mean.

The New-Car Caper

Margo and Rick were each faced with the identical task of buying a new car. What happened to each of them illustrates why, although very much in love, they were never fully at ease with each other.

Margo was a no-nonsense person. She started out her search for a new car by carefully analyzing her transportation needs, the precise amount that the monthly budget would allow her to spend on car payments, and the best time of year to purchase the sort of car she was interested in. She decided that a wise buyer would pick the most economical transportation possible, consistent with ease and economy of maintenance through the years. Margo knew that she was definitely not one of those frivolous "buy a new car every year" people. She comparison-shopped prices and loan terms, and even calculated the precise amounts to put down and to borrow to make the best financial use of a rising inflation rate. Having zeroed in on the make and model that would best suit her needs, she placed an order with her local dealer specifying precisely the options that she wanted, *and* those she would not pay for even if they were included. Margo's husband, Rick, looked on while she became a minor authority on automotive economics. His opinion fluctuated between awed respect for her systematic approach and irritation at her equally systematic skill in taking the fun out of one of life's more pleasant tasks, buying a new car.

Rick's approach, if it can be called that, was quite different. No long hours spent perusing specifications and comparative mileage rates for him. He had rousing conversations with friends about the newest models and their performance characteristics, then he toured the showrooms searching for that particular car that would appeal to his tastes. Every minute he spent trying out each high-performance, turbo-supercharged, engineered-for-the-future model was sheer pleasure. At length, he found his special beauty. It looked right and it felt right; it was "his car." Now Rick settled down for some serious haggling. He glanced at the want ads to get a feel for the highest possible value of his trade-in, and then took a tough bargaining position with the three automobile dealers in town who carried the model he wanted. How could he help but boast to Margo when a chastened dealer called to say he'd "take the deal."

"I told you it would work," Rick said proudly after the call. "My new Firestorm 5000 will be delivered next Tuesday, complete with a set of high-speed hubcaps, dealer's compliments. Pretty neat package, eh?"

"Sure," Margo replied, doodling on her manila folder, "I only hope you take better care of *this* new toy than you did the last one."

"What is that supposed to mean?"

"Oh, nothing. I suppose I can take in laundry to help you make the payments. And we'll have to get a lock for the garage door. You can't leave a car like that parked out on the street. I'm sure the two of you will be very happy."

"Why Can't You See Things My Way?"

As you can see, Margo and Rick were both concerned about satisfying their transportation needs, but *what* they each wanted and *how* they went about satisfying those needs were radically different. Given the same task (buying a new car), they searched out *different* sorts of information, made *different* judgments from the information, and came up with *different* solutions. No wonder, then, that the actions they took were quite different as well.

And no matter what the task we're engaged in, the same is true for each of us.

We all learn many ways to gather facts, weigh them, and draw conclusions, but most of us—like Margo and Rick—have one or two most-used ways of going about it. These preferred styles of thinking largely determine the sort of questions we ask ourselves, what sense we make out of the answers, and the methods we favor for making a decision. In a very significant way, they shape our entire outlook on life.

The car-buying adventures of Margo and Rick also illustrate one of the most frustrating things about being a person—your very strengths often turn against you.

Any human characteristic can be a strength or a liability, depending upon where and how much it is used. Even Rick had to admit that Margo's careful and methodical ways were eminently sensible. Certainly, he could have used more system in his own approach. But it was also true that her automobile, efficient and economical though it was, tied up a good deal of her income without adding much *pleasure* to her life. Rick could have told her (luckily, he didn't) that always being "sensible" may be very sensible, but it takes all the fun out of things. Does that mean he was right all along? After all, there was little doubt that Rick had *fun* before, during, and after buying his new car. The power and control that he felt whenever he drove to and from work added an exciting element to an otherwise uninteresting commute. And even Margo had to admit that Rick's ability to take and hold a tough bargaining stance was a strength. He acquired his bright new beauty at the lowest possible price, so in that sense he made better use of his money than Margo. But its equally true that Rick, not to mention wife Margo, must now scrimp and struggle to stretch a family budget that he overloaded. The salt in Rick's wound, and it must be said that Margo gets no little satisfaction reminding him of it, is the knowledge that his friend Harry found exactly the same performance qualities and even a good bit of dash in a model considerably less expensive than Rick's.

Our point here is twofold. First, it is obvious to anyone of common sense that differing situations call for different ways of thinking and acting. Be steady, systematic, and data-conscious when necessary; be fast-moving, direct, and risk-taking at other times. We all know this truth. The irony is that most of us aren't put together that way. Instead of flexibly shifting our thinking patterns from one appropriate mode to another, we tend to approach every situation using our own preferred ways of thinking. Like well-worn shoes, they are comfortable and feel right. In fact, our research indicates that about 85 percent of us tend to use the *same* one or two approaches to solve too many of the problems we encounter, even when those problems clearly call for alternative styles of thought. We chug along collecting data until the best decision time is long past. Or we make spectacular dives before checking on the presence of water in the pool.

Second, most of the trouble we make for ourselves doesn't come from lack of intelligence or from muddled thinking. We do ourselves in, rather, by bringing to bear too much of a good thing, the very strengths of our favorite styles. Once you are aware of this very human quirk, you can see it on all sides.

For example, there is certainly a place in heaven for those wonderful people who take life as it comes, fitting in with changing circumstances without a look backward. "Adaptable" and "fun to be with" are the terms usually applied. But when those same people shift their goals every week, or even every day, and try so hard to please that they seem not to have the strength of their own convictions, we then call them opportunistic will-o'-the-wisps with no backbone.

Fortunately, this predilection for spoiling a good thing by overusing it can be kept in reasonable bounds. The tool for doing so is a "mind map" that makes sense of ourselves and of those sometimes puzzling, but always interesting, people with whom we share our lives. The purpose of the next section is to give you just that.

STYLES OF THINKING

The names and style sketches that follow, along with a questionnaire called the Inquiry Mode Questionnaire (InQ, for short), are part of a program we and our associates have developed and tested as part of a larger study of differences between intelligence and competence. We sought to find answers to the question "How is it that very intelligent people can sometimes make phenomenally dumb decisions?" Since its inception, we have used the InQ with both individuals and groups to enhance their competence in making sounder decisions, communicating more effectively, and simply connecting better with others.* In our family it has been an argument preventer, a peacemaker, and a surefire cure to our taking ourselves too seriously.

But before we introduce you to these five styles of thinking, it is time for you to get an approximate fix on your preferences. Please read the directions given below and complete the abbreviated version of the InQ you'll find on page 135.

Before going further, make sure that your five total scores add up to 90. If they don't, reread the directions and go back and check your arithmetic. Also, check that you remembered that 5 meant most like you and 1 meant least like you.

We've already mentioned that there are five styles of thinking. Here they are:

The Synthesist
The Idealist
The Pragmatist

* The InQ Questionnaire is copyrighted (1977, 1980) by Bramson, Parlette, Harrison and Associates and reprinted by permission. For further information on its use in training, selection, and group development, write to BPHA, P.O. Box 10213, North Berkeley Station, Berkeley, CA 94707.

YOUR STYLE OF THINKING

DIRECTIONS: Each item in this questionnaire is made up of a statement followed
by five possible endings. In the box to the right of each ending,
fill in the number 5, 4, 3, 2, or 1, indicating the degree to which
an ending is most like you (5), or least like you (1). Do not use any
number more than once for any group of five endings. Each ending
must be ranked 5, 4, 3, 2, or 1.

A. GENERALLY SPEAKING, I ABSORB NEW IDEAS BEST BY:

1. Contrasting them to other ideas
2. Understanding how they are similar to familiar ideas
3. Relating them to current or future activities
4. Concentration and careful analysis
5. Applying them to concrete situations

B. WHEN I READ A REPORT, I AM LIKELY TO PAY THE MOST ATTENTION TO:

1. Whether or not the recommendations can be accomplished
2. The validity of the findings, backed up by data
3. The relation of the conclusions to my own experience
4. The writer's understanding of goals and objectives
5. The inferences that are drawn from the data

C. WHEN THERE IS A CONFLICT OVER IDEAS, I TEND TO FAVOR THE SIDE THAT:

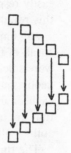

1. Identifies and tries to bring out the conflict
2. Best expresses the values and ideals involved
3. Best reflects my personal opinions and experience
4. Approaches the situation with the most logic and consistency
5. Expresses the argument most forcefully and concisely

D. IF I WERE TO BE TESTED OR EXAMINED, I WOULD PREFER:

1. An objective, problem-oriented set of questions on the subject
2. A written report covering background, theory and method
3. An informal report on how I have applied what I have learned
4. An oral-visual presentation covering what I know
5. A debate with others who are also being tested

E. WHEN SOMEONE MAKES A RECOMMENDATION TO ME, I PREFER THAT HE OR SHE:

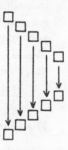

1. Take into account the drawbacks as well as the benefits
2. Show how the recommendation will support overall goals
3. Show clearly what benefits will be realized
4. Back up the recommendation with data and a plan
5. Show how the recommendation can be implemented

F. WHEN I FIRST APPROACH A TECHNICAL PROBLEM, I AM MOST LIKELY TO:

1. Look for ways that others might have solved it
2. Try to find the best procedure for solving it
3. Look for ways to get the problem solved quickly
4. Try to relate it to a broader problem or theory
5. Think of a number of opposing ways to solve it

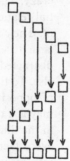

ADD SCORES VERTICALLY

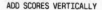

S   I   P   A   R

(IMPORTANT NOTE: This is an excerpt from the InQ questionnaire. It is not meant
to be an accurate measurement of your Thinking Style, but an approximation for
discussion purposes only.)

The Analyst
The Realist

Your highest totals represent your most preferred styles. Consider totals in the middle as backup styles which are available to you when the circumstances clearly call for them. (Some people have about even preferences for all five styles; they are lucky because they can more easily respond to the needs of the situation.) Now, on to understanding this rough map of your mind.

An important note about the brief descriptions that follow: They speak of the Synthesist, the Pragmatist, and t' ᵊ others as if individuals were solely guided by one Style of Thinking. While it is true that most people have a preference for one or two of the five Styles of Thinking, each of us has, to some extent, learned to use the thinking strategies that are characteristic of the other styles. That is why we all have the ability, although we may not always use it, to respond situationally.

The thing to remember as you read through our descriptions of each individual style is that people are really a mixture of styles, most showing a little bit of each and a whole lot of one or two. This explains why you may see some of yourself in every category, though one or two should seem like the most comfortable fit. Later in this chapter we'll touch on compatibilities and combinations, but for now try to get a feel for the essence of each way of thinking.

The Synthesist

Synthesists are creative, fascinating people who drive everyone else crazy. Their creativity and fascination comes from their quest for essential relationships, the basic inner core of almost anything you can think of. Their problem, although Synthesists never think of it as a problem, is that in their search for essentials, they don't allow themselves to be distracted by those concrete realities that are so important to everyone else. To the Synthesist mind, the essence of life is contradictory and full of opposites. There is always another way to look at any truth, and maybe a third or fourth as well. If there is any *reality,* therefore, it's not in the illusory nature of "facts" themselves, because they know that for every fact there is an equal and opposite fact. Synthesists believe that inferences and conclusions make the difference, not the facts on which they're based. Thus, Synthesists are abstract thinkers *par excellence.*

They love words, which, after all, are the ultimate abstractions, so it's not hard to understand why they are such ardent arguers. However, they argue not so much to win as to make sure you've been exposed to all the opposites and ambiguities inherent in your case. For example, if you were to say to a highly Synthesist thinker, "Hey, it's a nice day, isn't it," he or she would likely answer, "Yes, but I hope you don't have anything against clouds." This might then be followed by a delectable (to the Synthesist, that is) discussion about the value of rain to farmers or the quiet beauty of a shadowless day. Such comments aren't meant as obstinacy or resistance to sunshiny days, but merely a Synthesist calling the world as he or she sees it.

Synthesists often have a "distanced" view of the world, a consequence of their penchant for mentally moving from the concrete to the abstract. It can be disconcerting to have your fervent "I love you, dear" elicit an "Isn't that interesting" from your Synthesist mate. Oh well, the discussion that follows after you hit him or her probably will be.

Perhaps the most annoying characteristic of Synthesist thinkers (the fact that it is also a source of high creativity doesn't make it less annoying) is the way their minds branch. They are not, like most people, linear thinkers—that is, proceeding from one thought to the next in a reasonably logical sequence. Here is an example of what we mean. Suppose your Synthesist is preparing the evening meal and you ask the simple question "What's for dinner tonight?" Any other thinker would say, "Broiled fish," or "Roast chicken," or whatever was appropriate. Your Synthesist, however, might possibly say: "I wonder why we haven't heard from Aunt Millie recently?" Puzzling? Not when you understand how connections are made in a Synthesist's busy mind. On paper they would look something like this: "Aunt Millie hates fish. I wonder if she was offended by the fact that we forgot to send her a Christmas card this year?" Clear as a bell? It is to a Synthesist.

The Idealist

While Synthesists tend to believe that no one can ever fully agree with anyone about anything, Idealists tend to think that agreement is always possible if the parties are well-intentioned and the focus is on similarities rather than differences. Idealists are concerned with (and sometimes preoccupied by) goals and values. Consequently, they place morality and integrity very high in their personal priorities. They view such values not as abstractions (as your Synthesists might) but as the only real basis for caring relationships between human beings. They are usually good listeners and are receptive, even solicitous, of other people's ideas, searching among them for the common views which to them define the realities of the world. Idealists expect a great deal from themselves and apply those same high standards to others, often without those others knowing about them. Consequently, they are very disappointable people—disappointed in themselves for failing their own high expectations and in others when they behave expediently, produce poor-quality work, or wink at moral values.

Idealist thinkers are concerned about the future, perhaps more than any other style of thinker. They can feel lost if long-term goals have not been clearly articulated, or if once stated, they are not adhered to. They have deeply felt needs to be helpful to others and can usually be counted on for support or encouragement. Of all the Thinking Styles, Idealists alone value good intentions and valiant efforts almost as much as the results expected from them.

Wonderful as they are, Idealists can be hard to live with. Often they are so dedicated to the need to get agreement from everyone that they procrastinate, delaying the final decision interminably. When tough decisions are to be made, Idealists often stall as long as they possibly can. After all, whatever the solid reasons for moving to another city, how can we bring tears to the eyes of poor little Sally who "loves it here."

Idealists may even overdo their most wonderful quality, offering help to those who don't need it or want it. "Meddlesome" is the word most often heard. If a proposition is put in such a way as to tug at Idealist heartstrings, they often have trouble saying no, sometimes to the point of downright gullibility. Henry Barbour was such a fellow. He was chairman of the Scout parents' committee, active in the Dads' Club, treasurer of the local PTA, all of which interfered with his giving the proper after-working-hours time to mapping out the United Fund campaign. Not that Henry wasn't pained that he had little time to give to his family and none left for himself. It was simply that he could not say no to any of those truly worthy requests for his time.

The Pragmatist

Pragmatists believe that the world can be conquered one step at a time if one doesn't become too confused by looking too far into the future. That sort of incremental thinking gets them into action when more thoughtful souls are sidetracked. They don't wax philosophical searching for the "essence" of the problem as their Synthesist brethren might; nor do they become swamped by all of those unfillable needs looming on the horizon as do Idealists. They know that the way to get things done is to do them. As a result, most Pragmatists accomplish a lot.

Unfortunately, long-range planning is not the Pragmatist's long suit. Their concern is getting things started today, not keeping them going tomorrow. If you need a good job done, and you need it today, find a Pragmatist. But if the project is going to take longer than two weeks, don't be surprised if they haven't anticipated those three-week-away hurdles. You'll have to do that for them, unless you happen to be a Pragmatist, too. If so, you'd better bring someone else into the picture. Pragmatists succeed because they tend to be resourceful, innovative people who don't slow themselves down by trying to do something the "right way" or the "best way." They are perfectly willing to make do with whatever resources are at hand, testing those resources for service-ability and using whatever works. Obviously, Pragmatists make won-derful companions when you're lost in the woods or when you're trying to assemble a picnic for fourteen people on the spur of the moment. Not enough sandwich bread? Don't worry. Your Pragmatist can perform the "miracle of the loaves," even if it means inventing a few new colorful and innovative dishes out of scraps from freezer and cupboard. Pragmatists don't need to take on the whole world at once, as do those long-suffering Idealists. They're only concerned with the part of it that's confronting them at the moment. With the opposition thus scaled down to size, they'll provide enough enthusiasm to tackle what might other-wise seem an undoable job.

The take-it-as-it-comes approach of Pragmatists makes them awfully good at selling others on just about anything. With unclouded minds, they note what everyone is looking for and try to negotiate a win-win trade. "Let's compromise—one week in the mountains and one week at the seashore" is a Pragmatist solution to the usual vacation squabble. Not a bad one at that.

Sometimes Pragmatists seem too compromising to both Idealist and Realist family members. Flexibility can sometimes look suspiciously like opportunism when your spouse agrees with you tonight on the need for family rules and then agrees with your kids tomorrow that they're unnecessary. Pragmatists do that partly because they try to adapt and "fit in," and partly because they're willing to try anything to see if it works.

The Analyst

Analysts have the grandest grand strategy of all for nailing down the universe. It is simply this: There is, or at least there ought to be, one best way to do *anything*. To find that best way one rationally decides what the problem is, patiently gathers data, carefully searches for the "right" formula, method, or procedure. Of course, once that best way has been found, it's carved in stone and stays ensconced in the Analyst's mind forever. Well, at least until something better—and it has to be rigorously proved to be better—comes along.

Analysts are concrete thinkers (a material of which many non-Analysts think Analysts' minds are made). It is often difficult to get an Analyst to admit that anything that cannot be reduced to a measurable quantity is important enough to be given much weight, or even attention. Feelings, wishes, and fantasies are all right in their place, they believe, provided they aren't given too much sway when a decision is to be made. It isn't that Analysts don't have strong feelings, although others may see them that way. It's simply that they know how irrational and transitory feelings can be and are "logically" leery of giving them too big a vote. Besides, Analysts don't have time to waste on such speculative nonsense. They're too busy trying to contain a world that in good part persists in being whimsical. Anything that stubbornly refuses to submit to rational analysis must be ignored. If Margo struck you as the archetypical Analyst with her systematic, unemotional and no-nonsense approach to the problem of transportation, your judgment matches ours.

To Analysts praise and compliments seem to be so much window dressing, irrelevant to the real issues. Since they assume that others are like themselves, they tend to keep their positive feelings to themselves. Nice words aren't bad, they're simply extraneous. Carl, with whom we began this chapter, illustrates the problem side of this Analyst reserve too well. His useful concern with thoroughness and accuracy, bereft of the sweetening of a little honest praise, came through to his son Josh as oppressive nit-picking rather than a strength to be valued and emulated.

Realists and, to a lesser extent, Pragmatists can be reduced to frustrated spluttering by an ardent Analyst's endless insistence that the best method be found when one that will do is readily at hand. Such "analysis paralysis," they will tell you, is the sure sign of a rigid mind.

The Realist

For Realists whatever can be seen, felt, heard, smelled, and otherwise experienced is excitingly real. Everything else (if there *is* anything else) is either fanciful or theoretical and therefore of not much use. Realists like facts and accomplishments—things that can be sampled and savored. Of course, the facts they acknowledge are those that are sitting in front of them; they tend to mistrust third-hand knowledge from musty old reference books or brand-new recipe books. Interestingly, Realists will readily accept the testimony of those they accept as experts. (Naturally, the way to get Realists to trust you is to tell them to do something they've already decided to do.) Because these Realists assume the world is the way it appears (after all, it's *there* for everyone to see), they're baffled when other presumably intelligent people don't appear to see the "facts" that are so obviously apparent to that straightforward Realist mind. Therefore, they quickly conclude that those who disagree with them—especially if those bold, bare facts themselves are in dispute—must be deluded, dumb, or obstinate. As you might expect, Realists are uncomfortable with compromise, synthesis, analysis, idealism or any other "soft" world view. They see their objectives clearly and can't understand why everyone else doesn't see them as well. While Realists share with Pragmatists a willingness to get moving without too much soul-searching or analysis, they quickly part company when the conversation turns to compromise.

Our research with the InQ tells us that about 15 percent of the people you're likely to meet have no single, strong style of thinking, but show a wide range of responses that cover the entire spectrum. These thinkers are more flexible at matching mode of thought to a given situation, a clear advantage.

Many more—about 50 percent—have a single, definitely preferred style. They are thus more likely to find themselves solving the wrong problem in the wrong way. Those with very strong, single preferences have literally put most of their brainpower eggs in one basket. This, of course, makes their behavior much more predictable to others, since they are usually quite intense, often dramatic people.

The remaining 35 percent are *combination thinkers;* that is, they have a significant preference for two coequal styles rather than emphasizing one or utilizing all about equally. Such double-barreled thinkers have their own advantages and disadvantages. Take, for example, the Idealist-Realist thinker, one of the more common combinations our research has uncovered.

On the Idealist side, this thinker plans for the future, properly concerned for the needs of others and the world at large. As a Realist, he or she deals with the here and now in a strong and immediate way, still concerned with quality and doing a good job, yet perfectly capable of moving ahead boldly and forthrightly even in the face of obstacles.

If you are an Idealist-Realist parent, you are probably well tuned to the needs of your family (though perhaps not too well to your own needs) and proceed to do whatever it takes to satisfy those needs. You're chief chauffeur to Brownie Scouts and Little Leaguers, you volunteer for school activities, and you hold down the fort when your spouse or significant other is out of town. You listen to everyone's problems and aren't shy about giving good, solid advice and even seeing to it that it's taken. "Stop arguing and do it. It's for your own good!" is an admonition not unknown to your family.

You will continue to do all these wonderful things for a long time, perhaps a very long time, but the day will come when your circuits will overload. You'll begin to resent those things that, only recently, gave you so much pride of accomplishment. Your Idealist side will be embittered at those ingrates who don't appreciate you. Meanwhile, your Realist side is angry at those who passively wait for someone else (who else but you?) to take care of them. You will wake up, finally, in the middle of the night, angrily wondering "Just how did I get to be Atlas—holding the whole world on my shoulders? And more importantly, how do I get out from under it?"

Double-barreled thinkers are in fact looking at the world through binoculars whose lenses are each focused differently, a situation bound to produce inner tension and possibly uncertainty. Confidence can erode when one tries to cope with a world that is constantly shifting. For them, a greater sense of inner stability begins with understanding. First, they must recognize that they are indeed dual-minded. Then they need to gradually learn which kinds of situations can best be handled by each of their preferred styles of thinking. Finally with that in mind, the inappropriate lens can be consciously "tuned out" and they can move ahead confidently. Unfortunately, most combination thinkers are aware of the tension but not of its cause. They back and fill, or charge first in one direction, then in another. Their loved ones are baffled and at a loss about how to deal with such a puzzling family member. As an example, let's look in on Synthesist-Idealist Marty and his long-suffering wife Gloria.

One beautiful spring morning Marty awakened with Gloria and beheld a sparkling sky, the beginning of a wonderful day.

"Wow," said optimistic Pragmatist Gloria. "It's gorgeous outside. Let's go for a walk before breakfast."

Marty's Idealist side immediately heard its cue, "Gloria wants to walk—got to help her out." "You bet," he says with warmth, and then unaccountably he stops short. "Of course, we'll have to wear our ponchos." Suddenly, a simple hike along the seashore is no longer a matter for joyous impulse. It must be puzzled over and thought through.

Gloria sagged onto her pillow. "Leave it to Marty," she thought, "to turn a simple Saturday morning jaunt into Moses crossing the Red Sea."

"Well," he said, "spring showers can come up rather quickly around here. If we're going all the way to the pier, we'd better be prepared to come back in the rain."

"Oh hell," thought Gloria, who would have somehow dealt with the rain if and when it arrived, "do you always have to complicate everything?"

In this book we have been able to offer only a brief discussion of Thinking Styles. However, even an abridged understanding of how you and your family think can improve relationships more than anything else we know short of full-scale family counseling.* We use knowledge of each other's thinking proclivities all the time, and it never seems to lose its power to help us get the best out of each other.

In the next few pages you'll see how this understanding can reduce

* For those who wish a fuller and more accurate measure of their own (or others') styles of thinking, or who are as fascinated as we are with this new way of understanding yourself and others, we recommend *Styles of Thinking* by Allen F. Harrison and Robert M. Bramson (Garden City, N.Y.: Anchor Press/Doubleday, 1982). (Available in paperback under the title *The Art of Thinking* from Berkley Publishing Corp., 1984.) It includes the Inquiry Mode Questionnaire and completely describes the strategies for asking questions, making decisions, solving problems, and influencing others that we've only begun to introduce here.

friction in family decision making; help you to value different Styles of Thinking; and, perhaps most importantly, help you get important issues settled the "right" way (your way, of course) without manipulating or browbeating the people you love.

Finding the Right Way to Rub

Ever rub a cat the wrong way? They never appreciate it, and they let you know with a bite, a scratch, or a quick leap off your lap. Our fur is our inner conviction that the way we see the world is the way it is. When we're pushed to do things that violate our sense of how those things should be done, we feel just as Puss d⌒es. Our inclination goes one way while we're pressed to go another. Thus, when two fundamentally different modes of thinking interact on a regular basis, friction can occur. Here are a few examples:

1. *The Case of the Challenging Checkbook.* Analysts and Realists (Pragmatists, too) who live together often have checkbook problems. Analysts, for example, live in a world where everything adds up. Since they are careful, accurate, logical people, they are particularly irked by those who cannot (or *do* not) balance their checkbooks. To them, over-drawn accounts are clear signals of mental incompetence or sheer obstinacy, and unarguable evidence that Analysts alone can be trusted to handle money. Unfortunately, if the Analyst's partner is a Realist (maybe in truth a little obstinate but not at all incompetent), the checkbook situation will be sized up quite differently. Money, as every Realist knows, is simply an instrument of power to be used for getting things done. In the heat of battle, they will tell you, one doesn't stop to count one's bullets. Besides, those bean counters at the bank can always be put in their place, if and when it's necessary. Pragmatists also often play fast and loose with checkbooks. While they don't have a Realist's need to show the bank who's boss, they have sublime confidence that the account can always be reconciled if a need to do so should ever arise.

The problem comes from a very real difference in perspectives. To the Analyst the monthly bank statement is a goal unto and of itself, worthy of consideration and respect, a device for ensuring a stable and predictable world. To the Realist and Pragmatist, it is a window into a past which no longer interests them.

2. *"I'm Honest—Honestly!"* Realists and Idealists often squabble about integrity. Idealists, by definition, are true blue because they know

that's the way people should be. For them honesty is a universal truth, not unlike gravity. They know with deep conviction that human beings cannot live together in harmony unless they can trust each other's good intentions. Realists, on the other hand, believe that honesty is primarily a matter of power; in other words, one is honest when it is the most effective way to achieve results or to avoid punishment. Thus, some Idealists feel offended if their Realist partners or family members hide diaries, insist on seeing that all the doors and windows are locked at night, or proceed to confirm the "facts" that have been given them. To Idealists, all people are worthy of trust and respect until they incontrovertibly prove otherwise by their actions. Realists just *know* that this "soft" view of people just doesn't fit "the facts of life" (Realist phrase par excellence), so why set yourself up for a disappointment? Of course, Idealists have been known to cheat a little bit themselves on occasion but only for the *right* reasons. If the cause is just, they can bend a rule or forgive a trespass if it will further a worthy cause. Their Realist partners, of course, can only shake their heads and mumble about "mollycoddling" or "softheaded Idealists."

3. *Phooey on Fun.* Peggy the Pragmatist sat at her desk, chin in her hands, looking out of the window at the glorious spring morning. Allan, her Analyst husband, sat on the couch behind her, sorting the monthly bills.

"C'mon, Peggy, let's get with it," he said. "It's almost tax time and we've got a lot of paperwork to do."

Yes, the paperwork had to be done, but what Allan had overlooked was the fact that after three weeks of continuous rain *the sun was shining.* And it was a Saturday. As any adaptable Pragmatist will tell you, the time to have fun is when you feel like fun, not when the schedule says it's okay.

We don't know if Peggy succeeded in showing Allan the wisdom of taking the afternoon off for a trip to the park or the beach, but we hope she gave it a good Pragmatist try. Sure, the day could end with Allan even more convinced that Peggy can't plan past the end of her nose. Or Peggy might be more soured than ever about her capable, disciplined stick-in-the-mud. But it needn't turn out that way. After a little introspection on their diverse Styles of Thinking, they may come to realize that there are really no villains in the piece, just two interesting people with different views of the world. Analysts don't hate fun or frivolity— they just want to keep it in its place, and often properly so. Neither view is invalid; they are merely *different.* The moment you discover that those seemingly contrary people you live with have simply adapted to the world as they see it, your eyes will open to the how and why of harmonizing with them. Here's the way it happened for us:

Early in their relationship, Synthesist-Realist Bob frequently detected Realist-Pragmatist-Idealist Susan irritatingly interrupting him in mid-sentence. Worse, she often clearly tuned him out. "All right," he thought to himself, "she is pretty and charming, but she's not very bright." His assumption of her lack of brilliance showed through—he began to patronize her. Mutual frustration set in and flourished behind the scene. Then came the revelation: Not defective personalities but merely differently tuned thinking was the cause. Soon Susan came to understand that Bob's endless ruminating about all sides of any conceivable topic were a part and parcel of those same intellectual qualities which she had first admired. As she became less impatient with what had seemed like endless equivocation, Susan could see that some important decisions had actually been saved from disaster by Bob's "on the other hand" analysis. Set free from recriminations and not so subtle digs, both Bob and Susan found ways to deal with their own newly discovered liabilities. For example, Bob suddenly caught on that those blank expressions on others' faces came not from an inability to comprehend his deep thoughts, but from the impossibility of following his speculative flights of fancy. He began to sound less like the know-it-all his family had thought him to be. Susan began to use her practical Pragmatist thinking as a way of anchoring Bob's insights, to the benefit of both. To do that she had to listen, and somewhat to her surprise, found some gems of wisdom she'd previously thrown away. Best of all, they began to see each other with good humor and renewed interest. It all culminated in an admission from Bob to friends assembled for a dinner party that he had discovered that Susan was not only more intelligent than he had originally thought, she was actually as bright as he was. Susan's smile attested to the fact that she had known it all along.

Combinations and Compatibilities

Experience thus far with the InQ and other measures of other stylistic differences suggests these compatibility rules:

1. *People with at least one preferred thinking style in common have an easier time understanding each other.* For example, a Synthesist-Realist and a Synthesist-Idealist are likely to enjoy each other's speculations and not be bothered by jumping from one unrelated topic to another. They will enjoy each other's "brilliance," often excluding others from the conversation. True, when action is needed, they may not agree on the direction or force with which that action should be taken. Equally true, they will have to see to it that the Synthesist-Idealist doesn't too often give way to the Synthesist-Realist, resenting it later.

2. *When one partner's highest preferred style matches the other's lowest, they will chronically disappoint each other.* Marjorie and Frank were alarmed at the high level of conflict that seemed inherent in their relationship, even though they believed they shared comparable levels of intelligence, competence, attractiveness, and all the other "glue" that holds a partnership together. To better understand each other's styles of thinking, then, they took the InQ. Marjorie scored high as a Realist while Frank's Realist qualities barely registered. Quite possibly, Marjorie chose Frank as her life partner because she sensed in him those factors that she herself lacked. For his part, Frank may have made a similar choice, feeling their partnership as a whole compensated for their shortcomings as individuals. While, as you'll see in rule 3, there is wisdom in that notion, living with those who don't value your most conspicuous strengths can erode anyone's self-esteem. If, as rule 1 suggests, they had a second preferred style in common, their chances for a successful relationship would be much improved. Of course, their idealized view of one another—their romantic *love,* if you will—may still transcend the daily friction. But the havenly home they build will require a good deal of care and maintenance if it's to weather the storms intact.

3. *All other things being equal, the best decisions will come from a balanced mix of thinking styles.* Synthesists and Idealists can sometimes dream up fascinating, unworkable plans unless there is an Analyst and Pragmatist in their midst to keep them down-to-earth. Similarly, Pragmatists and Realists can quickly spend large amounts of time and money solving the wrong problem unless an Idealist or Synthesist is there to make sure that all the consequences are thought through. And of course, Analysts may never get started at all without

a Realist or Pragmatist around to push for action. If you're lucky enough to have a balanced mix of thinking styles in your family, and you can keep from beating on one another, be glad. You'll fill in each other's blind spots, bring a broad perspective to bear on any problem, and have a lively and interesting intellectual life. If you do not have that balance—if both of you are quick-on-the-trigger Realists, say— you'll feel more comfortable with each other's quality of mind, but will need to watch out for built-in biases in the way you look at things. Therefore, for example, take a hard look at the makeup of your own familial decision group. If you should discern a lack of the Analyst view, be wary of implementing decisions until you have run them by the eye of an Analyst-thinking lawyer, accountant, or family friend. In similar ways, plan to compensate for any other gaps in your decision-making resources.

Matching Styles of Thought to Kinds of Tasks

When possible, try to match job assignments to the thinking style of those available. A parent with a strong Analyst bent will be uncomfortable at setting up and supervising a family allowance system that delegates complete control of expenditures to the recipients. A consummate Pragmatist, on the other hand, would have little trouble giving the kids their allowance, no strings attached and no second-guessing either. Here are two examples of combinations that, whether embodied in a single person or a group, will maximize the return from certain kinds of jobs.

Analysts-Idealists. Design engineers, auditors, management accountants, and financial officers have by and large shown themselves to be skilled Analyst-Idealists, and the rest of us should be thankful that they are. After all, when you picnic in the shade of a reservoir or drive over a bridge it's nice to know that these structural marvels have been created by people who are motivated to achieve high quality and lasting results through thorough analysis and planning. Of course, if you should live with one of these careful people, don't expect rapid-fire decisions on important matters, or impulsive "to hell with the budget" vacations. By all means, however, assign to them any bookkeeping, accounting, planning, and data-gathering chores. They'll feel more secure knowing that such important functions are in safe hands, and once you think about it, you will, too.

Idealist-Pragmatist. Put your Idealist-Pragmatist in charge if your family is faced with a complex question, especially one that depends on the consensus of widely differing views, such as the relocation of the family. For that kind of question you'll need someone to keep the rest of the family zoo from stampeding to a too hasty decision. The Synthesists in the family will want to play "what if" forever, as may their Analyst compatriots, though for different reasons. The Realists among you, for reasons they think are plain to everyone, will want to get on with it, whatever "it" happens to be. But those sensitively strong Idealist-Pragmatists will stave off pressure to "get things decided" and keep the focus on family goals and the needs of all concerned. Still, a sprinkling of Realists and Synthesists can be useful, too, to make sure that fundamental conflicts aren't glossed over and that the family *really* has the resources it needs to make a go of it in a new environment.

The same principle applies to other qualities of mind. To match strengths with tasks answer these questions.

1. What qualities and skills are best suited for this job?
2. Who has them?
3. What is needed to keep the job on track?
4. Who can best do that?

In the next chapter we'll pursue the question of why some of us are too sensitive and others not sensitive enough. But before you move on, take the time to complete these exercises. They'll increase your understanding of yourself and your family, and even better, help you to use that understanding to build a better family team.

EXERCISES

1. What are your highest Thinking Style preferences? What are your lowest?

Highest_____, _____.   Lowest_____, _____.

2. List three or four tasks that are your responsibility—for example, assigning household chores, maintenance of the family car(s), paying bills.

Task	Strength	Liability
_____	_____	_____
_____	_____	_____
_____	_____	_____
_____	_____	_____

In the space provided alongside of each task, jot down a few words that characterize the way in which your thinking-style preferences influence the way you carry out that task.

Example: Your task is "paying bills"; your most preferred thinking style is Pragmatist. Under "Strength" you might list, "Don't get overwhelmed by the size of the pile." Under "Liability" your entry could be "If they're out of my sight, they're out of my mind."

3. List five ways in which your preferred ways of thinking add value to your family life. For example, "As an Analyst thinker I bring some order to the business part of our life," or "I'm the one who gets us moving again after something has gone wrong."

4. List five ways in which you overuse your strengths. For example, "I speculate forever about things that 'might happen' and drive everyone up the wall," or "I make up my mind too quickly and am often sorry afterward."

1. _____

2. _____

3. _____

4. _____

5. _____

Insight: When you acknowledge that the qualities of which you are most proud are precisely those that at times lead to your downfall, you set the stage for getting the best out of yourself. You will now find yourself increasingly aware of the point at which an appreciation for order and a constructive attention to detail turns into fussy nitpicking. When the voice in the back of your mind says, "You're doing it again, kiddo," you will collect yourself and get back on the strength side of the line.

5. In the matrix below, plot in the Thinking Style scores of each member of your family. Enter the scores one person at a time and then draw a line connecting that person's scores. You'll end up with a profile that looks something like the example shown below. You'll need to use a different color for each person in order to tell them apart (alternately, you can use dashed, dotted, spiraled, or wiggly lines).

If any of your family are too young to complete the abbreviated InQ Questionnaire we've included in this book, estimate what their scores might be. Accuracy is not as important as coming out with a profile that has the "peaks and valleys" in the right places.

When everyone's scores have been entered and the points connected, the group profile will look like this.

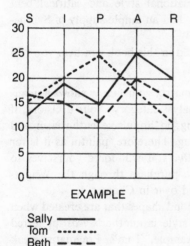

EXAMPLE

Sally ————
Tom ·········
Beth — — —

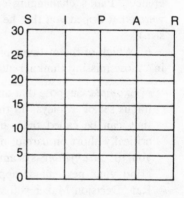

Note: the following questions work best when everyone in the family is involved in answering them. The answers themselves are not as important as the discussion that ensues.

6. Which Styles of Thinking are too well represented in the family? —that is, most of you show profile "peaks" in those styles. (For example, in the sample matrix above, Sally and Beth show peaks in the Analyst style.) Topics to think or talk about:

a. Does this style of thinking dominate your family discussions? For example, does impulsive fun *always* give way to cold rationality?

b. Are minority opinions often joked or explained away by those who "think alike"?

7. Are there gaps in the family's repertoire of thinking styles? (For example, in the sample matrix no one shows much in the way of Synthesist thinking.)

Topics to Think or Talk About

a. Who might you include in your important decision-making sessions that could bring to bear the perspectives that we lack? For example, could you ask your architect cousin Paul for his ideas on redecorating your home? (You chose Paul not just because of his profession, since architects come in all sizes and Thinking Style preferences. Paul's challenging conversational style and satirical bent were what tipped you that he likely had an ample supply of Synthesist.)

b. Which of the methods presented in this book can help you "fill in" those missing thinking qualities?

Example: Suppose that on the matrix your family shows a unanimous set of "valleys" in the Analyst category. Your decisions, if they can be called that, are long on impulsive enthusiasm and critically short on careful planning. Therefore, painful as it is for you to do *anything* systematically, you will force yourselves to grind your next major appliance purchase through the Weight-Rate Decision Maker you skipped over in Chapter 4.

8. Scan your family matrix for diamond shapes that are created when one family member's *most*-preferred style is another's *least*-preferred style. In the sample matrix, for example, Tom's Pragmatist peak matches Beth's Pragmatist valley.

Topics to Think or Talk About

People whose thinking styles are mismatched in this way often annoy or disappoint each other. They usually have no intention of doing so and little understanding of why it happens so often. Knowing the source of that contrariness often takes away some of the irritation. It can also help those involved make constructive allowances for each other.

CHAPTER 7

The Differing Worlds of
High Screeners and Low Screeners

Hal and Linda have finally arrived on the slopes for their first skiing vacation. Although they have over a week to play, Linda is out an hour after their arrival, eager to begin her lessons. In the lodge later that evening Linda is very animated, pink-cheeked from the unaccustomed snow. She responds quickly to the smiles of the other guests and is soon chattering about the "glorious day." With some displeasure she notices Hal stifling a yawn, nursing his cocktail, responding only minimally to the friendly overtures of the new friends she is making. That night in their room Linda makes no bones about how embarrassed she was by Hal's "anthropoid" behavior. She just hopes his lack of enthusiasm isn't going to ruin the entire trip.

Although neither knows it, Linda and Hal are living with the assorted problems, and excitements, that occur when a Low Screener lives with a High Screener.

We are all, at least in relation to everyone else, Low Screeners or High Screeners.

Imagine going through life with an amplifier built into your nervous system—every reaction magnified, bombarding you with unremitting sensation. Welcome to the world of the Very Low Screener.

Now assume that the amplifier has been replaced with a very efficient filter. Suddenly, your world is filled with hazy shadows, no more sharp spikes of feeling, only the strongest of stimuli catch your attention. You've met yourself as a Very High Screener.

Should you be a High Screener or a Low Screener?

The answer is: *It depends.* From birth, High Screeners reveal themselves as those proverbial "good babies." They sleep through the night and spare Mom and Dad that troublesome 3 A.M. feeding. Does this qualify them for sainthood? Of course not. It's simply that those high-screening babies don't feel as cold, hungry, or clammy as their low-screening fellows whose superefficient nervous systems give them no rest. When they grow to maturity, Low Screeners will likely have a lot more fun than High Screeners—when things are going well, that is. But if the atmosphere is negative, they'll also spend more sleepless nights and irritate everyone with their habitual "frazzled nerves." As we said, it all depends. The view through your sensory "window to the world" will tell you if your shutters need adjustment.

What Sort of Screener Are You?

You are probably already wondering if you tend to fit the High or Low Screener model. You can get an approximation of your screening level by taking the short quiz you'll find in the next paragraph. It is a much abbreviated version of a questionnaire developed by Dr. Albert Mehrabian, Professor of Psychology at the University of California, Los Angeles.* The results of this excerpt, while not as definitive as the full instrument, should give you an indication of your general position on the sensitivity continuum. All that's required is that you read each statement and think about yourself in relation to it, quickly and honestly. Don't spend too much time thinking about every aspect of each question and don't worry about what you think may be the "proper" way to respond: There are no right or wrong answers.

In the space provided for each item below, indicate on a scale of 1 to 10 (1 is least; 10 is most) the extent to which that statement describes you accurately.

_____ 1. My strong emotions in a situation carry over for one or two hours after I leave it.

_____ 2. I am usually much affected by the feeling of leather or upholstery on my bare skin.

_____ 3. Having heard a sound, I often lie awake at night for some time.

* You can obtain information on the Mehrabian Screening and Arousal Measure from Albert Mehrabian, 9305 Beverlycrest Drive, Beverly Hills, CA 90210.

_____ 4. When I walk into a crowded room, it immediately has a big effect on me.

_____ 5. Drastic changes in the weather can affect my mood.

_____ 6. I am tremendously affected by sudden loud noises.

_____ 7. I am excited or moved long after a good movie.

_____ 8. Sometimes if I have many things to do at once, I get rattled.

_____ 9. High-arousing stimulation affects me for a long time.

_____10. Sudden changes have an immediate and large effect on me.

Now add up your individual responses and subtract the total from 100 as shown below.

_____Total   100 − _____ = _____
                           (total)   *(your screening score)*

This latter value is your "screening score." Here are some guidelines for interpreting it:

Screening Score	Approximate Category
0–25	Very Low Screener
26–50	Moderately Low Screener
51–75	Moderately High Screener
76–100	Very High Screener

To get even more information from your questionnaire, cover up your own responses and ask someone who knows you well to rate you. Remember, they should respond the way they think you *really* are, not how they think you'd like to be rated or how they think you rated yourself. If they perceive you as being *less* sensitive (a Higher Screener) than your own evaluation, it may be that you are concealing too much of your inner reaction from others. If they consider you to be *more* sensitive (a Lower Screener) you may only be fooling yourself. Talking your responses over with those close to you can improve their understanding of why you react the way you do in family situations.

How Different Screeners Lead Different Lives

There is no "right" level of screening. First of all, it is the relative differences between screening levels that is the key factor in determining how any two people will perceive one another. In other words, if Dad is a Moderately High Screener and Mom is a Very High Screener, Dad will *seem* like a Low Screener to Mom even though he may rank well above Junior or Uncle Max (who'll seem like real rattlebrains to Mom). Second, the advantages and disadvantages of low screening or high screening depend a lot upon what's going on at the moment and whether it is seen as pleasant or unpleasant. To make this clearer, let's look at a few specific instances in detail.

There's no question that when pleasures are in the wind, Low Screeners simply have more fun. And why shouldn't they? They live in a world filled with subtle nuances and rich complexities that High Screeners seldom see. At parties, for example, they tend to enjoy themselves more and more as the action develops. Sure, they can easily overload themselves—"I could have danced all night" captures the Low Screener feeling nicely. For them the sudden letdown when the party's over is not too high a price for having scaled the emotional heights. They are first to see the potential of a beautiful day (sensing the warm sun and soft breeze on their skin) and can blossom like flowers when surrounded by good fellowship, turning chance acquaintances into instant friends. When someone says "I like you" to a Low Screener, they feel the warmth of the voice as well as the message in the words.

In Hal and Linda, whose skiing vacation opened this chapter, we see a High and a Low Screener in action. Because she is often on the verge of overload, low-screening Linda stretches to master her new skiing skills immediately. Early every morning she'll start a long day on the slopes, pushing herself to become at least minimally adept before the myriad of new things to learn overwhelms the fun and excitement of new sensations. "Learn it fast or drop it" is the self-protective motto of many Low Screeners.

In contrast, Hal is quite content to learn at a slower pace. Since he is less agitated by the multiplicity of unfamiliar experiences that characterizes learning a new activity, he is content to proceed one step at a time, acclimatizing himself to the mountain air and checking out equipment before he commits himself to lessons. While the after-ski activities around the fire are exciting for Linda, they are something of a bore for High Screener Hal—unless, of course, he happened to be surrounded by old friends whose behavior and reactions are more predictable and comfortable. Sensitivity to subtle friendly overtures by others is not likely to be Hal's strong suit. In fact, High Screeners are not quick to respond to *anyone's* attitudes and feelings. Small wonder that Hal was surprised at the vehemence with which Linda reproached him in their room.

Screeners at Work. Let's take Hal and Linda off the slopes now and put them back in the office. He is a successful salesman; she is an internal auditor for a large corporation. One of the secrets of Hal's success, his coworkers agree, is the single-minded doggedness with which he pursues a sale. "Nothing distracts the guy when he's on the trail of an order," one of them ruefully admits. "Mister Hard Sell—that's his middle name!" Clearly, sensitivity to polite indifference or customer procrastination is *not* the key to success in marketing the product that Hal's company produces. When he's traveling out of town, Hal's quite content to tell the desk clerk, "No, I don't mind having a room with no view." Why? Because he means exactly that. He's never understood how hotels could gouge their guests for a windowful of mountain or sandy beaches when all a traveler really needs is a place to sleep and hang his clothes.

Low Screener Linda, on the other hand, excels at her job precisely for the opposite reasons. Her sensitivity to detail, both on paper and in personal behavior, makes her the ideal auditor. Linda's ability to *sense* the discomfort in an employee's posture, to read the "body language" of anxiety and apprehension, give her a definite edge over her less observant compatriots in the auditing department.

True, sometimes she gazes distractedly out the window on a sparkling spring day longing to feel the warmth and the caress of breeze that portend a great weekend. When she arrives home, Linda is bubbling. It's been a great day with a brilliant sunset to bless the homeward commute. Good feelings ought to be nurtured and enhanced, she thinks. What better way than to manufacture some fun. "Let's call a few friends," she says to Hal the second she's in the door. "I feel like having a party."

Is the world always Linda's oyster? Unfortunately, no. When the news is bad, Low Screeners take it on the chin and High Screeners have most of the advantages. Here's an example.

The next morning Linda discovers that she will not get the raise she was counting on. When a coworker calls in sick, she is obliged to attend several important meetings for him, and her own workload piles up. In the afternoon the chief examiner tells her that the new procedure she had recommended was rejected by the auditing committee. Linda returns to her office and sits staring bleakly out of the window. Unable to concentrate on her work anymore, she leaves early. She tries to put together a nice dinner for herself and Hal—doesn't she deserve it after that trying day?—but she makes a mess of the chicken recipe and leaves the baking powder out of the shortcake biscuits. Nothing accomplished, feeling exhausted and depressed, Linda makes a last-ditch stand for her sanity—she sits down and tries to relax with the evening paper. Things being what they are in today's world, she feels worse than ever and seeks solace in a large gin. Finally, Hal comes home, and tosses his briefcase on the couch, narrowly missing Linda's stocking feet. Completely oblivious to her abraded ego, he brings her up to date on his own day.

"Hi, honey. Boy, what a day I've had. My train was late and I lost the papers to the Pringle account, and—wouldn't you know it—old George edged me out for Salesman of the Year. Oh well, tomorrow's another day, isn't it? What's for dinner?"

How Linda responded to this question is really beside the point (and is probably unprintable anyway). We would like to think, however, that Hal would not be put off by her ascerbic retort or her tears, knowing that Low Screeners do hurt more when faced with unpleasantness. Hopefully, he would chalk up weird chicken and stony biscuits to another Low Screener foible. When stressed, their level of performance decreases in both quality and quantity. They make more errors and they simply feel rotten. Consequently, Low Screeners sometimes seek desperately for relief. They show more psychosomatic symptoms than High Screeners, complain more often, and take more sick leave from work. And if the overload or unpleasant condition continues long enough, some of them seek more potent escape routes through the use of alcohol, drugs, excessive sleep, or psychological withdrawal.

To make matters worse, Low Screeners are prone to exaggerate the negative feelings of others, acting less like a mirror to those feelings than a magnifying glass. The conversation sounds like this:

Hal: You weren't home when I called yesterday, Linda.

Linda: Well, you can't expect me to be here every moment of the day and night waiting for the phone to ring while you're traveling.

Hal: Whoa! Hold on! Why are you being so defensive? All I did was state a fact.

Linda: Well, don't you think I know you like me to be home when you call?

Hal (after a thoughtful pause): Yeah, I guess maybe you're right. I suppose I was disappointed.

You can see that in this example we have given Hal credit for a lot more sensitivity than most High Screeners usually show. Such enlightened awareness doesn't usually occur when High Screener meets Low Screener in an emotional situation. More often, High Screeners, not completely in touch with their own subtle feelings will insist that they were "merely asking a question," leaving Low Screeners feeling hard-of-hearing (when they are in truth just the opposite), paranoid, or both. When faced with continuous and overwhelming bad news, such as unrelenting financial problems, Low Screeners tend to withdraw, and from the very people they'll wind up needing the most. Unless they're careful about it, High Screeners in the family can unknowingly contribute to a Low Screener's feeling of isolation by insisting that they are "overreacting."

This difference in sensitivity to both major and minor (to the High Screener, that is) irritants can provoke a multitude of minicrises without either party knowing why it happens. Picture Hal and Linda working side by side in a room with a fluorescent light that flickers with annoying (at least to Linda) regularity.

"That light is driving me crazy," complains Linda.

"Just ignore it, we've got to finish these bills— Hey, wait a minute, where are you going?" "What got into her?" thinks Hal as he watches Linda's angry back disappearing through the door.

While Hal may seem inordinately dense to his wife, his high-screening tendency has its good side as well. Because they're inherently less affected by bad news, as well as good, High Screeners can be as steadfast as the 7th Cavalry when things go wrong. So durable is their armor, in fact, that they can persevere—business as usual—until whatever unpleasantness that is around has been weathered. This quality makes them very handy people to have around when all about you has fallen to pieces—exactly the state in which Hal found Linda at the end of her bad day, reduced to tears on the couch. Isn't it splendid to see that Hal, not too pleased with his own day, can still take Linda in his arms and be calmly able to convince her that everything will be okay. Well, "splendid" may be a little strong, since to his well-insulated mind none of this was that bad to begin with. We also need to point out that this self-protective quality, while great in emergencies, can unfortunately let slowly deteriorating situations get out of hand as gradual turns for the worse escape the attention of confirmed High Screeners. One can hope that in those situations there will be a Low Screener or two around to act as an early-warning system, assuming—a perhaps not too hopeful assumption, albeit—that they will be heeded. Therein lies the chief liability that High Screeners carry with them. Suppose the atmosphere at his job has indeed turned a little sour. His "unlucky break"—loss of the best-salesman award—is. in truth, a sign that his employers are displeased with him. In that event it ought to signal him to reassess and do some useful problem solving. But Hal's equanimity, genuine because he is unaware that anything is wrong, can lead him to blithely allow a yet savable situation to fester under his nose until it becomes a full-blown crisis.

If overload is a Low Screener's burden, dullness is anathema for their high-screening fellows. For instance, they only enjoy sports, active or spectator, which force them to a high level of stimulation. When High Screeners do use drugs, it is to stave off boredom. While Low Screeners may drink to find some needed relief from overload, their high-screening partners may match them drink for drink simply to get a little fun out of life.

If we've left you with the impression that there's little you can do to cope with your "dolts" or "ditherers," we'll correct that right away. Coping with higher or lower Screeners in your family is largely a matter of awareness and practice. In the next section you'll find some pointers for minimizing family stresses and helping both High and Low Screeners get the best from each other.

Before you proceed with the next section, however, a reminder, and an important one. As family members, the important question is not whether you are a High Screener or a Low Screener, but whether you are a higher or lower Screener than those with whom you live. Therefore, in reading the next section where we provide helpful hints for both High and Low Screeners, you may need to think of yourself in both categories. For example, your spouse or housemate may seem to you to be a constant backseat driver who loves parties but fades away when the atmosphere is depressing. Think of him or her as a lower Screener than yourself and attend to the pointers for High Screeners. At the same time, you may be acutely aware that your supposedly fragile daughter ignores sultry heat and biting cold with equally annoying stoicism, and is bored by movies that you find full of subtle humor or sentiment. Plan to relate to that one as if you were a Low Screener and she a High.

Pointers for High Screeners

If you are a High Screener, consider the following:

Set Up and Maintain Special Channels of Communication. For example, a regular family meeting every month can give lower Screeners a chance to complain about mishaps that you are certain could never happen in your family. Slights (real and imagined), parental favoritism, unrealized but important personal sensitivities, and violations in family agreements, may all have escaped you or may have been dismissed as trivial. Put into place, and invite others to use, a variety of other communication devices—personal notes, corkboard messages, candid asides over coffee—whatever it takes to make sure that important messages penetrate your efficient sensory armor. If it helps to salve your self-esteem, remind yourself that businesses use this tactic all the time, relaying vital employee information through the mixed media of memos, bulletin-board notices, public-address-system announcements, company newsletters, and formal meetings.

Learn to Ask Questions and Then Watch for Reactions. Are you a perpetual High Screener? If so, admit that Mother Nature hasn't exactly armed you with the acute senses of a wary deer, and compensate by asking questions and then paying hard attention to what happens. Alternately, use both specific and general questions, and be ready to follow them up with prompts such as "Tell me more." Start with "How are things going?" Then switch to "How did you do on that last math test?" Remember, once you've found the right water hole, there's no telling what sort of fish you'll catch. The simple inquiry "Any big social events coming up?" followed by an attentive and expectant silence on your part may help your taciturn (and sensitive) seventeen-year-old admit that "Nobody likes me at school," or "I thought all you cared about was grades." You can help this process along by watching for nonverbal signs that more is happening than you thought. High Screeners often miss important clues that something has gone wrong in a relationship. Once you accept that lack in yourself, you can compensate by looking attentively at those with whom you're talking. Tears starting, a slight quiver of the lips, and eyes flickering rapidly back and forth are a few indicators of inner turmoil. When they are noticed, an "I can see something is on your mind" may start a conversation that will both alleviate Low Screener overload and get to the heart of whatever the matter was.

Listen (Sigh) to those Whiners and Complainers. Whiners and complainers, odd as it sounds, usually have something worth saying, though their manner of saying it can sometimes drive you into not listening. Perpetual whining comes from people who see things that are wrong but feel powerless to fix them. Complaining is a *reaction* to an insufferable problem, not the cause of it. Take the wind out of complainers' sails by showing them that you're listening, just what they want, but least expect because you've been so dense before. You may find behind that plaintive emoting nothing more than a long-suffering Low Screener frantic because you haven't responded with action to hints (or even matter-of-fact requests) to "please fix that dripping faucet."

Legitimize Goofing Off. While most of us need some way to let off steam from time to time, Low Screeners need more of it and they need it more frequently. Everyone will benefit when this need is openly recognized, perhaps by an "officially" sanctioned mental health break. Giving your permission for such "inefficient" use of time is often hard for High Screeners to do, since they've survived everything the Low Screener has and don't understand what the fuss is about. If you happen to be a higher Screener, remind yourself that when your spouse or partner or other low-screening family member curls up with a book or crossword puzzle in the midst of a thousand things that need doing, it's precisely what they ought to do. Recall that while discipline and fortitude are great virtues, having to vacuum around your low-screening spouse's twitching body is itself not too efficient. Better by far to suggest a little relief before collapse—often a twenty-minute "read" or nap will do—and you will be rewarded by enthusiastic, high-quality work later. Since your Low Screener may feel ashamed of needing such "pampering," it will help if you are its sponsor. Start with "Why don't you sit down with that new paperback, dear?" and work up to "Oh hell, let's forget about the yard work this afternoon and take in a movie." (First, make sure the movie is relaxing and not stimulating.) If the overload justifies it and the pocketbook permits it, weekend jaunts to a quiet out-of-town hideaway can recharge low batteries. The bedrock reality is that for Low Screeners, time off for mental health is a necessary cost of doing business. If you scrimp in paying it, the results will show up where you least want them. Do we need to remind you that an irritated and depressed Low Screener can drag everyone down?

Pointers for Low Screeners

If you're a Low Screener, here are a few suggestions that will help you retune your sensory apparatus to a wavelength less likely to overload.

Put a Fuse in Your System. As a Low Screener, you know that when things are going well, when you're feeling good and doing the things that you enjoy, anything's possible. You take on more and more responsibilities, glowing with accomplishment until *bam*—overloaditis! Crises demand attention, problems mount, and frazzled nerves demand retreat. Somehow, someway, you've got to build in a protective fuse in this cycle, a little circuit breaker to stop you before your emotional reserves are overcommitted. In other words, what you need, NEED, NEED, is to learn to say *no* to that seductive request, explicit or implied, that you say yes. We suspect you've tried to do just that but have overlooked this fact: The best time to reduce an overload is before it hits, just when you feel least like doing it. For to you as a committed Low Screener, when the day is bright, and your energy is bubbling, the sky's the limit. To aid you in getting around your better (and worse) nature, here are some thoughts about saying no.

1. *Pause before saying yes.* Respond to any request for your time with "Maybe, but I need to think about it. I'll call you in ten minutes." In the interval, mumble to yourself, "I'm a Low Screener, I'm a Low Screener." Recall past bouts with the results of taking on too much.

2. *Be decisive.* If you decide to say no, say it at once, loud and clear, without equivocation. The longer you wait, the harder it will be to stay convinced that you're doing the right thing. Remember, most people will assume that if you haven't said no you are probably going to say yes. Clear up any potential ambiguity so you won't be stuck filling a gap left by someone who "was sure you'd be able to make it."

3. *Don't give reasons for saying no.* As we have previously noted, many Low Screeners often feel they need "permission" to take care of themselves. Without it they feel a need to justify their refusals to be overloaded. When you give reasons why you can't or don't want to do something, you solicit the asker to come up with helpful thoughts on how to get around the obstacles you've cited. In addition, "reasons"

signal your ambiguity and invite further efforts to persuade you which will prolong your agony. Merely say, "I'm sorry, I just can't help you today." Period. If you're asked why or to reconsider, your standard reply *must* be "Sorry, but it's just not possible."

Prioritize Your Problems

One of the signs of overload is a plethora of problems that all appear to have the same menacing overtones. You are literally unable to discern the little ones from the big ones, and squander your efforts on frantic attempts to juggle everything at once. The way out of this self-made dither is to put some of the tasks aside for the time being, by deciding which ones is not your cup of tea. For while High Screeners have priority systems built into their anatomies, Low Screeners must purposively compensate for that which nature has shortchanged them. A priority-setting device, such as the Paired-Comparisons (Noah's Ark) Matrix described in Chapter 2 may be just your ticket. Or a quick assessment of the Big D, Middle D, and little d dimensions of the responsibilities on your list may reduce the strain in your mind immensely.

Learn to Fight Feeling Frantic

When a surfeit of problems has overtaken you too quickly to manage, when your circuits are overheated, High Screener or Low you'll need a kind of safety valve that you can put into play just when you are least capable of doing anything sensible at all. Since the prime purpose of your safety valve is to stop you in your own tracks, you'll only want to set it going as a last resort. Therefore, you'll need to recognize the unique signs that mean that you're overloaded. Here are some examples of common indicators of overload tension: You start snapping at the kids when they're only acting like kids. You throw your mostly innocent dog out in the snow. You start five separate projects in as many minutes. You feel so restless when you sit down that you have to stand up; and when standing, so jumpy that you have to sit down? Whatever your own signals are, you must learn to recognize them and immediately summon into play an unthinking, automatic set of responses. Here they are.

1. *Stop dead in the water.* Assuming you're not piloting an airliner on

final approach, stop whatever you're doing—totally—and bring yourself to a complete halt. Picture yourself driving frantically through traffic to an appointment for which you are already fifteen minutes late. Your heart pounds, you are panicked, angry at yourself, utterly frantic. Immediately, without further thought, pull off the street, park, and shut off the engine. The important thing is to break the cycle of events that is putting you into a panic. A year from now you won't even remember to which meeting you were late.

2. *Relegate your panic to a ritual.* Our forebears knew the power of rituals to contain and then release tension. When something beyond their coping occurred—flood or solar eclipse—they designed a new tribal dance and felt once more in command of the universe. Find your own private ritual for dissipating your frantic feelings. Some people find that touching wood helps. Europeans have relied on worry beads for hundreds of years to help when they've tripped over one of life's sudden hurdles. There are dozens of other methods, many of which you can learn from instruction, such as breath control; repetition of a familiar verse; tensing and relaxing neck, back, arm, and leg muscles. Whatever method you choose, be sure to follow through until it's served its purpose. In other words, ritualize it. If nothing else, it will give you something positive to do until the frantic feeling passes.

3. *Announce your plight.* This, perhaps, is easiest of all. Turn to someone—your own reflection in a mirror will do if no one else is available—and say, "Hey, I'm really feeling pushed (rushed, frantic, in a panic)!" This formal announcement to the world at large can help you get a bit of perspective on the ridiculous state of affairs in which you find yourself. It may even provoke a tension-dissipating chuckle or two, and who knows, an offer of help.

4. *Take things one step at a time.* One of the stress-producing realities of having a hundred things to do is that it's clearly impossible to do them all simultaneously, so why try? Instead, do them deliberately one step at a time. You've pulled off the road, late as you are for that appointment. You've evoked your own relaxation response and shouted "I'm absolutely frantic!" into the traffic noise. Now what? You're still late, right? And getting later. Not to worry. There's a telephone at that corner service station, and like all good Low Screeners, you have a little change in your pocket or purse for just such emergencies. Step One for you will be to find a *telephone.* Great. You're out of your car and by the phone, dimes in hand. The phone, and only the phone, has been your

focus up to this point, your life raft in a sea of hysteria, and now you've found it. Then and only then do you think about what you'll say. Continue climbing up the ladder, one rung at a time, toward a feeling of control.

5. *Reduce outside demands.* Whenever possible, temporarily postpone immediate demands on yourself. For example, suppose yourself at that telephone. How might you get some temporary relief? Here are some options. Call ahead and give your proxy to a friend or ally at the meeting. Or ask if the meeting can be postponed. If none of these steps are possible, inform whoever answers the phone that you'll be there in twenty minutes. Resist the temptation to promise a too optimistic arrival time; doing so will merely put you back into the stew. This is not an optional step; it is essential, and often lifesaving. Driving under an overdose of adrenaline can be just as lethal as alcohol, and what sort of meeting—PTA, business, or otherwise—is truly worth that kind of risk?

Learn to Speak the High Screener's Language

Have you ever watched two people of different nationalities try to communicate? Usually, they begin by making friendly gestures—nods and smiles—after which they point to common objects, making numerous literal gestures, latching on to whatever fragments of their native tongue the other seems to recognize. This is your model for communicating with a die-hard High Screener. Since they live in a world of their own, buffered from life by a layer of insulation, your job is to penetrate that layer using a language your less sensitive counterpart can understand. Here's how to begin:

1. Don't interpret your High Screener's lack of response as an indication that he or she is trying to block your efforts to resolve the problem. Remember, it often takes an atom bomb to make some High Screeners understand there is any problem other than how to make you stop fussing.

2. Understate the problem. This is necessary because your High Screener has likely tuned out all your best adjectives and hyperbole as overemotional exaggeration. Instead of "Nobody gives a damn about how much I do around here," try, "You know, I could use a little more help in the kitchen right now."

3. Use visual aids when spoken, shouted, or whispered words, how-

ever choicely phrased, draw only glassy-eyed inattention. For example, leave written notes at the family information center, but be sure to edit out accusatory, complaining, or too strongly worded statements. Some spouses have even resorted to formal stamped letters delivered in the office mail or declaratory banners stretched across the garage to get the necessary attention. The key idea here is to use your imagination, tempered by a little patience and restraint, to penetrate that thick screen.

Do these suggestions mean that you should pretend that you don't feel the way you do? Not at all. You need to acknowledge those feelings to yourself loudly and clearly. If that's insufficient for the occasion—that is, you're still boiling inside—don't keep it a secret. A short blast may be the two-by-four that gets your "Missouri mule's" attention. As soon as you are able, however, return to communicating in the most effective way you can to capitalize on the breakthrough. Once your High Screener has gotten the message about how important the matter at hand is to you, you'll find your agenda has moved higher on the list of his or her priorities—where it belongs.

Screening Modes and Styles of Thinking

Is there an interaction between one's preferred styles of thinking and position on the high- and low-screening continuum? We think so—it certainly explains why all realists are not the same. It also sheds light on one sort of human behavior that otherwise is hard to understand, a self-defeating response to stressful conditions that worsens things just when we really want to make them better. The sequence of events goes this way. When stress hits the family system, Low Screeners not only feel it first, but they will be sensitive to the stress that builds up in High Screeners long before the High Screeners, themselves, are aware of it. The Low Screeners will react to that double dose of stress by overusing whatever their natural strengths are, a common tendency when under emotional pressure. Analysts will tend to become even more stubbornly analytical, Realists even more hardheaded, Pragmatists a little too expedient, Idealists too understanding and noble for words, and Synthesists infuriatingly detached and pompously "philosophical." The dumping of these personal liabilities on others in the family eventually brings everyone into the game. They end up doing just those things that they like least in themselves, and in turn get from others what they can't stand in them. But this terrible circle need not occur. If you know how and why it happens, if you can be alert to the signs that overloading stress is creeping in, then you can take hold of yourself, use every active communication device you can muster, and head off the escalation before it gets out of control. That is the power that knowledge of ourselves and our loved ones gives to us.

We hope this chapter and Chapter 6 have accomplished several things for you.

First, we hope you have a deepened understanding of yourself and your family as unique, valuable human beings, each wanting love, affirmation, and secure contentment, but pursuing them in quite different ways.

Next, we hope we've given you a framework that will help you to individualize the methods we've presented in the previous chapters and will present in the chapters ahead.

Finally, we hope we've helped you discover your *own* ways to use those differences positively to build a happy, havenly home, multiplying each others' strengths while buttressing each all-too-human weakness.

EXERCISES

These exercises can help you in several ways:
1. They can help you identify the most comfortably practical methods for taking advantage of your screening level, whether high or low.
2. They can alert you to subtle ways in which your screening level is affecting your family life.
3. They can show you how to minimize any burdens that you or your screening level may inadvertently be imposing on others.

1. On the line below, place the initials of each member of your family at the point that represents his or her screening score. Your line should look something like this:

0	SG		RG	50	PG		NG	100

Low Screener   *High Screener*

Remember: If you are PG, SG will see you as a High Screener, while NG will wonder why you are always so sensitive, if he (masculine pronoun intended) is aware of you at all.

If You Are a Low Screener, Answer the Following Questions:

2. What are the signals that tell you that your circuits are overloaded? Identify at least three. For example, awaken at night feeling panicky; feel uneasy when I come into the kitchen; snap at George when he mumbles something.

_____

_____

_____

3. In the left half of the spaces below, describe situations or activities that seem innocent at the time but tend to result in a feeling of overload. For instance, do you accept discretionary assignments when you're feeling great that will combine, along with all those nondiscretionary things you have to do, to leave you feeling oppressed, depressed, or frantic.

Overloading Situations	*Ways to Manage*
_____	_____
_____	_____
_____	_____
_____	_____
_____	_____
_____	_____
_____	_____
_____	_____

4. To the right of each of the activities or situations you described in question 3, write at least one thing that you intend to do to prevent or minimize its effect on you. For example, "The next time I'm asked to take on a voluntary assignment, I will reply, 'I'll let you know tomorrow' (or 'in ten minutes' or 'by tonight,' etc.)."

5. In the left-hand portion of the following spaces, describe those circumstances in your family life that overwhelm you even though "they shouldn't because they're trivial and unimportant." Some examples: Clutter in the living room depresses you; You're furious because everyone else seems oblivious to the bellowing of the TV that was turned up to drown out squalling kids, screeching cat, and hysterical dog.

Overwhelmers	*Preventive Maintenance*
_____	_____
_____	_____
_____	_____
_____	_____
_____	_____
_____	_____
_____	_____
_____	_____

6. To the right of each of the circumstances you've listed for question 5, describe one action on your part that might decrease its overload quality. For example, establish a Saturday morning "pickup party" so that Saturday night accumulation of debris will be of less massive proportions.

If You are a High Screener, Do the Following Exercises:

7. Commit yourself to start two open-channel mechanisms that you are not now using. Examples: Stop reading the morning newspaper at breakfast; Spend some time alone with each member of the family; Say "How is it going"; Pay attention to what happens; listen hard.

a._____

b._____

8. Convene a family meeting (call it what you like) and ask for comments on anything that family members find irritating or annoying. Invoke a rule that all reactions to what is said must be saved for the discussion time coming up later.

CHAPTER 8

The Gentle Art of Containing Chaos; or, Recipes for Rattlebrains

"Hi, Pop," said twelve-year-old Bert. "Wanna shoot some baskets?"

"Sure," replied Pop. "We've got a few minutes yet till dinner."

"Oh, by the way, somebody called for you about an hour ago, but I don't remember who."

"Whoa! Wait just a second. He didn't leave his name?"

"Yeah—but I forgot it—"

"Well, was it important?"

"He didn't say. But he wanted you to call him back real soon."

"Did he give you his number?"

"He said you had it. Hey, are we gonna shoot baskets or not?"

"Well, can you *think* of his name? It might be important."

"I think it was Fred or John or Bob or something like that—"

"Why didn't you write it down? It might have been a customer or my boss. How do you expect me to earn money for things like basketballs if you don't remember to write down important messages?"

"Gee, Dad, what do you think, I'm *stupid* or something?"

No, Bert, Dad doesn't think you're stupid. But he *is* beginning to suspect that you're a full-fledged member of the Society of Rattlebrains (we would have said "dues-paying," but they seldom remember to pay them), an august group whose numbers include some of the most talented and successful people around. In fact, our research into individual styles of thinking shows that six out of ten of the people you're likely to live with are scatterbrained enough, one way or another, to qualify.

WHAT MAKES A RATTLEBRAIN?

Since rattlebrains can be creative, resourceful, and even practical thinkers, what makes them rattlebrains? The answer, as you might have guessed if you live with one, is that they simply do not sort the world into orderly categories and then deal with them one step at a time. It is precisely this unpredictability that makes them such fascinating, if sometimes disconcerting, people to know.

Rattlebrains have been accused, usually quite appropriately, of these sins: They tend to be pack rats, moving little piles of belongings from one open space to another. They tend to forget phone messages, as Bert did, important or not. They stash away important documents (such as bills) until the day before they need them and then can't remember where they are. They cover every inch of any available flat surface, tabletops, bookshelves, and floors, for example, with an interesting assortment of objects.

This is only a partial list, but it serves to make the point. We have not made it longer because an honest look at the full extent of rattlebrain sins is very depressing to both of us. The fact is that, in quite different ways and for different reasons, we are both eminently qualified for scatterbrain honors. As a Realist-Pragmatist thinker, Susan's forte is *getting things done*. However, as is the wont of such rapid-fire thinkers, her wake is often strewn with the tools and materials needed to accomplish these tasks.

Bob, on the other hand, trains his Synthesist-Realist mind on wry solutions to cosmic problems, leaving such humdrum tasks as filling the gas tank and telling Susan he'll be in Chicago to other, more prosaic minds.

This chapter will give you a potpourri of methods we've found useful in saving rattlebrains from themselves. There are two pledges, however, that all conscientious rattlebrains must make before beginning.

First, you must acknowledge your sins of rattlebraining before the Altar of Chaos. You must admit (privately is okay) that you are sick and tired of inconveniencing yourself and your loved ones through more-than-occasional acts of forgetfulness.

Second, you must dedicate yourself to thinking about and talking about how important it is to bring law and order to the wild frontier of your life. You will be trying to undo and repair not just bad habits, but habits that have their seat in some faulty way you have learned to think about the world. It will take concentration and all the motivation you can muster, but it does not require that you change your ways of thinking or any other aspects of your personality, merely that you acknowledge who you are and that being that way gets you into trouble.

It's only fair to tell you that you will face a couple of immediate hurdles. Most people feel insulted when the quality of their memory or their ability to control a situation is questioned. After all, you, your rattlebrained significant other, or delightfully "spontaneous" child are bright, intelligent people who just happen to "forget things once in a while." If the thought of remediation is too depressing, tell yourself (or your partner) that these methods *also* help efficient, well-organized people operate just that much more efficiently. Besides, most of the methods, in somewhat different form, of course, are used in most well-run business organizations to great advantage—which is what led us to try them out in our own home.

A particularly insidious form of sabotage derails rattlebrains who are employed outside the home in tough, demanding, competitive jobs. These people frequently look at their havenly home as the one place where they *don't have* to be careful and conscientious and always on top of things. This quite understandable wish is based on the patently false notion that what goes on at home is somehow less important than what happens in office or factory, or on the concert stage. The opposite is true, for your home is, or ought to be, your source for energy renewal and rejuvenation. Disorder and uncontained chaos are the enemies of reenergizing; they produce overload and tension, not relaxing fun or excitement.

For convenience' sake, we've grouped our suggestions for reforming rattlebrains into five general categories: using Information Centers; handling Mail and Rememberables; relying on Memory Helpers; cutting mental clutter through Planning Networks; and generally improving tempers with Catchalls for Containing Chaos.

INFORMATION CENTERS

Messages are nothing more than carriers of information. Too often people confuse the medium of the information (message form) with the message itself. That is why businesses are rife with pointless memos and meaningless accounting data. What the derattlebrained home needs is more and better *information*—not bigger and grander messages.

Information Centers can be anything you want them to be. We have elected to use the refrigerator door for our main message center, but anywhere or anything else will work provided it meets a few minimum requirements:

1. *It must be hard to ignore.* Rattlebrains are famous for overlooking the place where they've been told something important will be waiting for them. Your Information Center should be prominently placed, yet not so decorous and formal that people are reluctant to touch it.

2. *It must be within easy reach of everyone who will use it.* This is not so obvious as it appears. We have seen message boards placed atop counters or behind appliances (or in other places a gorilla would have problems reaching) where seven-year-olds could never post their own information. The center must be low enough to allow children to participate but high enough to preclude toddlers and other prerattlebrains from swallowing thumb tacks, chalk, magnets, or other hazards. Naturally, physically disabled or infirm individuals ought not to be denied their right to live an orderly life as well.

3. *It must be easy to add, remove, or change messages.* "Hot" messages and reminders have a way of piling up, and people must be encouraged to keep the Information Center current. Some workplace organizations have a "bulletin board committee" whose job is to police the company's message centers and make certain that outdated material or improper material is removed. On the other hand, your message policy shouldn't be so strict that this creature becomes a sacred cow. You may want to make Information Center supervision a formal chore as discussed in Chapter 3.

4. *It must be the only Information Center in the house.* This doesn't mean that family members shouldn't be encouraged to keep their own engagement calendars or bulletin boards, etc.; it simply means that all "official" information will be found *only* in one, authoritative place. If the refrigerator door is the approved information center, then messages should *not* be left on the dining table just because that was where you were sitting when you thought of leaving them.

What should your Information Center look like? Again, use whatever works best for your family, both from an aesthetic and a utilitarian standpoint. Our message center (the fridge), in addition to its central location in the kitchen, is in the direct line of sight of anyone looking for something to eat or drink to assuage a nervous system abraded by school or a tough day on the job.

Papers of assorted sizes and shapes can be affixed to it using those little decorator magnets or magnetized clips you see in department and hardware stores. (Attractive, humorous, or personalized magnets also promote interaction with the center and keep people feeling good about using it.) Blackboards have been used, but with mixed results, largely because messages *must* be entered with chalk, and chalk has a way of breaking into tiny pieces that wander off to the corners of the house. Magnetic blackboards are available, of course, for that multimedia effect, as are newer, wipeable vinyl boards using special pens. We tend to shy away from methods, however, which require unique or costly apparatus. Remember, the effectiveness of your center will be measured by swift, clear communications rather than awards for arts and crafts.

Finally, no discussion of Information Centers would be complete without mentioning that great link between sonic vibrations and indelible memory, the telephone message pad. The lesson here is: Have one. Preferably, it should be permanently (or semipermanently) fixed near the phone and have a supply of writing instruments nearby. We recommend ballpoint pens (cheap is just fine) since pencils wear down and points break. Who ever heard of walking all the way to the study to sharpen a pencil and returning to the phone in the same motion, or even the same day or month? The laws of nature seem to say that he or she who must look for pen and paper to take a message, won't. After all, they can always make a mental note to remember to tell you that the boss called and wants you to call back immediately. Just like Bert.

MAIL AND REMEMBERABLES

Most mail is the dandruff of life. Except for dividend checks, tax refunds, and love letters from missing persons, most of ours used to collect in unsightly piles on the flat surfaces of every room: on the dining table, kitchen sideboard, bookshelves—even the sacred family washbasin was not immune to this creeping disease. It's not that we were ungrateful for all those helpful coupons, free samples, and offers to subscribe to obscure (but no doubt worthy) specialty magazines. And Heaven knows our creditors deserved their time to remind us of past bouts of profligate abandon. But we have always believed in the sound administrative maxim that a letter should be touched only once: picked up once for inspection and then immediate disposal—to an action step, to the wastebasket, to a file, or to another person. The problem arose with those pieces of mail which were neither fish nor fowl, deserving neither an honored place in the "bills to be paid" (or other pending files), nor a summary heave-ho. They needed thought, or fact gathering, or mutual discussion. They were the flotsam that ended up on the dining room table, the drainboard, etc.

After our third disastrous attempt to stem this paper avalanche by teeth-gritting determination to "keep up with the mail," it dawned on us that we were somehow missing the point. We had simply underestimated the degree to which our home, not to mention our office, had been taken over by the "paper revolution." The mail was getting through all right, and it had flooded out all of our intentions. What we needed was a system, similar to the one we used in the office, to handle these invaders from the "age of information." Here's the three-pronged attack we wound up launching.

1. *Set up individual mailboxes.* How does your mail get to you in the first place? The post office puts it into a little box marked with your address, the same way incoming letters are sorted in office mail rooms. To replicate this simple system, we purchased or made a variety of desk organizers (flats used for holding beer or soft drinks make great substitutes for official-looking In baskets). The person whose chore it is to bring in the mail simply sorts the items into the appropriate mailbox (including a place for "Resident"). Our absolute rule was that each mailbox had to be emptied each day or on the day the person returned from traveling. Mail that is continually left in the box and unclaimed "Resident" mail is dumped by our household postal inspector; as yet, there has been no apparent effect on the earth's rotation. A tougher problem was what to do with all of those items that looked really valuable and interesting but pertained to no particular member of the family at the present time. This led us to our second innovation.

2. *Get lots of little folders for one big filing cabinet.* Being at times frugal (we won't comment on the other times), we didn't want to invest in too many capital improvements just to lick the mail problem. We did find, however, that since our problem was lots of little, unrelated things all searching for a common roost, purchase of a good-sized filing cabinet was in order. In it we placed folders for each family member, along with general folders for recurring events and activities—entertainment, vacation, hobbies—as well as folders for essential family records, such

as for insurance, taxes, and automobile service. We had finally recognized a momentous fact but one *not* previously obvious to us: Every family accumulates a great deal of paper that it needs to keep or wants to keep. The alternative to a proper filing arrangement will invariably be nondescript boxes of paper stashed in the basement, attic, or apartment storage room.

3. *Give all magazines a "destruct date."* Your dentist isn't the only person who offers visitors a three-year-old copy of *Newsweek*. Since much of our excess paper is in the form of outdated magazines, we mutually decide how long a given publication should be kept. Any copy of that magazine found lying around with a date beyond this limit is either thrown away or put into the charitable contribution box, as appropriate. Issues to be kept permanently or for indefinite periods are treated like any other valuable resource and placed in proper receptacles (stand-up files) and put on the shelf. This has not only cleaned up the clutter but has turned our trove of previously disorganized back issues into a considerable reference library.

MEMORY HELPERS

Memory Helpers are devices that substitute for the real thing. Simple as a blackboard on the wall or complicated as a computer, they hang on to ideas, feelings, or facts so that you won't have to. The human memory can be a deceptive thing. Even highly intelligent people can forget things as fast as they see or hear them. The transfer of data from our short-term memory banks to long-term memory is fraught with all of the bugs of any complex information processing system.

Because of these characteristics, human memory needs all the help it can get. Memory Helpers as we describe them, are devices that remember for you. Here are three that have been of immense help to us: a telephone message board, stick-on notepads, and a calendar of events.

Let Your Fingers Do the Talking

To make sure no important messages slipped through our memory noose, we picked out the most popular telephone extension in the house (the one near the entrance to the TV room) and mounted a blackboard and a notepad and pen holder. We figured this space-age level of redundancy would allow a message to be saved successfully even if a single system failed. Admittedly, the blackboard is a "minus ten" from the interior decorator angle, but it is a great attention getter. The effort to overlook it clearly exceeds the energy saved in declining to write (or read) a message.

Stick It on Your Nose

Adhesive (stick-on) note pads are another great memory-helping invention. They are available at most stationery stores and can be applied not only to message or information centers but to anything else as well, such as an automobile steering wheel ("Get gas before you get on the freeway"), the front door knob ("Don't forget your umbrella") or the inside of an overnight bag ("Don't forget I love you").

Master Calendar of Events

Norm and Alice were a successful young couple. Though they had worked together in the same advertising agency before marrying, their lives since then had gone ahead on different but parallel paths, equally as exciting and creative. Norm continued advancing his reputation as a top-flight account executive while Alice left the agency to have their first child and pursue her career as a highly paid free-lance designer. With the coming of their second child and the pressures of Little League and a rising interest in community affairs, Alice had begun working closer and closer to home. Her children were very important to her and she chided Norm sometimes for his hectic, unpredictable schedule.

One day Alice returned home from an appointment, her arms full of trimmings for little Brad's eleventh birthday celebration. She was greeted by a note signed by Norm which read, "Don't forget, airport on Friday, United flight 207 at 3:00 P.M."

What airport and *what* Friday? she wondered, dialing Norm's office. His secretary told her that Norm was off on a two-day trip, scheduled some months ago, and would be returning as he had indicated on the note. Since he went to the airport with another executive, he would be needing a ride home Friday afternoon. "Why?" the secretary asked. "Didn't he tell you?"

Sometimes, synchronizing life's major and minor events can seem like a hopeless task.

A sure cure for such foul-ups as Norm's is the family's master calendar of events ("that damned calendar" for short). It is simply a garden-variety planning calendar (with spaces for each day of the month big enough to allow handwritten notations on each) posted in a place where everyone can see it and write on it. Near the family's Information Center is a good place. At a convenient time, usually near the first of a new month, the powers that be sit down and go through their respective appointment books, message files, PTA announcements, season ticket schedules, or other relevant records and jot down who's doing what to or with whom and on exactly what date. Yes, it's a nuisance to write everything down twice, but not doing it is worse.

From time to time the extra work of writing in our master calendar has seemed just another demanding job to be done, and we have let the whole thing slide. Invariably, we have fallen flat on our forgetters and lost control of our five-ring circus. Without the overview afforded by that unforgiving calendar, we are tripped up by schedule conflicts that surprise us, baby-sitting arrangements not made, and frantic last-minute phone calls to work out transportation arrangements. If this still seems like an exercise in needless double bookkeeping, consider some of the potential catastrophes this system has helped our own family avoid:

— A father on the road on a flexibly scheduled business trip during a son's Boy Scout awards banquet.
— A spouse's birthday dinner not planned.
— Overlapping trips out of town (with no baby-sitter) or too many events, recreational or otherwise, coming up on the same weekend.
— Too many activities scheduled for too few automobiles.

The list could go on and on to include notations for the due dates of important bills, follow-up enquiry calls about ongoing problems, and— as is appreciated by even the most devoted parents—those blessed nights to ourselves when the kids are on pack trips or visiting their grandparents. Such moments, while appreciated as pleasant surprises, are much better when planned in advance.

Our Memory Helpers have helped so well, in fact, that we have been able to distill a few immutable laws about memories and remembering from them:

1. *Always assume that if something can be forgotten, it will be.*
2. *Memory devices that depend upon your remembering to look something up should be returned for your money back.*
3. *Write down whatever you need to remember as soon as you think of it, not when it's convenient.*
4. *Don't accept reminders from others that are not written down.* This is especially true of anything said to you that begins with "Oh, by the way, would you please remember to . . ."
5. *Remove old reminders as soon as possible.* Human beings are a fickle bunch. A reminder left tacked to the wall very soon comes to look just like wallpaper.
6. *Memory Helpers must be at the right place at the right time to be of any help at all.* Reminding a child at bedtime to remember his or her house key has a very low chance for success at eight o'clock the next morning. A note left on the dining table is better but can still be ignored. A self-sticking reminder affixed to the handle of the front door, however, is much harder to overlook.

PLANNING NETWORKS

Everyone knows that a schedule is something that tells you what you're supposed to do and when you're supposed to do it. In other words, it takes a task list and spreads it out against time or the calendar. This is fine as far as it goes. But most schedules tell you little or nothing about the *sequence* of tasks, or task dependency. For example, if I have four things on my list of tasks for Saturday:

— Go to the Wilsons' barbecue
— Do the laundry
— Get the groceries for the week
— Wash the car

I know *what* I have to do and I know that I'm supposed to have them all completed by the end of the day on Saturday. What do I know about sequence? Well, I know that I can only go grocery shopping when the local market is open and that is from 8 A.M. to 9 P.M. I know, too, that the Wilsons' party starts at 3 P.M. and will run well into the night, so if I'm going to go to the store, it will have to be between 8 A.M. and 1 P.M. (I will need some time to put the groceries away and get cleaned up before the party.) The laundry I can do anytime, but I would rather wash the car later in the day when the temperature outdoors warms up. So from a sequence standpoint, my list now will look something like this:

1. Get groceries for the week
2. Wash the car
3. Do the laundry
4. Go to the Wilsons' barbecue

Now what about task dependency? How will the prerequisite needs of one task affect the sequence of the others? To answer this I need to look a little further beneath the surface. In order to go to the party, I'll need to have clean clothes, so task 3 *definitely* must precede task 4. That is, they are hooked together now with an unseen line, a tether if you will, that means laundry comes before barbecue. No matter what else I choose to do, I cannot reverse this sequence. Now how about washing the car? If it is currently full of sporting equipment from last week's softball game, I will probably *have* to unload it before I can fit a week's worth of groceries into the trunk. Since I must park the car in the driveway to do this, I might as well give it a wash at the same time (good planning is just a "legal" way to be lazy). Therefore, my new list, ordered for dependency, would look like this:

1. Wash the car
2. Get groceries for the week
3. Do the laundry
4. Go to the Wilsons' barbecue

So task 1 and task 2 are linked by an unseen "arrow" as are tasks 3 and 4. Can we now infer that task 2 must come before task 3, or even task 4? No. There is no direct relationship between getting groceries and going to the Wilsons'. In fact, if the party breaks up early enough, I could do the weekly shopping in the evening, as long as it was begun before nine o'clock.

This somewhat laborious example reveals a common problem to planning in most unhavenly homes. Much thought is given to *what* we have to do and even *when* it has to be done, but very little to which tasks are directly dependent on another. When projects become quite lengthy and complicated, such as planning for a full-scale, formal wedding, the interlocking, interdependent chains of tasks can daunt the most intrepid seat-of-the-pants scheduler.

The solution, as you may have guessed, is something called a Planning Network. Planning Networks can be plain or fancy; we prefer plain for use in the family and fancy in the office, where they make a great impression on visiting firemen. The version that we will describe to you here is plain and straightforward an example for just about any family project.

A Planning Network Is:

— A visual display of all the things you need to do to undertake a project in a successful, orderly way.

— A device for showing you which things need to get done in order for other things to get done. As an example, you can't go to Europe without a passport and you can't send in an application for a passport until you've obtained the forms and had passport-sized photographs taken. You also need a copy of your birth certificate. Therefore, the first inexorable steps to going to Europe are to write away for your birth certificate and make an appointment with a photographer even though these are not directly related to your trip.

— A method for *scheduling* your interdependent tasks so that everything will be accomplished not only in the proper sequence but also according to some overall date of completion. A Planning Network for our passport project would therefore show that it takes two weeks to get a birth certificate, and an additional thirty days for processing the paperwork in the local regional office of the State Department. You can conclude, then, that you should not pack your bags for Paris sooner than six weeks from the date you sent off that first letter to your place of birth.

— A Memory Helper in that it reminds you to do certain critical things at the proper time and shows you graphically what will *not* be happening if you fail to do them.

— A valuable tool for coordinating the efforts of others in projects that depend on several (or many) people doing separate but important tasks independently. It clearly shows, for all to see, who is responsible for carrying out each step along the way. It thereby prevents—well, almost prevents—later comments beginning "For God's sake, why didn't you remember to . . ."

To illustrate the steps required to prepare a Planning Network, you'll find on pages 184–185 the full-blown version that we constructed and assiduously used for our younger daughter's formal wedding. It worked so well at getting things done, *and* easing the tensions that so often afflict what should be fun, that we took the lesson back into our consulting practice, where we now use these nerve-preserving devices for almost every important undertaking.

(This is an excellent example of a point that has long puzzled us about methods like these: We had *known about* Planning Networks for years, in fact we had taught others to use them. However, we did not begin utilizing them in our own work until, prompted by an associate with planning skills, we actually, and quite easily, constructed one of our own for an event of real meaning to us.)

How to Construct a Planning Network

Many books about management and management science will give you guidance on how to build and use Planning Networks. Most of these are way too formal and elaborate for our purposes here, though you should consult them if you ever plan to build a moon rocket or nuclear submarine, projects for which they were developed. The important thing to remember about Planning Networks as we employ them is that they are nothing more than a list of tasks (which you would probably make anyway) laid out on a calendar (to make sure you finish by the time you need to) and rearranged to show the sequence or dependency of the tasks you've scheduled. Follow along with our network on pages 184–185 as we show you, step by step, how a Planning Network is built.

Step #1: Obtain a huge piece of paper. You'll need plenty of elbow room, since building a network involves not only listing many tasks but positioning them spacially through something of a trial-and-error process. Good working materials are large sheets of newsprint (such as those available at stationery and art stores for making flip charts), butcher paper (which comes in long rolls), or even rolls of brown wrapping paper. If nothing else is available, tape ordinary typing paper together to form a flat surface of at least thirty by forty inches. In our office, we use a seamstress's cutting board, obtainable at most fabric stores.

Step #2: Obtain marking and writing materials and notepads or cards. Veteran network makers may work directly on the planning surface, but we strongly recommend (and still use ourselves) movable slips

by January 20	February 20	March 20
Start guest list	Look over and add to the preliminary guest list	Complete invitation list
Call photographers for prices		Order invitations
Develop food list	Make final decision on photographer	Final decision on bridesmaids' dresses
Call and interview caterers; pick one	Meet with caterer	Final decision on menswear
Get prices for invitations and announcements	Check out bridesmaids' outfits	Let mothers and grandmothers know color scheme for dresses
Check out possible honeymoon sites	Check out menswear	
Check on number of chairs at reception location	Choose rings	
Choose and confirm all attendants	Make honeymoon arrangements	Final decision on florist and flowers
Check out music possibilities		Make final decision on music
Final decision on wedding dress design; purchase all material and get to dressmaker		
Decide on clergyman		
Reserve Piedmont Community Center for outdoor wedding and reception		

April 20	May 9 (6 weeks prior to wedding)	June 1
4/1 Shower given by aunts in Los Angeles	Mail invitations	Julie's shower
4/20 Write and mail thank-yous for shower gifts	Set date for wedding portrait	Start moving into apartment
	Finish wedding dress	

Address invitations	Mothers' and grand-	Complete arrange-
Make direction signs	mothers' dresses cho-	ments for out-of-
	sen	town guests
	Final decision on	Meet with clergyman
	time/place bachelor's	for counseling
	party	
	Register bride at de-	
	partment stores	
	Have blood tests	
	Choose and purchase	
	attendants' gifts	
	Make arrangements	
	for bridesmaids' lun-	
	cheon	

June 6 (2 weeks)	June 13 (1 week)	June 16
Write thank-you notes for Julie's shower	Finish all thank-you notes for Julie's shower	Pick up rental menswear; check for correct sizes
Obtain marriage license	Pack clothes for honeymoon	Pack emergency repairs kit (thread, safety pins, etc.)
Change name on all important papers	Mail wedding announcements	Arrange for rehearsal dinner
Final apartment moving and decoration	Call Community Center to remind them *not* to water lawns the day before the wedding!	
Check with caterer for final coordination, food/flowers	Bridesmaids' luncheon	
Wrap gifts for attendants	Bachelor party	

June 19	June 20	
Pick up out-of-towners at airport	8 A.M., post signs with directions to wedding	
3 P.M., wedding rehearsal	9 A.M., wedding parties get dressed	
6 P.M., rehearsal dinner	10 A.M., STARTING TIME	

of paper for our tasks. Be sure your writing instruments will leave a good, contrasting line on the paper surface, since hard-to-read marks (such as pencil marks on brown paper) will make your network all but unusable. We favor felt tip pens and the adhesive-backed note pads mentioned earlier in the chapter. The size you use will depend on how much room you have and how many people are involved. We found that two-by-two-inch slips were easiest to work with. We also wound up listing each individual's tasks in a different personal color, so that responsibilities could be picked out at a glance. If color is not available, be sure to place the responsible person's name or initials someplace prominently on the sheet.

Step #3: Draw the calendar you will work with. This is not the box-like calendar you're used to seeing in the home or office, but simply a straight line running across the top of the planning sheet divided into months, weeks, and/or days, depending on the overall length of the project. In our example, we laid out a six-month period beginning in January and ending on June 20, the date of the wedding. Be as cavalier about the time units you select as you wish. For example, you'll notice that we started off with monthly time intervals until April 20, then through June 6 we switched to two-week intervals. Anticipating a potential "Panic City" from June 6th on, we used one-week intervals.

Step #4: Finalize your task lists. Now is the time to bring in everyone involved in the project. Give them a sheet of writing paper and a pencil and ask them to list all the tasks they think they will have to accomplish to uphold their end of the job. For example, if Dad's job is to arrange for a photographer, he knows he will have to shop around for quality and price, sign an agreement, coordinate the wedding portrait, and see to it that the photographer is present for the rehearsal and/or the ceremony. These are the things he would be expected to write down as separate entries on his task list.

Step #5: Lay out all the tasks on the Planning Network according to the dates when they must be finished. This is where your movable, stick-back note squares become invaluable. Write each task onto a single note square and position it on the calendar according to the approximate date by which it will have to be finished.

Step #6: Rearrange your tasks on the Planning Network as required to show the sequence of dependent tasks. As you work your way across the calendar, starting at the near future (or the present) and ending at the target deadline, ask the person responsible for each task what they will *need* to have that task completed. As we saw in the earlier example, the wedding dress must be available for the wedding portrait; therefore, that seemingly separate task must be done before the date for the wedding portrait. You know from this that the portrait cannot be taken without the dress (although the wedding *could* proceed if it had to without the portrait).

Step # 7: Periodically update and evaluate the network. From time to time, get all those involved in the project together and review your progress. If dates or plans or tasks have changed, be sure to reflect the changes in the chart. Since all the ramifications of that task are clearly visible "down the road," and a participant is overloaded, it is now an easy thing to transfer part of his tasklist to someone else's to even out the load. Above all, do not become a slave to the chart. Like the genie in a magic lamp, it's there to serve you, not the other way around.

Obviously, Planning Networks are most useful for projects that you don't carry out frequently, are costly and time-consuming, or have a high emotional stake. In other words, when everyone cares a lot about whether or not they turn out well. If you perform the project often enough (for example, if you have five marriageable daughters!), you will come to learn the tasks and critical junctions by heart, although the particulars in each case will be different. In either event, you will have an orderly, logical guide to help you through the roughest parts as well as the easiest. It goes without saying, too, that the first network you make will be the toughest, since you're learning the method as well as solving the problem at hand. You will then have under your belt a technique that turns big project lions into pussycats, eliminating or minimizing unpleasant surprises, reducing stress, and saving everyone's time, effort, and energy.

CATCH-ALLS FOR CONTAINING CHAOS

Originally, we thought about calling this section "If You Can't Beat 'Em, Join 'Em," since it puts forth some handholds for those who have accepted ambiguity and disorder as a fact of life, or at least the lives that they currently lead. Often that acceptance is realistic and wise, an acknowledgment that paves the way to positive action. For example, all parents of families with several youngish children live buzzing lives which defy orderliness and method. However, recognizing that some situations are inherently chaotic doesn't preclude trying to contain that chaos. Certainly, each of the gems described below has added to our enjoyment of an exciting but often hard-to-corral life.

The Bounty Basket

If there is a better thing to do with baseballs, footballs, mitts, bats, day packs, and sweaters than dropping them inside the front door, our children were late in learning it. Requests for them to "put your stuff away" were greeted with pained looks of incomprehension. "Why hang it up, or worse, carry it *allllll* the way to the bedroom if we'll just have to get it out again?" If energy conservation is the goal, the children we've known are experts.

Since this retort was puzzlingly rational, we were convinced that the only way to assuage the doorside clutter was to accommodate it. We did this by finding the least unattractive laundry basket we could buy and putting it by the front door. All household efficiency experts were instructed to dump whatever could not reasonably be carried to their rooms into this receptacle (some articles have remained there long enough to sprout mushrooms, but most are used repeatedly throughout the week or for weekend sport). While the Bounty Basket was clearly a surrender to fate, we saw two immediate benefits: First, the entryway really *was* less chaotic. (The kids soon found that they preferred to deposit their personal stuff safely in their rooms rather than beneath a pile of communal equipment.) Second, when quick cleanups of the hallway were needed, there was no doubt where odd-lot items could go— right into the Bounty Basket—considerably reducing the number of stormy searches for "lost" articles.

Saved by the Person Box

Sports equipment and parkas and other large items are one thing; calculators, personal letters, library books, model airplanes and other personal effects are another. When a maximum-effort picking-the-place-up drive surges through the house, the clean*er* has a strong impulse to simply throw away anything found out of place that belongs to a "clean*ee,*" even if the penalty in money or inconvenience is excessive. The only alternative previously was to hand-carry the offenders' personal effects to their bedroom doors and fling the stuff onto their beds. Since a physical counterattack usually resulted (further diminishing the impulse to do a really good cleaning job), a better system was needed. We solved this with the Person Box.

A Person Box is nothing more than a shallow box with the person's name on it. When a cleaner circulates through the house, any item suspected of belonging to a cleanee is picked up between thumb and forefinger and deposited into the appropriate box. The boxes are all kept in the same place and the owners are expected to look there first for missing articles and to clean them out periodically (or whenever nothing else could be stuffed into them). Person Boxes not only organized what had been scattered, they reduced squabbles and frustrations over who does the cleaning and how it is done. Some items, it is true, submerged into the Person Boxes never to be seen again. We have been careful not to enquire too closely about what happened to them.

Paper Bag Pickup

Our household has always operated in compliance with the Law of Flat Surfaces: *Any available space on a flat surface will be filled with objects.* This pervasive principle of human nature applies to dresser tops, floors of children's bedrooms, all tabletops of any size and shape, garage floors, and desks, especially if they are placed where every visitor to the house can see them. Normally, this law of household physics is not life-threatening—until unexpected guests require a rapid cleanup. To accomplish this we have devised a system that gives the uncanny illusion of order without having to combat a reality of the universe (or, at least, of our universe).

First, assemble at the site of the flat surface a large paper bag (grocery bags are excellent for this) and put everything not assigned to that flat surface into the bag. Then fold the bag and label it with the place from which the objects came and the date they were removed. Finally, remove the bag to some out-of-the-way place where you have previously determined such bags will be kept, and forget about it. When curiosity finally gets the better of you, or the habitués of the room in which the bags were stored, (we have some bags that have gone unopened for years, like Egyptian crypts), you will either rejoice over rediscovered treasures or you will no longer remember why you were saving them in the first place, which makes throwing them away very easy.

Occasionally, important items such as car keys and eyeglasses find their way into the bags. They, of course, must be recovered right away, and the offenders will know just where to look, won't they? This brings out an insidious effect of Paper Bag Pickup. The more people play it, the more careful they are of keeping track of the important items (such as checkbooks and bus passes) they formerly scattered around the house; and that, after all, is the *real* name of the game.

There is a variation to Paper Bag Pickup we like to call the Four-Bag Sort.* It's a technique to use whenever you would like to ensure that your effort results in something more than tossing back into your closet a large number of objects that you've just tossed out. In this game, four bags are used, labeled "Keep," "Dump," "Repair," and "Give Away." The rule is that each time you pick up an object you place it in one of those four bags (if you are applying this method to cleaning out the garage, you will obviously need very large bags). You will note that even if you then simply put all four bags back in the closet, at least some of the disorder will have been contained. Actually, we have found that the process does provide a considerable amount of forward motion. Whatever is in the Give Away bag at length reaches one of those worthwhile agencies that utilize salvageable articles, the Dump bag moves on to the trash can, and the contents of the Repair bag move into an automobile for eventual distribution to repair places. The Keep bag is on its own.

Peekaboo Toy Baskets

We firmly believe that neatness and happiness cannot exist in the same kid, at least not for more than twenty minutes tops. However, we have found a technique that gives the illusion of order to a child's room. The tools are a collection of brightly colored plastic laundry baskets. The method is described below. It all happened when we realized that our previous feeble efforts at uncluttering had inevitably caused any toy that was wanted *right now* to have moved mysteriously to the bottom of the box. This meant that any child who wished a toy naturally had to find the nearest available parent to aid in the search. An expedition would be formed to make the rounds of all of the toy boxes, dumping out the contents of each in turn until the desired toy was found, invariably in the last box rummaged through. At this exact moment the child would grab the toy with a whoop and be instantly out the door, leaving one or both parents to (1) either patiently replace all of the toys in the

* We found this method also mentioned in two references: *Sidetracked Home Executives* and *How to Organize Your Work and Your Life.*

toy box, (2) cry, or (3) both. This toy box problem was complicated by the fact that they all had flat tops, which meant (please see preceding discussion of the Law of Flat Surfaces) that even getting into the toy box at all required a good deal of work. One very fortunate day one of the kids, under orders to "Clean up your room," and finding every other possible repository already piled high or stuffed full, heaped his toys into an empty laundry basket. The advantages of that system became immediately clear: (1) one could tell at a glance (usually) whether a desired toy was in the basket; (2) toys piled into a laundry basket do *not* make a flat surface; (3) since there is no lid to be raised, it is easier, after a chosen object has been pulled out, to simply dump things back into the basket; (4) it is much easier to find the loose sock (never socks) that find their way into a basket along with toys, games, stuffed animals, and other essentials for living; (5) there are fewer messes because there is always a yawning mouth open to receive any item (sometimes shot from across the room, basketball style); (6) picking up becomes so easy that the kids involved just *may* learn that keeping a room neat is not an unnatural act.

Communal Cleanups

What is work for one person can sometimes be fun for two. Do you have a particularly difficult job to be done? Let's say your full-to-overflowing garage has come up first on your priority list, or perhaps it's a hall closet that bulges at the seams. Make a deal with a friend, neighbor, or relative to jointly and reciprocally tackle such disagreeable duties. We've found these advantages to Communal Cleanups:

1. The social aspects somehow make a dreaded job more palatable. The commitment to meet someone at a certain time to do a certain thing also limits your opportunities to procrastinate.
2. Some tasks are just more efficiently accomplished if two people do them. Working in a tiny closet may preclude assistance, but moving furniture does not.
3. Some people have special resources you might need. Many folks are reluctant to lend out a special tool or vehicle (say you need a pickup truck to move a mattress) but would be more than happy to operate it themselves in exchange for future favors.
4. Shared communal cleanups strengthen and deepen relationships.

After some initial reservations about inviting a "stranger" to share your family's most cluttersome secrets, you will discover that more than likely they, too, have chaotic closets and unobservable flat surfaces. They might even appreciate some of the hints you'll share with them from this book. In any event, you'll find you feel less guilty about your own state of affairs and that your shared frustrations are a good source of future private jokes and reciprocal gestures of trust.

Start out with a cleanup or task that is not your worst and see how it goes—and don't forget to plan a nice treat for yourselves afterward!

RULES FOR RATTLEBRAINS

For many years we have worked with clients whose work and family relationships have suffered from their inability to lead more orderly lives. Far from being trivial, these "minor irritants" and "personal foibles" have a way of undermining efforts to maintain a growing relationship. At the least, they may leave both parties with a feeling that family life somehow just wasn't what it should be. From reflecting on such professional work and on our own successes and failures in reducing the ambiguities in our lives, we have come to some conclusions about the art of reforming and redeeming rattlebrains.

Rule #1: Work for incremental rather than a once-and-for-all improvement. Don't try to remake your entire life in a single weekend, month, or summer. Start first with a small area of your life and try to keep that clutter-free, a calm oasis of quiet and order. When you've got that under reasonable control (say a 75 percent success rate), start on another area, and so on until the household seems closer to the way you want it than it was before.

Rule #2: Remember that the opposite of "perfect" is not "failure" but "imperfect." Studies of procrastinators, and others whose lives are out of control, have shown a common scenario, which might be called *Determination to Disaster in Three Acts.* In the first act, the hero or heroine makes an impassioned commitment to completely turn over a new leaf, never again to be late for any appointment, never again to be remiss in paying bills. As Act 2 begins, heroic efforts keep all appointments on time and all creditors paid early. Then, inevitably, a slip occurs. One payment is late, a single meeting is forgotten, all is lost. As Act 3 begins, the orchestra swells in a symphony of self-blaming; "I've failed, I'll never be any good," is the refrain. Promptly forgotten are the appointments that *were* kept, and so further efforts to do anything about the problem float away on a sea of guilty tears. The motif of this sad little play is this: Many troubled people who try to get their lives in hand fail because they strive for perfection. Since human beings are never perfect, they never succeed.

Rule #3: Don't be surprised when your new systems need plenty of maintenance. As we mentioned previously, an executive's job consists largely of setting up systems for getting things done and then correcting them later when things go wrong. This definition applies even more to the executives in the havenly home. The difference is that in the workplace managers are (or ought to be) less surprised for they have elaborate information systems to tell them when plans are going off track: quality control reports, accounting data, and sales reports, to name only a few. At home, however, your only notice that a system needs refurbishing is a dining room table piled with mail, as the Law of Flat Surfaces once again prevails. Simply take these rattlebrain alerts as valuable reminders that nothing works forever. Quickly review how well your chaos containers have worked for you. Devise any refinements that might prevent, or at least put off, future problems. Then get things back on the track again.

Rule #4: Use your imagination. Use your own ingenuity to find methods, techniques, and systems that work for you. Walk through a large office supply store occasionally, looking for ideas that you might apply at home. Take a look at your own place of work. What systems are working well there? Ask yourself why. Can you modify whatever it is that is being done right for use where it really counts, your home?

Finally, never forget that your ultimate goal isn't reducing those lovable rattlebrains to fearful, compliant robots, but reducing the level of tension in a far too stress-filled life. Nailing down even a little corner of that world can be more helpful than you think.

EXERCISES

The following exercises are best done as part of a family discussion.

1. On a scale of 1 to 10, rate yourselves in "rattlebrainedness": 1 = little or none, 10 = lots.

2. For each of you, what are the indicators that you are at times scatterbrained. For example: Items (letters, bills, car keys, etc.) are frequently lost; Important dates forgotten; I seldom return *anything* to its proper place, etc.

3. Now each person select one, and only one, of the methods described in Chapter 8 for trial during the next month. Jot down who is to do what in the spaces below.

_____

_____

_____

_____

_____

Suggestion: Authorize each other to remind ("remind" is *not* just another way of spelling nag) whenever a slip occurs, the reminder to be followed by renewed commitment, not discouragement. Remember, none of us is perfect although it's fun to try to be.

CHAPTER 9

Cycle of Change, Cycle of Growth

Mom: Johnny, how many times do I have to tell you to stop teasing your brother?

Johnny: If that little linthead would just stop that crazy hopping around, I'd leave him alone.

Tom: Betty, our bedroom is a shambles. Your clothes are everywhere. Why do we have to live in such a mess?

Betty: I know I've slipped a little this last week, Tom, but I've been busy.

Elaine: I don't like being overweight, but I just never had any willpower. I can't seem to resist good food, and then I feel guilty as hell.

Joan: I know what you mean, Elaine. Still, you do carry your weight well.

If there are echoes of these dialogues in your own lives, have courage. For Johnny, Betty, and Elaine have one thing in common: They're all on the way to a change for the better. To be sure, they are not there yet, but everything we know about the way people change and grow shows them well on the road to a better grasp of their lives. In this final chapter we'll walk you through the process of change. You'll find that simply understanding how it works will give you heart to set reachable goals and pursue them. We will also point out ways in which you can help yourself and your family move through the phases that character-ize all personal growth to a new, more satisfying, and less stressful life.

The path of personal development is never a slow and steady climb to glory. It is far more like an obstacle course replete with tiger traps and seductive side roads. The fact that the pitfalls are mostly self-constructed is what makes the whole thing so interesting. We call this series of psychic hurdles the Cycle of Change.

Here is a picture of the Change Cycle. You can see that it's a road which ascends to heavenly learning or hellish frustrations through a series of separate phases (for literary buffs, the resemblance to Dante's downward and upward journeys will come to mind). The phases, in the order in which one encounters them, are:

Dissonance, an unpleasant, sometimes nasty experience in which you see yourself too clearly.

Denial, which sometimes sounds like "The house isn't a wreck, it just has that lived-in look."

Blaming, others or yourself, to show how futile it would be to even try.

Acknowledgment, in which you see that you are indeed part, but only part, of the problem.

Problem solving, which will not work at all until acknowledgment has occurred.

Action, without which the whole thing has been an exercise in wishful and self-deceptive thinking.

Checking it out, in which you make sure that you've done what you promised yourself to do.

Evaluation, which ends in a momentary pat on the back, fading into awareness of a new challenge.

Here is what each of these phases looks like when found in the family setting.

Dissonance

Dissonance is a musical term. It refers to sounds that are discordant and out of harmony; in other words, they don't fit well together. The dissonances that start you on your Change Cycle are jarring thoughts, sights, and sounds that tell you, often without warning, that your current image of yourself is slipping, that you are not living up to your own expectations, or that the act you're putting on isn't really fooling anyone. The experience is not unlike being smacked in the face with a wet fish. The size and general odor of that fish are a rough indication of the speed and dedication with which you'll move on to the next phase. For example, dissonance is that sudden glimpse in the mirror that tells you that you are no longer slim and twenty, and probably never were. Here are some of the wet fish that have hit us, forcing us into sometimes painful periods of growth for which we are now grateful:

— Sleepless nights and twitchy muscles that made us see that we were *not* the cool, calm copers we imagined ourselves to be.
— Frequent half-hour searches for "mislaid" documents that belied our assumptions that we were basically well organized and in full control of our domain.
— Unwise purchases that shook, if only for a moment, our assurance that we were emotionally mature and self-controlled adults.
— Sudden awareness of ourselves whining out petulant complaints at our "unappreciative" children which eroded our self-satisfied opinions of ourselves as superior parents.

Denial

Denial is a bit of psychological magic by which you make the evidence of your senses disappear. It can occur at any level of your nervous system. For example, imagine Ralph and Sybil are walking to their car after a painful meeting with a bank's loan officer. "You looked so unsure of yourself in there," remarks Sybil. Before that unflattering "unsure" has gotten past Ralph's protective middle ear, it will have been miraculously abbreviated to "sure." If, however, "unsure" should penetrate the bulwark of perceptual distortion, Ralph can always explain it away. Here is a sample of rationalizing phrases that may sound familiar. As you can see, they serve rather well to impeach the evidence that he may not be quite the hero that he would like to be:

— "Nah, I was just anxious to get out and get going."
— "Well, I *was* worried that the kids might get home from school before we did."
— "I've never felt that way before; it must have been what we ate for lunch."
— "I wasn't unsure, I was just showing him that we couldn't be pushed around."

The fact is that most of us are so consummately skillful at denial that we can take the sting out of, or at least decently bury, those missives that might have disturbed our view of ourselves. With our dissonant tension dissipated, we are free to continue with the illusions of ourselves that keep us from changing. Sometimes, however, try as we will, our efforts at denial just don't do the trick; the dissonance continues to intrude, and we are forced to fall back on the second line of defense: blaming.

Blaming

Blaming can take two forms: blaming others and blaming yourself. Each serves the function of getting rid of the dissonance, but in quite different ways.

"It's All Your Fault." Blaming others rids you of irksome dissonance, not by rationalizing the data as its cousin Denial does, but by artfully dumping it at someone else's door. If poor Ralph had not been able to fully deny the reality of Sybil's insightful "unsure of yourself" comment, these blaming tactics, used singly or en masse, might have served him well.

— "Well, what did you expect? That guy came on like Attila the Hun."
— "You should talk, Sybil, I was just embarrassed by some of the stupid questions you asked."
— "If you'd done a better job of getting our papers together, we wouldn't have had all that trouble."
— "My father always told me to watch out for bankers, and I've never been able to get over it."
— "You're a fine one to talk, you were petrified."

Clearly, he would like us to believe, if anyone should change and be different, it ought not be Ralph.

"You're Right, I'm Awful." Blaming yourself is a third line of defense usually called into play only when blaming others doesn't work, or you happen to enjoy feeling guilty. Self-blaming gets rid of dissonance by harmonizing your view of yourself with that nasty information that has intruded itself. Remember that it is not the negative information that causes the pain, it is the lack of fit of that information with your own perception of how you are, how you ought to be, or how you want to be.

Self-blaming, in other words, works in a sense by "joinin' 'em" rather than "fightin' 'em". Say that Sybil has stuck to her guns, brushed aside Ralph's best denial efforts, and overturned each of his "it's all their fault" attempts. Now the dissonance is too sharp to bear, and strong measures are called for. They might sound like this:

— "Oh God, I'm so sorry, Sybil. I'm just no good at talking to bankers, or anyone important."
— "You'd better handle these things from now on, Sybil. I just can't handle money, and these guys see it every time."
— "Yeah, hon, you're right. I'm always so nervous, I'll never be a success."

The sequence of events is this: First, Ralph's image of himself is shaken, in part by his own glimpse of himself as hesitant and fumbling, and even more thoroughly by Sybil's calm refusal to be talked out of what she saw. Then Ralph's valiant efforts at denial fail and he cannot even fix the blame on others. Finally, as a last resort he does more than accept the verdict—he aligns himself with it in spades. He is not just a bit unsure when talking with bank officials, he is absolutely and forever hopeless. In one stroke Ralph has rid himself of the acute and disturbing tension that accompanies an out-of-tune self. To be sure, the cost is high—guilt, the acceptance of future ineptness, and even depression. That anyone resorts to self-blaming as a defense at all is a tribute to the painful power of dissonance.

No one knows precisely why, or how it happens, but some people, some of the time, move on beyond denial and blame to the next phase in the change cycle: acknowledgment.

Acknowledgment

"Acknowledgment" means "to show, often grudgingly, by word or deed, that one knows or agrees with something." It does not imply simple acquiescence without agreement, nor acceptance that things are as they should be. You acknowledge yourself when you see yourself in nakedly full array—strengths and weaknesses, beauty and blemishes, assets and liabilities. Such an unflinching gaze at a person that does not match up too well with the ideal you cherish for yourself is never easy. Once again, picture Ralph as he sees himself in that banker's office: wanting to be confident and in control, and knowing that he should be, yet not able at that instant to deny or blame away the vision of himself staring at the floor, mumbling excuses, shuffling nervously through the pile of papers in front of him. For Ralph, and for Sybil who loves him, the moment is cruel indeed. Yet (hear the background music rise in a triumphant crescendo), painful as it is, that unvarnished view of himself is Ralph's open door, his only open door to gaining the self-confidence that he wants so much.

Acknowledgments are emotional affairs, although the kind of emotion that accompanies them can differ widely. They are often helped along by self-directed but perspective-giving humor: "You know, I must have looked pretty funny in there when I was telling him how organized we were, and then couldn't remember just how I'd gotten that gross income figure." Or "You know, I don't understand how someone as smart as I am could go into a meeting like that with so little real preparation." At other times the rush of feeling is naked and unadorned, a kind of cold anger directed straight at the unwanted behavior. "I know I sounded like a stupid ten-year-old, and if you think I like to be that way, you're crazy." Note the lack of any whining, self-blaming quality. What distinguishes acknowledgment from slicked-up self-blaming is the absence of those conditional words that give the appearance of adamant commitment while providing in advance an easy way out. Be wary of "oughts" and "shoulds," "mights" and "woulds." Behind the mask of active acknowledgment they imply passive self-blaming. Thus, "I should really be better prepared" always carries with it the unspoken parenthetical phrase "but I never will be."

Acknowledging statements are usually followed by realistic commitments to do things differently.

Problem Solving

Perhaps it was an intuitive knowledge of the fact that acknowledgment opens the door to realistic problem solving that prompted Sybil to give Ralph a kiss when he looked her in the eye and said, "Let's go to the office supply store *now*. We need as many aids as we can find to get ourselves organized." Sybil may have thought to herself, "Where do you get that 'we,' Buster," but she didn't say it. She knew that acknowledgments are so valuable they should always be rewarded with a hug.

Until you have looked at yourself with the clear if somewhat jaundiced eye of acknowledgment, all of your efforts to solve long-standing problems will avail you little but discouragement and further fuel for any self-blaming you might be engaged in. You can attend three time-management courses in rapid succession, taking careful notes at each, thoroughly convinced of the applicability of the dandy methods you are learning. But if you have not yet said to yourself, "I, and only I, am the one who is frittering away my time on unimportant things," and "I don't want to be that way, and I don't have to be that way, and I won't be that way," you will not manage your time one whit better than you did before. But—and praised be those who watch over us complex and crazy human beings—the reverse is also true. Once you have acknowledged that you *are* part of the problem, your efforts will pay off handsomely. You will eagerly seek advice that you formerly disdained. Not only will you listen, but you will take it very seriously. Here's the way it worked for uncertain Ralph and his Sybil. They drove to a nearby park and sat for an hour under a tree. Ralph talked about how vulnerable he felt when he was caught in an error. "When that banker told us that our figures didn't add up and then showed us, I felt so *dumb*. Then when I couldn't find last year's tax return, it was all downhill." Ralph readily acceded to Sybil's suggestions that they: (1) reorganize their files; (2) assign to her, the Analyst in the crowd, the job of keeping the files current; *and* (3) set themselves to plan better for their next encounter with the bank. Solutions without action, however, are worse than no solutions at all.

Action

Most of the pages of this book have been devoted to explaining a variety of ways to solve problems. We've described techniques for accomplishing tasks that may be as difficult for you as they were for us; we've suggested tricks that you can play on yourself to help you evade, or avoid, the tiger traps that you've dug in your own front yard; and we've proposed effective approaches to organizing your time, energy, and money. But even these tested problem-solving methods will accomplish little if they are not put into effect. Therefore, every time you decide to try one out, never end that discussion, whether it was just with yourself, or included others, without having clearly stated what, when, and how you're going to get started. For our friends Ralph and Sybil, it would sound like this: "Our next meeting with the loan officer is set for a week from Thursday. So on Tuesday night at 6 P.M. we sit down and complete the paper work, separate every piece of paper we'll need, and rehearse in advance how to answer those tough questions. We'll check it out at Wednesday breakfast."

Checking It Out

Action plans that go awry are usually only temporary roadblocks. But action plans that go awry and are then ignored can lead to major setbacks. Good intentions not withstanding, Ralph let Tuesday night come and go without preparing for their confrontation with that tough banker. It just happened that Ralph brought an old school buddy home for dinner, and good fellowship, lubricated by a great red wine, defeated responsibility. Ralph's awareness that he'd slipped didn't come, or so he told Sybil, until he saw the expression on her face—"grim" was the word that came to him.

Well, it certainly wasn't a step forward, but not a catastrophe either, for they'd thought ahead and allowed a little time for slipups. Even if Sybil hadn't remembered—after all, every house doesn't have a resident Analyst—their preplanned Wednesday breakfast would have set them on course again.

Keep in mind, especially if you're inclined to become easily discouraged with yourself, that it's even more important to build into your plans some ploys that will keep you from doing what comes naturally: deciding that since you're not perfect, there's no sense trying at all. Remember that denial and blame are always lying in wait for you. Are you trying to get yourself consistently to work on time? If so, develop a morning schedule for yourself and ask your ten-year-old to remind you (ten-year-olds may forget what *they* have to do, but they seldom forget what you have to do). Avoid, at all costs, letting mornings come and go with you and your spouse *ignoring* the fact that you did not implement your action plan. When you look the other way, you dig yourself into a rather deep hole from which you must then clamber to stay on your developmental path, not impossible but much more painfully difficult.

Well, you've looked your shortcomings squarely in the eye, you've selected problem-solving methods, put them into action, and checked yourself out to make sure you were doing what you intended to do. You're ready now for the last step in the change cycle: evaluation.

Evaluation

Periodic evaluation provides a basis for reassessment and renewal. It also sets the stage for refocusing on a new area of dissonance, one that perhaps you've purposely ignored with the not unwise notion of taking on only one tiger at a time.

Family holidays are easy-to-remember stopping places for review and evaluation. A good time to sit together and revisit such questions as "What's happened to us and with us during the past year?" "How are we doing in terms of our goals?" "What's missing from our lives?" These are bold, sometimes intimidating questions, but deliberating over them even a little helps to close the circle of meaning that every person, young or old, needs. If the answers are in themselves troublesome and dissonant, that only serves to give notice that a new cycle of growth is beginning.

Understanding the nature of the Cycle of Change through which you or your family members must travel can aid you in two ways.

First, by helping you to anticipate some of the rough weather that plagues any serious effort at changing old ways. When your commitment to become neater, thinner, or more confident once again drifts away on a sea of rationalization, guilt, boredom, or any of the other manifestations of denial and blame, you will catch yourself at it, smile knowingly, and turn back into the wind.

Second, understanding change can arm you with some powerful techniques for helping those you love move from one step in the cycle to the next. The following exercises will help you to identify where you presently are in your own efforts to change. Read through the exercises now, fill in the blanks in your mind but don't pause to commit your thoughts to paper. Then continue on through the balance of this chapter to a look at how to help others to change. Return to the exercises when you are ready to develop a solid change plan.

EXERCISES

1. In the spaces below list three of your favorite ways of denying that anything is wrong. For example: "I feel tense a lot of the time, but it's just the nature of the business I'm in" or "If we spend all of our time wondering what's wrong with the family, we'll never have any fun."

_____
_____
_____

2. In the spaces below list your three most used "blaming" techniques. For example: "When I was young, teachers really cared about how kids were doing in school" or "I'm just one of those people who can't keep a checkbook straight."

_____
_____
_____

3. In the spaces below briefly describe a problem area in which you are in the "denial" phase.

_____
_____
_____

4. In the spaces below briefly describe a problem area in which you are in the "blaming" phase.

_____
_____
_____

5. Now, in the spaces below, check the phases of development you find most difficult to deal with. For example: Do you content yourself with laying blame and never get on to looking for ways to make things better? Or do you keep thinking of useful solution steps but never take them? Have you actually had some success at solving a problem but can't seem to find the time to sit down and congratulate yourself? I keep myself from changing most by:

Denial _____
Blaming others _____
Blaming myself _____
Not reinforcing my own efforts to change _____

HELPING OTHERS TO CHANGE

To help someone to change (whether that someone is yourself, a member of your family, or of your work group), you must do two things: Rub his or her nose in the disagreeably dissonant information that he or she is trying to avoid, and lather on as much support as you can muster while you are doing it. Both must be done, and in about equal amounts. Let's examine why.

Too much unrelieved dissonance can overload any but the most saintly of individuals, pushing that person deeper into denial and blame until the hot seat gets too hot and he or she runs away, gets drunk, or gets divorced. To keep them in the fray, you'll need to balance bad news with encouragement, caring, and support. Here are some rules of thumb for doing that.

Being Decently Dissonant

Don't Overload. Suppose that your spouse or partner is a beloved rattlebrain. That is, he or she consistently forgets to deliver messages, loses important papers, leaves clothes and other debris everywhere but where they should be. Choose one, perhaps two, of those annoying habits of life on which to focus, clothes on the floor and forgotten messages, perhaps. You will then bite your tongue when the impulse hits to complain over lost checkbooks, misplaced keys, and overdue library books. Be especially wary of an urge, especially when confronted by a relapse, to overkill by reading off a long list of sins which includes every felony and misdemeanor committed over the last two years.

Be Descriptive. Describe, don't judge. You will provoke less denial or blaming if you say "Dear, your clothes are on the floor," rather than "You're being sloppy again!" "Clothes on the floor" are facts which you are describing; "sloppy" is an indictment of your loved one's inner soul, which no self-respecting inner soul will put up with, not when there's plenty of denial and blame lying around.

Be Specific. It's even better to say, "Your yellow shirt, gray scarf, and one tan sock are lying on the floor." For one thing, it saves a lot of argument over whether one shirt, one scarf, and one sock constitute "clothes." Second, the more your dissonant noises sound like data rather than interpretations of that data, the harder it is to deny them.

Be Matter-of-fact. Matter-of-factness is easier to describe by saying what it isn't. It is not accusing, nagging, sarcastic, superior in tone, or patronizing. On the other side of it, a matter-of-fact quality is not hinting or beating around the bush. Try for the tone you might use when telling someone their shoelaces are untied—a simple matter of stating a fact.

Don't Overstate. Be careful not to overemphasize your dissonant point. While dropping a shirt on the floor for the eighteenth time this week may be annoying, it is not a monstrous crime against nature.

Persist Through Denial and Blame. The good news about the change process is certainly the fact that when the target for all this effort is in a state of flaming denial, or is blaming everyone under the sun for every problem on the horizon, or is sinking into a sea of guilty tears, he or she has already started on the road to change. When you hear that wonderful sound of "It must have fallen off the bed" or "If you hadn't rushed me so much in the morning, I would have had time to put it away," you know you're making progress. That knowledge will help you to continue to state (and restate) your perception of what is happening, to point out that it doesn't match your own expectations of a spouse, child, partner, or the standard of performance you've already agreed upon, or the expectations your loved ones have for themselves.

Don't Be Afraid to Make It Personal. Don't shy away from clearly stating your own disappointment, anger, or frustration if agreed-upon standards are not met. When you say with firmness and undisguised feeling, *"I* expect you to live up to what you've agreed to do," you do two valuable things for yourself and your backslider. First, you relieve feelings that might otherwise erupt in a less useful way. Second, such loud and clear statements have the best chance of breaking through your darling's ever present denial.

Standing Up to Blame. Since you are the one who is insisting on being disagreeably dissonant, you will be a ready target for blaming. Expect an angry accusation which combines an attack on you as the bearer of bad news with a justification that excuses the problem behavior. For example, "Dammit, I'm not the only one who's not compulsive about neatness—your shoes have been sitting in the family room for two days!" Your response should have this quality: "Whether or not I'm neat enough, or too neat, we can talk about later on. Right now my point is that you haven't done what you said you would do." Try something similar if others get the brunt of the attack. "Who's to blame isn't really the question. Let's look at your part in what happened," should do.

When to Quit. When one is not about to change, denial or blame are not forthcoming; indifference is. If, in response to your facing your rattlebrain with the evidence that he or she is indeed one, the reaction is an offhand "So what's new?" you might as well stop your efforts at changing and switch to something else. At that point you have four reasonable courses of action: Ignore what you don't like, learn how to handle yourself better in the face of it, choose to live with it, or literally leave it behind. Those who would like to know more about dealing with impossible behavior patterns are referred to *Coping With Difficult People* (Robert M. Bramson, Anchor Press/Doubleday, 1981; in paperback from Ballantine Books, 1982).

ACKNOWLEDGING ACKNOWLEDGMENT

Never ignore an acknowledgment even if it's only partial ("Well, I can see that I was partly to blame"), tentative and wavering ("Did I really say I'd be home at nine o'clock?"), or even slippery ("Maybe I *could* have taken another minute to straighten things up"). In whatever form you find them acknowledgments are worthy of as much support as you can muster. A warm smile, vigorous head nodding, friendly humor, and enthusiasm (remember *My Fair Lady*'s "You've got it! By George, you've got it!") can all help to solidify and reinforce self-acceptance. Watch out, however, for an excruciating temptation to pounce with an "I told you so" on that miscreant who, after three years of nagging, *finally* accepts responsibility. There is no better way to quench the fire. In contrast, a solid matter-of-fact "It looks as if we both agree on what we want out of this" can set the stage for productive problem solving.

PRODUCTIVE PROBLEM SOLVING

Acknowledgment feels so good, it can tempt those wanting to change, and their helpers, into a rapid-fire and enthusiastic commitment to a plan that is not well thought out. Before you can solve a problem, you have to know what it is. Reasonable as that statement is, its truth must escape many people much of the time, for they (at least all but died-in-the-wool Analyst thinkers) seem perfectly content to plunge ahead with any sort of plausible-sounding solution, figuring to somehow make it work. That system works fairly well with easy problems, not so well with complicated ones—that is, with anything having to do with personal change.

Here is the kind of useless exercise that can result from quick and easy answers to behavior problems:

Mark's problem: Often late for work.

Wife Geri's solution: Set the alarm earlier.

Frustrating result: Mark awakens earlier, eats breakfast earlier, reads the paper twice as long as usual—and is s ll late for work.

Impact on Mark: Disheartened and tempted to give up.

Plausible as it is, Geri's solution to Mark's tardiness missed an important point: Mark's problem was not *when* he awakened, but what he did after he awakened. She could have helped more by asking him problem-exploration questions.

Here are some examples of questions we've found useful:

— "When did you notice you first had a problem with this?"
— "Is it any better any particular days of the week? Is it worse?"
— "What have you tried before that didn't work? Would it have worked if you had done it better?"
— "What runs through your mind when it's happening?"
— "What ideas do you have?"

Think of yourself as a consultant to your family member; that means that you'll do your best to listen hard, and keep both of you from charging off with a quick and dirty idea that may not work. However, those ideas need not be lost for good. Since you're the "consultant," you can also be the note taker. Jot down whatever thoughts arise and then say, "I've got that down; let's move back to talking more about what happens on those mornings you're late." Expect to feel impatient yourself, but sit on it. Remember from our discussion in Chapter 5, time spent in explicating the problem pays off.

When at length the problem-analysis well begins to run dry, move on to the next step: looking for alternative solutions to try out. You'll find that sticking with the problem analysis to the point of boredom will have paid off. It did for Geri and Mark, at any rate. Their analysis brought out these specifics:

— Mark needed thirty minutes each morning to shower, shave, and get dressed.
— He loved to read the paper from cover to cover.
— He had a poor time sense and would "lose himself" while reading or talking to others.
— If Geri reminded him of the time, he accused her of nagging.
— The idea of a morning "schedule" made him "feel like a prisoner."

Having pinned down the problem, you're now ready to solve it. If asked, feel free to give advice. While it's true that your "consultee" is more likely to fully accept solutions that he or she thought of, two heads *are* often better than one. For one thing, the fact that you are not the one presently on the hot seat may give you a clearer view of what can work. Then, too, the different modes of thinking that you bring to the problem can make you an exceptionally valuable resource for filling gaps in the joint supply of brains.

However, keep in mind that it is that other struggling person who is trying to change, not you. An action that would be well suited to you might be difficult, even impossible, for your loved one. It's his or her troublesome inner programming, perhaps leftover from a childhood quite different from yours, that needs to be worked through or gotten around.

HELP TO IMPLEMENT THE ACTION PLAN

Geri and Mark finally heaved a satisfied sigh when, at the end of their hour-long problem-solving session, they'd come up with these ideas:

Problem: Often late for work.
Solution Plan:
— Change subscription from morning to afternoon newspaper.
— Write out "getting ready schedule" for morning.
— Set kitchen timer to ring at 7:30 A.M.
— Mark will respond to reminders from Geri by saying "Thank you, dear" and nothing more.
— Talk to Geri about feelings of resistance to the schedule the moment they occur.

But solutions without action, while interesting, are not enough—somebody has to do something. Not that words themselves don't have power, for verbal commitments do make action more likely. Nonetheless, your job as helper is to make sure that no discussion ends without someone asking, "What are the action steps, who does them, and when do they start?" Mark's action plan looked like this:

Action Plan:
— Mark telephones both morning and evening newspapers by next Monday evening.
— Mark and Geri write out morning schedule by end of next Sunday.
— Geri purchases kitchen timer during next Tuesday's shopping.
— Check out how it's all working next Saturday over lunch.

REINFORCE IMPROVEMENTS

A curious thing about people who have changed is that they do not always know it. As their behavior changes, their outlook on the world changes as well. Memories fade of how frustrated, ashamed or defiant they felt each time they sneaked into work late. Be ready, therefore, to emphasize the positive and reinforce any forward steps that have been taken. For example, "Do you realize that you were only late for work once during this last week?" or "I've appreciated it very much that you haven't growled at me when I've reminded you to set the timer." Add "I feel good about the serious way you're tackling this problem," and you will have built a bridge across whatever emotional pitfalls your "changee" needs to struggle.

SUPPORTING IT ALL THE WAY THROUGH

People who care for each other often respond to their loved one's efforts to change with understandable but debilitating inconsistency. When the target of their concern is backsliding, they scold and complain. At other times, when the mood is bright and optimistic, the erstwhile targets of abuse are "supported" in being their usual deficient selves. When you love someone, it is very easy to be co-opted into saying, "I love you the way you are," when that loved one begs for your help in denying the mirror by saying, "I really should lose a few pounds." When tempted by either of these extremes, remind yourself of the twin pillars on which change rests: continued dissonance *and* equally continuing support. For it is caring support that enables us all to face the sometimes grinding, sometimes laughable differences between our expectations and our achievements. At base, support is the affirmation of the essential goodness, power, and lovability of the self. At times when self-esteem is high, we can affirm ourselves, infuse into our hearts the courage to face our human imperfections and yet not give up the search for the best we can be. But at other times, when doubts are high, we can gain strength from others who tell us in many different ways, "I see the positive side of you. I believe you can be different, and as long as you'll work at it, I'm with you all the way."

Remember always that learning is never a steady uphill climb. Expect rapid progress; but also expect regressions, creative denials, furious blaming, and boasts about progress that may seem minuscule compared to the ground yet to be covered. Be comforted by your knowledge that growth and development are always possible; they occur all around you, everywhere you look. Know, also, that by your willingness both to mention cheerfully just what your beloved targets of change are trying hard to forget and to continue strong and caring support, you are doing everything you can to help them on their way.

REFERENCE LIST

BIRD, CAROLINE. *The Two-Paycheck Marriage.* New York: Rawson, Wade Publishers, 1979.

BRAMSON, ROBERT M. *Coping with Difficult People.* Garden City, N.Y.: Anchor Press/Doubleday, 1981.

BREECH, H. R., L. E. BURNS, and B. F. SHEFFIELD. *A Behavioural Approach to the Management of Stress.* New York: John Wiley & Sons, 1982.

CHURCHMAN, C. WEST. *The Design of Inquiring Systems.* New York: Basic Books, 1972.

COREY, GERALD. *I Never Knew I Had A Chance.* Monterey, Calif.: Brooks/Cole Publishing Co., 1978.

DOYLE, MICHAEL, and DAVID STRAUS. *How to Make Meetings Work.* Chicago: Playboy Press, 1977.

ERIKSON, ERIK. *Toys and Reasons.* New York: W. W. Norton & Co., 1977.

FROMM, ERICH. *Man for Himself: An Inquiry into the Psychology of Ethics.* Greenwich, N.Y.: Fawcett Publications, 1947.

GALL, JOHN. *Systemantics.* New York: Quadrangle/The New York Times Book Co., 1977.

GARDNER, RICHARD A. *Understanding Children.* New York: Jason Aronson, 1973.

HALL, F. S., and D. T. HALL. *The Two-Career Couple.* Reading, Mass.: Addison-Wesley Publishing Co., 1979.

HARRISON, ALLEN F. and ROBERT M. BRAMSON. *Styles of Thinking.* Garden City, N.Y.: Anchor Press/Doubleday, 1982.

HOLMSTROM, L. L. *The Two-Career Family.* Cambridge, Mass.: Schenkman Publishing Co., 1972.

JONES, W. M., and R. A. JONES. *Two Careers—One Marriage.* New York: AMACOM, American Management Associations, 1980.

KANTOR, DAVID, and WILLIAM LEHR. *Inside the Family.* San Francisco: Jossey-Bass, 1975.

KEPNER, CHARLES H., and BENJAMIN TREGOE. *The Rational Manager.* Princeton, N.J.: Kepner-Tregoe Associates, 1976.

LEBOEUF, MICHAEL. *Working Smart.* New York: McGraw-Hill Book Co., 1979.

LEDERER, WILLIAM J., and DON D. JACKSON. *The Mirages of Marriage.* New York: W. W. Norton & Co., 1968.

LIEBERMAN, MENDEL, and MARION HARDIE. *Resolving Family and Other Conflicts: Everybody Wins.* Santa Cruz, Calif.: Unity Press, 1981.

MEHRABIAN, ALBERT. *Public Places and Private Spaces.* New York: Basic Books, 1976.

MORRISEY, GEORGE. *Getting Your Act Together.* New York: John Wiley & Sons, 1980.

MOSKOWITZ, ROBERT. *How to Organize Your Work and Your Life.* Garden City, N.Y.: Doubleday & Co., 1981.

O'TOOLE, PATRICIA. "Choosing the Perfect Partner." *Savvy,* Jan. 1982, pp. 61–72.

PORAT, FRIEDA. *Creative Procrastination.* San Francisco: Harper & Row Publishers, 1980.

SATIR, VIRGINIA. *Peoplemaking.* Palo Alto, Calif.: Science & Behavior Books, 1972.

————, and MICHELLE BALDWIN. *Satir Step by Step.* Palo Alto, Calif.: Science & Behavior Books, 1983.

WATSON, DAVID L., and R. G. THARP. *Self-directed Behavior: Self-modification for Personal Adjustment.* 2nd ed. Monterey, Calif.: Brooks/Cole Publishing Co., 1977.

WILLIAMS, R., and J. LONG. *Toward a Self-Managed Life-style.* Boston: Houghton Mifflin Co., 1975.

WINSTON, STEPHANIE. *Getting Organized.* New York: W. W. Norton & Company, 1978.

WRIGHT, LOGAN. *Parent Power.* New York: William Morrow & Co., 1980.

YOUNG, PAM and PEGGY JONES. *Sidetracked Home Executives.* New York: Warner Books, 1981.

INDEX